CW01082162

Speak out

3RD EDITION

B1

Student's Book and eBook

CONTENTS

LISTENING/VIDEO	SPEAKING	WRITING
Listen to people talking about the people and activities that are important to them	Use a diagram to describe people who are important to you	Write a personal profile page
	Tell a news story	
Listen to three conversations between strangers	Roleplay conversations with people you don't know **FUTURE SKILLS** Communication **MEDIATION SKILLS** Agree on a community project	
B B C Street Interviews about lifestyle	Interview your partner about their lifestyle	Write a blog post about a day in your life
Listen to a story about two friends travelling in India	Tell an anecdote about a personal memory **FUTURE SKILLS** Communication	Write a story about a memorable experience
	Complete a class questionnaire	
Listen to six conversations about problems	Conversations offering and accepting apologies **MEDIATION SKILLS** Solve a problem between work colleagues	
B B C Documentary *Mediterranean with Simon Reeve*	Talk about a place that is special to you	Write a review of a place
Listen to two friends discussing a quiz	Ask your partner quiz questions **FUTURE SKILLS** Communication	Write an email asking for information
	Talk about future plans and intentions **FUTURE SKILLS** Leadership	
Listen to three conversations in which people make inquiries	Roleplay two situations and make inquiries	**MEDIATION SKILLS** Give a friend advice about where to study English
B B C Street Interviews about what's important in life	A conversation about what is important to you	Write an online forum comment
Listen to a podcast about rules for success	Discuss advice about success at work and your personal goals **FUTURE SKILLS** Goal-setting	Write an email/letter giving advice
	Discuss your use of social media	
	Give a presentation about a sport or game **FUTURE SKILLS** Communication **MEDIATION SKILLS** Help someone understand a game	
B B C Entertainment *Top Gear*	Talk about a memorable journey	Write a travel writing competition entry

CONTENTS

LISTENING/VIDEO	SPEAKING	WRITING
	Retell a news story	
Listen to a podcast about young people in the news **FUTURE SKILLS** Social responsibility	Present a campaign to solve a local problem	Write an online comment offering a solution to a problem
	Share good and bad personal news **MEDIATION SKILLS** Agree on a plan	
B B C Street Interviews about types of news	Plan and present an idea for a news app	Write a webpage about a news app
	Talk about a hobby you used to have	
Listen to four people talking about creativity	Discuss ways to become more creative	Write a review
	Discuss your favourite things in art and media **FUTURE SKILLS** Critical thinking **MEDIATION SKILLS** Agree on a book to read for a book club	
B B C Documentary *What do artists do all day?*	Nominate someone for a creative genius award	Write a nomination for an award
	Discuss solutions to problems with tourism **FUTURE SKILLS** Social responsibility	
Listen to someone talking about about moving to Brazil	Talk about new experiences	Write a description of an experience
Listen to a conversation about visiting Shanghai	Talk about a place and make recommendations **MEDIATION SKILLS** Tell someone useful information	
B B C Street Interviews about travelling	A discussion about travel	Write an essay about why we travel
Listen to four people talking about their practical skills	Ask and answer questions about your abilities	Write an anecdote about learning a skill
	Plan or present a video or video channel **FUTURE SKILLS** Creativity	
Listen to three conversations about technical problems	Roleplay two conversations about technical problems **MEDIATION SKILLS** Make instructions easier to understand	
B B C Documentary *Inside the Human Body*	Discuss the best ways to learn a language	Write a forum comment about language learning

AUDIOSCRIPTS p158   **VIDEOSCRIPTS** p170   **IRREGULAR VERB TABLE** p174

GRAMMAR

1 A Choose the correct word to complete the sentences.

1 **Do / Are / What** you studying at university?
2 What **do / have / did** you eat last night?
3 How many countries **do / have / did** you been to?
4 What **are / will / do** you doing next weekend?
5 Where **has / does / is** your best friend live?
6 I **not / wasn't / didn't** working when she arrived.
7 I'm sure the school **doesn't / isn't / won't** be open tomorrow.
8 She **is / has / did** worked in several cities.

B Work in pairs. Check your answers, then choose two questions to ask and answer.

2 A Read the text. What do you have in common with Yusuf?

Hi, I'm Yusuf. I'm from Turkey, but at the moment I'm living in London, which is an amazing city. I'm going to stay here for six months so that I can improve my English. I love getting to know new cities, and I'm really happy that I chose to come to London. I've been to seven or eight fantastic museums and art galleries, and I also really like the parks. The best thing about London is that there are so many interesting things to do, especially for someone in their twenties, like me. The worst thing is the weather. I really hate cold weather. I arrived in January and it was freezing!

B Read the text again and find examples of

1 a present continuous verb.
2 a past simple verb.
3 a present perfect verb.
4 a verb form for future plans.
5 a superlative.
6 a modal verb.
7 a relative clause.
8 a verb + -*ing* form.

PRONUNCIATION

3 A Find pairs of words in the box that have the same vowel sound.

> bar boat fight heat heart mail oil put queue
> seen show shy take through took toy

bar, heart

B 🔊 **L.01** | Listen and check your answers.

C Work in pairs. Think of other words in English that use the same vowel sounds.

COMMON ERRORS

4 A Correct the mistakes in the sentences.

1 My sister don't like football.
2 Which film you watch last night?
3 I'm from france.
4 We love listening music.
5 Let's discuss about this later.
6 When I can go home?
7 I'm teacher.
8 I live here since 2018.

B Decide which mistakes in Ex 4A are connected with these things.

1 a missing preposition
2 an extra preposition
3 a verb tense
4 word order
5 a missing auxiliary verb
6 punctuation or capitalisation
7 verb–noun agreement
8 a missing article

VOCABULARY

5 A Complete the common phrases with the verbs in the box.

> chat   do (x2)   go   ~~have~~   listen to
> post   send   take   watch

1 _have_ a meeting
2 _____ out with friends
3 _____ a photo on social media
4 _____ to a colleague
5 _____ some work
6 _____ an email
7 _____ a film
8 _____ some music
9 _____ some sport/exercise
10 _____ a break

B Complete the table with the phrases from Ex 5A.

work	free time
have a meeting	

C Work in pairs. Can you add any more phrases to the table in Ex 5B? Which of these things do you do in a normal day?

people

1

BBC

VLOGS

Q: How would your friends describe you?

1 ▶ Watch the video. Note down some of the adjectives that you hear. Compare in groups.

2 How would your best friends describe you?

GSE LEARNING OBJECTIVES

1A LISTENING | Understand people talking about the people and activities in their life: people and relationships; personality adjectives

Talk about different people and activities in your life: present simple and present continuous; state verbs; adverbs of frequency

Pronunciation: connected speech: *do you*

Write a personal profile; use linking phrases

1B READING | Read a news article about people with unusual jobs: jobs; work

Talk about jobs and work: verb patterns

Pronunciation: syllable stress

Invent a news story

1C HOW TO ... | start and end a conversation; keep a conversation going: conversation topics

Pronunciation: rhythm and intonation

1D BBC STREET INTERVIEWS | Understand people talking about their lifestyles

Talk about your lifestyle: modifiers

Write a blog post about a day in your life

1A Who are you?

GRAMMAR | present simple and present continuous; state verbs; adverbs of frequency
VOCABULARY | people and relationships; personality adjectives
PRONUNCIATION | connected speech: *do you*

Pedro

VOCABULARY

people and relationships

1 A Work in pairs and discuss the questions.

1 What different groups of people are there in your life? Think about work, college, family, hobbies, etc.
2 How often do you see each group?
3 What activities do you do together?

B Look at the photos. Which different groups of people and activities do you think are important for Pedro?

2 A Read what Pedro says about the different people and activities in his life. Find them in the photos.

B Complete the table with the words in bold in Ex 2A. Can you add more words for people to the table?

work	sport	friendships/ personal life	family

C Match the highlighted phrases in Ex 2A with the meanings (1–4).

1 have a good relationship with someone .... and ....
2 be similar to a parent or relative ....
3 respect someone ....
4 see, talk or write to someone ....

D Use the words in Ex 2B and the phrases in Ex 2C to talk about people you know.

I look up to my grandfather because ...
I get on well with my partner because ...

1 I'm part of a football team and I get on well with my **teammates**. We usually go out together after a match. I think it's really important that teammates can get on with each other on and off the pitch. It helps you to play a better game.

2 Every day I work with the same people. Luckily, I'm friendly with most of my **colleagues**. I also have a really good **manager**. I look up to her.

3 I message my parents a lot. I like to stay in touch with them by video call, too. My **grandparents** were very important to me so I want my children to have a good relationship with my parents. My daughter takes after my mother. They're very similar in many ways.

4 I would say my **partner** is my best friend, but I also have a group of **close friends** and we sometimes play music together. We try to meet once a month.

LISTENING

3 A 🔊 **1.01 |** Listen to three people talking about their lives. Who talks about each idea in the box?

parents   studies   work   a sport children   a grandparent

Tomasz: <u>studies, ...</u> ....
Michaela: ....
Jo: ....

B 🔊 **1.01 |** Work in pairs. Answer the questions. Listen again and check.

Tomasz
1 What is he studying at the moment, and where?
2 Who does he live with?
3 How often does he see and speak to his parents?

Michaela
4 How often does Michaela play hockey?
5 Why does she admire her grandmother?
6 Where did she meet her group of close friends?

Jo
7 What is Jo's job?
8 Why is her work busy at the moment?
9 What three jobs does she mention doing at home?

C Work in groups. Discuss the questions.
1 Do you have a small group of close friends, or a large group of friends?
2 How good are you at staying in touch with old friends and family members?
3 How important is your work or studying to you? Why?
4 What 'jobs' do you do at home?

4 A Work in pairs. Read the descriptions (a–c) that the speakers use. Which people are they talking about? Then answer the questions (1–3).
a They're so **funny**, and great to be with.
b She's such a **kind** and **generous** person, and she's always **cheerful**.
c They are **hard-working** and very **reliable**.
1 Do the adjectives in bold have a positive or negative meaning?
2 Who in your life would you describe with these adjectives?
3 What other adjectives can you use to describe personality?

B Learn and practise. Go to the Vocabulary Bank.

▶▶ page 136 **VOCABULARY BANK** personality adjectives

GRAMMAR

present simple and present continuous; state verbs; adverbs of frequency

5 A Look at sentences 1–6 from the listening. Which tenses are the verbs in bold?
1 I'm **studying** design and I **love** it!
2 I'm **living** with a few of the people on my course at the moment.
3 We **study** during the day and then we usually **cook** together in the evening.
4 My parents **live** back home in Poland.
5 When they **come** home, we always **try** to meet up.

B Look at the verbs in bold in Ex 5A again. Answer the questions.
1 Which verb describes a fact or something that is always true?
2 Which verbs describe a temporary situation or something happening around now?
3 Which verbs describe a habit or routine?
4 Which verb tense do we use with adverbs of frequency, e.g. *sometimes*, *often*, *never*?
5 Which verb in the present simple describes a feeling that is true now?

C Learn and practise. Go to the Grammar Bank.

▶▶ page 104 **GRAMMAR BANK**

PRONUNCIATION

6 A 🔊 **1.02 | connected speech: *do you* |** Listen to the question. Notice how the words *do you* are joined together.

Do you cook for your family?

B 🔊 **1.03 |** Listen and write the questions that you hear.

C Work in pairs. Ask and answer the questions in Ex 6B.

7 A Make six true sentences about your life, job and studies. Use words and phrases from box A. Use the ideas in box B or your own ideas.

A
always   at the moment   hardly ever   occasionally never   nowadays   often   sometimes   usually

B
| cook dinner   do sport   eat out in a restaurant go on holiday   stay in touch with friends visit my grandparents

enjoy my job   get up before 6 a.m.   go out with colleagues   learn something new   start a new project

enjoy my course   find my course difficult study for exams |
| --- |

B Work in pairs. Compare your sentences. Ask more questions.
A: I hardly ever eat out in a restaurant. I always cook dinner for my family at home.
B: Really? What kinds of things do you like cooking?

SPEAKING

8 A Look at the diagram about Kasia. Who is Kasia's best friend? Who does she work with?

Ela: teammate at volleyball, friendly, fun

Alice: best friend, funny, good at languages, tidy

Filip: brother, bossy!

Shaun: my partner, charming and kind

Maria: work colleague, journalist, friendly

B Think about the important people in your life. Make a similar diagram for yourself.

C Read the questions (1–4) and prepare your answers. Make some notes for each of the questions.

1 How do you know each person on your diagram? What is their relationship to you?
2 How can you describe them?
3 How often do you see each person and how do you stay in touch?
4 What things do you usually do with each person, and what things are you doing with them at the moment?

D Work in groups. Tell others about the people in your diagram. As you listen, ask one or two questions about each of the people that your classmates talk about.

A: Alice is my best friend. She's really funny, and she's a bit crazy sometimes. That's why I like her. We get on really well. I see her every week, and we often go shopping together. At the moment, we're planning a holiday. I can't wait!
B: What does she do?
A: She's a designer.

WRITING

a personal profile

9 A Read Matt's personal profile. Where do you think you might read this profile?

a in a job application
b on someone's professional website
c in an application to college or university

Matt Erbrich
About me ...

I believe photographs have the power to show emotion and character **as well as** beauty. I am a portrait photographer and I love taking photos of people.

I was born in Germany and grew up in the UK, but now I'm living in New York. I love travelling, especially in Europe **because** there are so many interesting countries to visit. I enjoy working on city scenes and travel photography, **too**, and at the moment I'm working on a travel book. I work on photo projects around the world and I have **also** won awards for my work. I love taking photographs of people in their daily lives, **for example** colleagues working together or grandparents playing with their grandchildren. I'm quite patient and easy-going, so I'm happy to wait to get the right photo! I hope you enjoy my photos. If you need a photographer, get in touch!

Contact me: MattErbrich22xx@gmail.com

B Work in pairs. What information does Matt include in his personal profile?

address   age   awards won   current projects
education   family   hobbies   home town   job   name
nationality   personal beliefs   professional experience
roles in life   work skills

10 A Look at the linking phrases in bold in Matt's profile. Notice how they connect two ideas together. Which linking phrase:

a gives a reason?   b adds a similar idea (x3)?   c gives an example?

B Complete the sentences with the linking phrases in the box.

also   as well as   because   for example   too

1 I occasionally write articles for a local newspaper, and contribute to their online blog, ...
2 I sometimes do different jobs. .... , I work as a waiter, a lifeguard and also a delivery person.
3 I'm studying biology .... I love learning about nature.
4 I really enjoy surfing .... skiing.
5 One of my passions is cooking, but I .... really enjoy music.

C Imagine you are setting up a new website based on something you are interested in. Write your personal profile page for the website. Use Matt's profile as a model.

1B Good people

GRAMMAR | verb patterns
VOCABULARY | jobs; work
PRONUNCIATION | syllable stress

VOCABULARY

jobs

1 A Write down five jobs that involve helping other people.

Medical workers save lives.
Teachers help us to learn.

B Work in groups. Compare your ideas. Then decide which jobs help people the most.

2 A 🔊 **1.04** | Listen to eight people talking about their jobs. Match the speakers with the jobs (a–h).

a musician **b** mechanic **c** shop assistant **d** financial consultant **1**

e plumber **f** chef **g** gardener **h** journalist

B Look at the jobs in Ex 2A again. In which jobs do people
1 work with numbers or words?
2 sell objects or food?
3 sell a service?
4 help people?

C Work in pairs. Discuss the questions. How can you describe the jobs in Ex 2A? Which would you like to do? Why?

A chef is responsible for planning the menu and creating new dishes.
I'd like to be a financial consultant because they earn a good salary.

D Learn and practise. Go to the Vocabulary Bank.

▶▶ page 136 **VOCABULARY BANK** work

PRONUNCIATION

3 A | **syllable stress** | Work in pairs. Which syllable is stressed in these words? Which word has a different stress pattern?

> assistant   consultant   journalist
> mechanic   musician

B 🔊 **1.05** | Listen and check. Is this statement true or false?

The stress on three-syllable jobs is usually on the second syllable.

C Make sentences about the jobs in Ex 3A, then read your sentences to a partner. Remember to stress the correct syllable.

My brother is a journalist.

READING

4A Work in groups of three. Student A: Read text A on this page. Student B: Read text B on page 146. Student C: Read text C on page 148.

B Complete the table with information from your text.

	Text A	Text B	Text C
Who is the text about? Where?			
What is their job? What do they do for other people?			
Why do they do it?			
Do they run an organisation?			
What do they say about what they do?			

5A Use your notes to tell the other students in your group about your text. Complete the table for the other two texts.

B In your groups, discuss the questions.

1 What do you think the three people enjoy about what they do?

2 Which person do you admire the most? Why?

C Find words or phrases in bold in your text to match the meanings (1–5).

1 a list showing how much you have to pay

2 behaviour that shows you care for and want to help others

3 the money that someone earns or receives regularly

4 to become popular

5 to do something so you can be certain of the result

D Work with other students. Read the Future Skills box and discuss the questions.

> **FUTURE SKILLS**
> ### Social responsibility
>
> The media often describes people like Lou, Zeal and James as good people or heroes. Define a good person. Are the people in the texts good people? Which famous people do you think are good? Why?

A

Food is Free

Lou Ridsdale loves gardening. In a small space next to her home in Ballarat, Australia, she grows vegetables. One day, she heard about a man in Los Angeles who grew food to share with the community. He belonged to an organisation called Food is Free. Ridsdale saw that she had more vegetables than she needed and decided to give them away, like the man in Los Angeles.

In Ballarat, just 6.4 percent of people eat the recommended amount of vegetables. A lot of people in the city have low **incomes** and the city has many problems connected to what people eat: lack of affordable food and lack of education about healthy eating. Ridsdale wanted to change this.

After leaving the food outside her home, she put up a sign inviting people to help themselves. Soon volunteers were bringing food for those in need. People usually bring fruit and vegetables but sometimes plants and seeds, too. There is no money involved, no food **bill** to pay, only **kindness**. Helping people is what Ridsdale does. She says that no one is judged on what they bring or take as long as they leave with a smile. She **makes sure** they always do.

Apart from feeding people, Ridsdale understands that education is the other important part of the programme. Once the programme was established, she began to go into schools to talk about food. She believes that young people need to learn about healthy eating. This will help to make their lives healthier and better. She hopes to see her idea **catch on** all over Australia.

GRAMMAR

verb patterns

6A Look at the highlighted words in your text. Find …
1 an *-ing* form as the subject of a sentence.
2 a preposition + *-ing* form.
3 four verbs + *to* + infinitive.

B Correct the mistakes in the sentences. One sentence is correct.
1 After leaving school, I decided do a plumbing course.
2 She hopes for become a chef.
3 You need to speaking to a financial consultant.
4 Working here is great – I love it!
5 Before study to be a doctor, he worked as a volunteer in a hospital.

C Learn and practise. Go to the Grammar Bank.

▶▶ page 105 **GRAMMAR BANK**

SPEAKING

7A Work in pairs. Choose one of the headlines and invent a news story. Answer the questions (1–5) to help you.

100-year-old walks his dog and raises €1,000,000 for hospital

WOMAN PLANTS A TREE EVERY DAY FOR A YEAR

Recycling hero builds parks for kids

1 Where and when did it happen?
2 Who was involved?
3 Why did they decide to do this?
4 What difficulties did they have?
5 How did people hear about the story?

B Work together and prepare to tell your story. Make notes, using at least five phrases from the box.

after + *-ing* form   agreed to   before + *-ing* form   decided to   helped to   needed to   realising   wanted to

C Tell your story.
1 Work with your partner. Use your notes and practise telling your story together.
2 Work with a different partner. Tell your story again without using your notes.

D Work in groups. Do you know any real stories like the ones you heard?

1C Let's talk!

HOW TO ... | start and end a conversation; keep a conversation going
VOCABULARY | conversation topics
PRONUNCIATION | rhythm and intonation

VOCABULARY

conversation topics

1 A Look at the photo. What do you think a 'Happy to chat bench' is? Who do you think might use it?

B Read the text to check your ideas.

The benefits of talking to strangers

Most of us spend part of our day surrounded by strangers, perhaps when travelling to work, sitting in a park or a café or visiting the supermarket. We are together with other people, but nobody talks. However, research shows that starting up a conversation with a stranger can make you feel happier and enjoy your day more.

When Allison Owen-Jones saw a man sitting alone on a bench in the park, she wanted to talk to him, but she felt uncomfortable because she wasn't sure he would want to chat. Then she had an idea: 'Happy to chat benches'. She made a sign to put on park benches which said, 'Happy to chat bench. Sit here if you don't mind someone stopping to say hello.' The idea was a success. Now 'Happy to chat benches' can be found in several countries including Canada, the USA, Australia, Switzerland and Ukraine.

So, the next time you see someone sitting alone, give them a smile and say hello. You never know: they might be happy to talk.

C Work in groups. Answer the questions.

1 How often do you talk to people you don't know? In what places?

2 Do you think 'Happy to chat benches' would be a good idea where you live? Why/Why not?

3 Which topics do you think are suitable or not suitable for talking to people you don't know?

2 A Match the questions for starting a conversation (1–9) with the topics in the box.

> clothes and fashion   food and eating out
> hobbies and free-time activities
> holiday experiences   politics
> sport or music events   the news
> the weather   work or studies

1 Did you hear about the fire in town? It's terrible.

2 That's a nice jacket. Where did you get it?

3 Lovely day, isn't it?

4 So, who do you think will win the election?

5 Astrid tells me you like painting. What kinds of things do you paint?

6 It's the *Big Music Live* this weekend. Are you going?

7 I hear you have a job in finance. Do you enjoy it?

8 Have you tried these pastries? They look delicious.

9 We've just got back from Corfu. It was wonderful.

B What other questions could you ask about the topics in the box to start a conversation?

How to ...

start and end a conversation; keep a conversation going

3 A 🔊 **1.06** | Listen to three conversations. Where are the people? What topics do they talk about? Make notes.

B 🔊 **1.06** | Are the statements True (T) or False (F)? Listen again to check.

Conversation 1

1 The man has never been to the music festival before.

2 The woman is going to see a family member at the festival.

Conversation 2

3 Kate prefers the coffee from the coffee machine.

4 Kate started work two weeks ago.

Conversation 3

5 The man is on holiday.

6 The woman likes the city.

4A Work in pairs. Complete the extracts from the conversations with the missing words.

Woman:	Excuse me, ¹_____ sitting here?
Man:	No, go ²_____ .
Woman:	Thanks.
Man:	No ³_____ .

Woman:	Have you been to the festival before?
Man:	Yes, I go every year. How ⁴_____ you?
Woman:	Oh, it's my first time.

Kate:	I'm Kate, by the ⁵_____ .
Justine:	Hi, Kate. I'm Justine.
Kate:	Great. Well, Justine, I've ⁶_____ go. Nice to meet you.
Justine:	Yes, nice to ⁷_____ .

Man:	Excuse me, do ⁸_____ if I charge my phone here?
Woman:	Not at all. ⁹_____ my guest.
Man:	Thanks. That's very kind.

Woman:	Oh, that's my train. Nice ¹⁰_____ to you.
Man:	Safe journey home!

B 🔊 **1.07** | Listen and check your answers.

5A Match the sentences (1–8) with their uses (a–c).

1 Nice talking to you.
2 Do you mind if I charge my phone here?
3 Help yourself.
4 I've got to go.
5 Is anyone sitting here?
6 Do you know if there's a café near here?
7 What about you?
8 Nice to meet you.

a starting a conversation
b responding/keeping a conversation going
c ending a conversation

B Can you think of any other phrases for each of the categories (a–c)?

C Learn and practise. Go to the Grammar Bank.

▶▶ page 106 **GRAMMAR BANK**

PRONUNCIATION

6A 🔊 **1.08** | **rhythm and intonation** | Listen to the phrases we use for responses. Notice that they all follow a similar rhythm and intonation pattern.

Not at all.   Go ahead.   Help yourself.   Be my guest.
No problem.

B Try saying these phrases. Do the phrases follow the same or a different pattern?

See you later.   Nice to meet you.   I've got to go.
Enjoy your weekend.

C 🔊 **1.09** | Listen and check.

D Work in pairs. Make three short conversations using some of the phrases in Ex 5A. Choose from the situations in the box.

first day at work   in a café or canteen
meeting in a park   on a bus or a train

E Practise the conversations. Focus on the rhythm and intonation in the phrases.

SPEAKING

7A Work in pairs. Read the Future Skills box and discuss the question.

FUTURE SKILLS
Communication

To keep a conversation going, it is important to listen actively and show you are interested in what the other person says. Ask questions like 'How about you?' or other questions that encourage the other person to talk.

Look at the audioscripts on page 158. What questions do the speakers ask to encourage the other person to talk?

B Work in pairs.

Student A: You are sitting on a 'Happy to chat bench' near the station. Think about where you are and why you are sitting there. Someone comes to the bench to talk to you. Continue the conversation.

Student B: You see someone sitting on a 'Happy to chat bench' near the station and decide to talk to them. Think about why you are there. Then start a conversation.

C In your pairs, reflect on the activity in Ex 7B. Was it easy or difficult to start the conversation and keep it going? Why?

D Work in a different pair. Think about a different place for your 'Happy to chat bench', and think about why you are there. Then have a conversation. Talk about different topics.

MEDIATION SKILL
managing turn-taking
agree on a community project

▶▶ page 150 **MEDIATION BANK**

1D BBC Street Interviews

Lifestyle

GRAMMAR | modifiers
SPEAKING | an interview about lifestyle
WRITING | a blog post about a day in your life

Vambai   Philip

PREVIEW

1 Work in pairs. Which of the following words would you use to describe your lifestyle? Give reasons for your answers.

1 busy or relaxed?   3 normal or alternative?
2 quiet or social?   4 healthy or unhealthy?

BBC

Q1: How would you describe your lifestyle?

Q2: Is there anything you would like to change about your lifestyle?

VIEW

2A ▶ Watch the interviews. Note down:

1 some of the words the speakers use to describe their lifestyles.
2 some of the things they want to change in their lives.

B ▶ Watch the first part of the interviews again. Who does the following things? Write the names of the speakers.

1 lives with their parents
2 cooks for herself
3 works in an office, in finance
4 does quite a lot of studying for university

C ▶ Watch the second part of the interviews again. Are the statements True (T) or False (F)?

1 Elliot would like to go for a run every day.
2 Vambai would like to visit different places.
3 Tom would like to spend more money.
4 Kayla would like to travel more.
5 Jack would like to work more.
6 Philip would like to have a more exciting job and live somewhere warmer.
7 Adam would like to have more time to himself.

GRAMMAR

modifiers

3A Read the sentences from the first part of the video (a–e) and answer the questions.

a I would describe my lifestyle as **quite** normal.
b I have **quite a** normal lifestyle.
c My lifestyle is **pretty** normal.
d I think my lifestyle is **relatively** normal and conservative.
e I guess my life is **fairly** comfortable.

1 Is 'quite normal' more than very normal, or less than very normal?
2 Do 'pretty', 'relatively' and 'fairly' have similar or different meanings in the sentences?

B Read the sentences from the video (a–d) and answer the questions.

a I'm doing **quite a lot of** studying for university.
b I would like to … explore the country **a bit more**.
c I want to travel **a bit more**.
d … maybe having **a bit more** time to myself as well.

1 Does 'a bit more' mean a small amount or a large amount more?
2 Does 'a lot' mean a small amount or a large amount?

C Learn and practise. Go to the Grammar Bank.

▶▶ page 107 **GRAMMAR BANK**

Tom

Kayla

Jack

Elliot

BBC

Alice

Lotte

Saffi

Adam

SPEAKING

an interview about lifestyle

4 A You are going to interview your partner to find out more about their lifestyle. Use the topics in the box and write six questions about their lifestyle now and things they would like to change.

> books   food   free time   friends/family
> health   hobbies/interests   music
> social media   sports   TV

1 Do you spend your free time with friends or with family?
2 What does your social media tell us about your lifestyle?

B Work in pairs. Take turns to interview your partner about their lifestyle. Make notes on their answers. Use the Key phrases to help you talk about your lifestyle.

> **KEY PHRASES**
>
> I think I'm quite/relatively/fairly healthy because …
> My lifestyle is quite normal/alternative because …
> I spend quite a lot of time …
> I'd like to … a bit more.
> Something I'd like to do is travel more/work less/be a bit more healthy.

C What kind of lifestyle does your partner have? Tell the class about the person you interviewed.

WRITING

a blog post about a day in your life

5 A Read the blog post. In what ways is Kim's lifestyle similar and different to yours?

A day in my life
Kim, games designer (UK)

I'm a games designer and I live in Hackney in London. On a typical day, my alarm goes off at 6.00 a.m. and I try not to look at my emails or start work immediately. First, I do a bit of yoga and make a cup of green tea. I have a fairly healthy breakfast – some cereal with milk, or some toast, and then I cycle to work. It takes about twenty minutes and I find it really relaxing. At work, the first thing I do is switch on my computer and read my emails. For lunch, I get some noodles or something from one of the Vietnamese cafés or restaurants near to where I work. After work I like to meet up with friends for dinner, or go out somewhere. I love going to the cinema or the theatre or just staying at home listening to music.

B Write a blog post about a day in your life. Use some modifiers and write about:

- what time you usually get up.
- what you do first in the morning.
- how you travel to work or college.
- what you have for lunch.
- what you enjoy doing in the evenings.

GRAMMAR

adverbs of frequency

1 A Match the questions (1–6) with the answers (a–f).

1 Do you usually go to bed after midnight?
2 How many texts do you send per day?
3 Do you regularly phone friends?
4 How often do you cook?
5 How frequently do you read novels?
6 Do you ever play ball sports?

a Usually about twenty, but sometimes more.
b Yes. Once in a while I play tennis.
c Rarely. I prefer books about history.
d Yes. Sometimes I only sleep for four or five hours.
e Hardly ever. I'm terrible in the kitchen.
f Yes. I speak to Janet every day.

B Work in pairs. Take turns to ask and answer the questions in Ex 1A.

present simple and continuous

2 Work in pairs. Look at page 149 and follow the instructions.

verb patterns

3 A Choose the correct verb forms to complete the sentences.

1 He promised **to give** / **giving** me the money.
2 Everyone agreed **to work** / **working** together.
3 I spent a whole day **writing** / **to write** my essay.
4 We'd like **to create** / **creating** an app.
5 They don't mind **studying** / **to study** together.
6 This hotel seems **to be** / **being** very luxurious.

B Work in pairs and discuss. When was the last time you:
• finished making or doing something difficult?
• decided to try something new?
• spent time visiting friends or family?

modifiers

4 A Complete the sentences with the words in the box.

a bit more	fairly	lot more	quite a	quite an

1 I would say that I lead _____ unhealthy lifestyle because I don't do a lot of exercise or eat healthily.
2 I work hard but I never seem to finish things on time. I would like to be _____ productive.
3 I have _____ good social life. I enjoy spending time with friends and going out.
4 I would love to have a _____ time for travel.
5 My work is usually _____ relaxed, so I'm not stressed.

B Change the sentences in Ex 4A so that they are true for you. Compare your ideas with a partner.

VOCABULARY

5 A Add the missing vowels to complete the words in the sentences.

1 It's important to g_t on w_ll with your c_ll_ _g_ _s.
2 I'm a teacher, and in my pr_f_ss_ _n, you need to be very p_t_ _nt.
3 I l_ _k up t_ my gr_ndp_r_nts – I respect them.
4 The most important quality of a p_rtn_r is that they're f_nny!
5 In my country it's difficult for a m_s_c_ _n to work f_ll-t_m_ even if they're good!
6 A f_n_nc_ _l c_ns_lt_nt must be r_l_ _bl_.

B Work in pairs. Do you agree with the sentences in Ex 5A?

C Choose four of the sentences in Ex 5A. With your partner, add an opinion to each sentence, beginning with *and* or *because*.

I look up to my grandparents because they are good, hard-working people.

6 A Choose the correct options (A–C) to complete the text.

VSO

VSO (Voluntary Service Overseas) is an organisation that sends people to foreign countries to work as [1]_____ . They work on community projects and spend time [2]_____ about the culture and language of the host country. [3]_____ a lot of them help to build houses or public buildings or work in education or healthcare. The [4]_____ they earn is small, but it's enough to live in the country. The people on the programme [5]_____ end up becoming [6]_____ friends. When they return to their country, their time abroad is like a [7]_____ that they have gained. The skills they have learnt can help in many different [8]_____ . An employee who has been [9]_____ for organising a project in another country often has an open mind and good problem-solving skills. One VSO volunteer said, 'A lot of what I [10]_____ about the world comes from my time living in Mozambique. It was amazing.'

	A	B	C
1	volunteers	part time	salaries
2	to learn	learn	learning
3	Enough	Quite	Very
4	finances	dollars	wage
5	often	ever	at the moment
6	tight	close	near
7	job	qualification	course
8	work	employment	careers
9	responsible	in charge	managing
10	am knowing	knew	know

B 🔊 **R1.01** | Listen and check your answers.

tale tellers 2

B B C

VLOGS

Q: Tell me about a happy memory.

1 ▶ Watch the video. Tick the topics the people mention.

> birthdays   new possessions
> pets   relationships   school
> travel and holidays

2 Which memory did you enjoy the most? Why?

GSE LEARNING OBJECTIVES

2A LISTENING | Understand a sequence in a narrative: adjectives for feelings; -ed/-ing adjectives

Tell an anecdote: narrative tenses

Pronunciation: weak forms of *was*, *were* and *had*

Write a personal story; use linking phrases

2B READING | Read an article about storytelling: story words; types of film

Talk about films, books and plays: past simple and present perfect

Pronunciation: contracted *have* in the present perfect

2C HOW TO ... | apologise and give reasons: collocations with *get* and *make*

Pronunciation: intonation for apologising

2D BBC PROGRAMME | Understand a TV travel programme telling the story of a place

Talk about a place and how it is changing: prepositions of time

Write a review of a place

2A What happened?

GRAMMAR | narrative tenses
VOCABULARY | adjectives for feelings; *-ed/-ing* adjectives
PRONUNCIATION | weak forms of *was*, *were* and *had*

VOCABULARY

adjectives for feelings; *-ed/-ing* adjectives

1   Work in pairs. Discuss the questions.

   1   Do you share stories on social media? What types of story?

   2   What stories do you enjoy telling friends and family (about work, studies, travel, other people, etc.)?

   3   How do people tell stories differently on social media and face to face?

2 A   Read the story. Choose the best final sentence for it (a–c).

   a   He still hates painting now!

   b   I was sure it could never happen again!

   c   He's still got photos to show our 'artwork'!

This happened when my sister and I were three and four years old. It was the summer holidays and my granddad was looking after us. We were **bored**, so we went into the garage and were really **excited** when we found all dad's paints. We decided to surprise him by painting the house while he was at work. We managed to paint a big area of wall blue before my granddad noticed. I think he found it a bit **embarrassing** that he wasn't watching us carefully enough. He said to us, 'Your dad is going to be really **annoyed!**' My sister and I were **frightened**, but when dad came home, all he said was, 'I'm **surprised** you chose blue. I thought you two preferred red.' Now I look back, it's **amazing** that he was so calm. He was probably **disappointed** with us, but he didn't show it. ....

👤 **Andy**   ✏ 2 reviews   ⊙ GB   A day ago

B   Complete the meanings with the words in bold in the story.

   1   When you are afraid of something, you feel ....

   2   If something is very good, it is ....

   3   When you feel unhappy because something is not interesting, you are ....

   4   When something is not as good as you hoped, you feel ....

   5   When you feel angry about something, you are ....

   6   When you are looking forward to something in the future, you are ....

   7   When a situation makes your face go red, it is ....

   8   When you are not expecting something to happen, but it does, you are ....

C   Look at the pictures. Which adjective ending do we use

   1   to talk about how a person feels: *-ed* or *-ing*?

   2   to talk about what causes the feelings: *-ed* or *-ing*?

I'm bored.

It's boring.

3 A   Complete the adjectives in the questions with *-ed* or *-ing*.

   1   What's the most amaz............ book you have read?

   2   Can you remember a time when you were really bor............?

   3   What's the most embarrass............ thing that has ever happened to you?

   4   What sorts of things do you find annoy............? Why?

   5   Have you ever been surpris............ on your birthday?

   6   When did you feel really excit............ about something?

   7   Have you ever been very frighten............ by something? What was it?

   8   Can you think of a time when you were disappoint............?

B   Work in pairs. Ask and answer the questions in Ex 3A.

C   Do you know any more adjectives for feelings? Learn and practise. Go to the Vocabulary Bank.

▶▶ page 137 **VOCABULARY BANK** adjectives for feelings

LISTENING

4 A Work in pairs. You will listen to a story about two friends, Beth and Jane, travelling in India. Look at the pictures (A–F) showing six events from their journey. What do you think happened to them?

B 🔊 **2.01** | Listen and check your ideas.

C 🔊 **2.01** | Number the events from the story (A–F) in the order they happened. Listen again and check.

A ....
B 1
C ....
D ....
E ....
F ....

D Work in pairs. Answer the questions with as much detail as possible.

1 How did Beth and Jane feel when they were by the lake?
2 What did they think the journey to Varanasi would be like? Were they correct?
3 How did they feel on the train?
4 Why was Beth worried?
5 What happened to Jane?
6 Who helped Jane? How did he help her?

5 Work in pairs. Discuss the questions.

1 Would you like to go on a long train journey? Why/Why not?
2 When was the last time you made a long journey?
3 Was the journey easy or difficult? Tell your partner about it.

GRAMMAR

narrative tenses

6 A Read the sentences from the story. Answer the questions.

They **were sleeping** on the floor.
Suddenly, the train **stopped** in the middle of nowhere.

1 What tenses are the verbs in bold in the sentences?
2 Which tense do we use for background information to the story, or to set the scene?
3 Which tense do we use for the main events in the story?

B Read the example sentences and look at the verbs in bold. Answer the questions.

Jane **woke up** on the railway track. She **had fallen** off the train.

1 Which event happened first, Jane waking up or falling off the train?
2 Which tense do we use to describe an earlier event in the past?

C Look at the audioscript on page 159 and find more examples of the three narrative tenses.

D Learn and practise. Go to the Grammar Bank.

⏩ page 108 **GRAMMAR BANK**

PRONUNCIATION

7 A 🔊 **2.02** | weak forms of *was*, *were* and *had* | Listen to the sentences. Notice how *was*, *were* and *had* are pronounced as weak forms.

1 I <u>was</u> beginning to get really worried.
2 They <u>were</u> sitting on the roof.
3 She <u>had</u> fallen off the train.

B 🔊 **2.03** | Listen and write the three sentences. Then practise saying them.

C Work in pairs. Ask and answer the questions. Focus on pronouncing *was*, *were* and *had* with weak forms.

1 What were you doing at this time yesterday?
2 Where were your parents living when you were born?
3 How many places had you lived in by the time you were fifteen years old?

SPEAKING

8 A You are going to tell your partner an anecdote about a personal memory. Choose one of the situations below, or your own idea, and plan your anecdote. Answer the questions below to help you.

Talk about a time when ...

- you visited an amazing place.
- you went to a fun event, e.g. a sports or music event, or a party.
- you saw or met someone famous or interesting.
- something unusual happened to you.
- something went wrong, e.g. you lost or forgot something.

When was it?

Where were you?

Who were you with?

What happened?

How did you feel?

What happened in the end?

B Read the Future Skills box and plan some phrases you can use in your anecdote.

FUTURE SKILLS
Communication

When you are telling an anecdote, it is important to think about the order of events. You can use phrases to help you organise the anecdote, e.g. 'The next thing I knew, ... ', 'And then ...', 'In the end, ... ', 'Finally, ... '.

Look at your plan and think about how you can use phrases to make the order of events clear in your anecdote.

C Work in groups. Tell your anecdotes. Add as much detail as you can. Ask questions about your classmates' anecdotes.

9 🔲 Bring a photo to the next class showing an important event in your life. Share it with other students and tell them why it is important to you.

WRITING

a personal story

10 A A magazine has asked its readers to send in stories of memorable experiences. Read about what happened to Rob. How was he left on the island off Okinawa?

Left on an island off Okinawa

This happened when I was travelling in Japan. ¹_____, I decided to visit one of the small islands off Okinawa on a jet ski. I'd never been on one before, so I was really excited. The weather was beautiful and we had an amazing journey to the island. ²_____ we arrived, the jet ski driver left me on the beach and we arranged a time for him to collect me. I spent an hour walking around the island and taking photos. The only problem was that ³_____ I was walking around, I got lost and couldn't remember the exact beach where we had arranged to meet. I walked up and down the different beaches, getting very hot and thirsty . ⁴_____ I found the right place, the driver had already left. I could see him in the distance, so ⁵_____ I tried shouting from the beach, but he couldn't hear me. ⁶_____ I tried to call his mobile, but there was no signal. I couldn't swim back to the larger island because I had my phone, a camera, and a fear of sharks! So I just had to wait. ⁷_____, I was saved by a passing boat. But I had spent six hours without water in the very hot sun, so it wasn't a great day!

B Read the story again and complete it with the correct linking phrases in the box.

> after that   as soon as   at first   by the time
> in the end   one day   while

C Match the linking phrases in Ex 10B with the meanings (1–7).

1 This describes two actions that were happening at the same time: ....
2 This describes something that happens at the end of the story: ....
3 This describes something that happens immediately after another action: ....
4 This refers to the action that happens next: ....
5 This refers back to an action that happened previously: ....
6 This sets the scene at the beginning of the story: ....
7 This refers to the action at the beginning: ....

D Write your story to send to the magazine. Use narrative tenses and some of the linking phrases in Ex 10B.

2B Storytelling

GRAMMAR | past simple and present perfect
VOCABULARY | story words; types of film
PRONUNCIATION | contracted *have* in the present perfect

VOCABULARY

story words

1 A Work in pairs. Read the 10-word summaries of famous films. Which films are they about? Go to page 147 to find out.

1 Boys go on long journey to throw away dangerous ring.
2 Girl travels to find sister who can stop ice age.
3 Great-grandma remembers the worst, most famous boat trip in history.
4 World's best theme park becomes world's most dangerous theme park.
5 Boy accidentally misses family holiday. Helps catch burglars at home.

B Work in pairs. Write a summary of a well-known film in 10 words. Read it to other students. Can they guess the film?

C Work in groups. Discuss the questions.

1 Which of the films in Ex 1A have you seen? Did you enjoy the story? Why/Why not?
2 What kinds of film do you enjoy most?
3 Do you like seeing films of books you have read? Why/Why not? Give examples.
4 What do you think makes a good story?

2 A 🔊 **2.04** | Listen to three people talking about what makes a good story. What ideas do they mention?

B 🔊 **2.04** | Complete the sentences the people said with the words in the box. Listen again and check.

> characters   ending   fairytales   hero
> performances   plot   storyteller   TV shows

1 I think having an exciting _____ is important.
2 You need a _____ that you like.
3 I like a happy _____, too.
4 My grandmother told me _____.
5 It's the same with _____ and films.
6 Everything depends on the _____.
7 I love the actors' _____.
8 They bring the _____ to life.

C Match the words in Ex 2B with the meanings (a–h).

a the main person in a story hero
b the people in a story
c when people act or sing in front of people
d the way a story finishes
e a person who tells the story
f programmes which are shown on television
g traditional stories for children
h the main events in a story

D Work in groups. Think of a book, film or TV show that you like. Tell other students why you like it. Use some of the words from Ex 2B.

READING

3 A Read the article. What is the main topic?

1 ways in which storytelling has changed over time
2 differences in the way different cultures tell stories
3 how heroes are different in traditional and modern stories

B Read the article again. Tick the ideas that are mentioned.

1 Storytelling is a very old art.
2 We can learn a lot from stories.
3 Schools don't usually teach fairytales.
4 People who play video games help create the story.
5 Technology has changed the way we tell stories.
6 Writers spend a lot of time writing TV shows.
7 Some stories remain popular for a long time.

C Work in groups and discuss the questions.

1 Do you agree that 'good stories last forever'? Can you think of any old stories that have lasted a long time?
2 What types of storytelling do you like best, and why? Which do you like least? Talk about the ideas in the box, or your own ideas.

> books   films   theatre performances
> TV shows   video games

D Find two types of film in the final paragraph of the article. What other types of film do you know?

E Learn and practise. Go to the Vocabulary Bank.

>> page 137 **VOCABULARY BANK**
types of film

GRAMMAR

past simple and present perfect

4 A Read the extracts from the article. Which verbs in bold are in the past simple and which are in the present perfect?

1 In December 2019, researchers in Indonesia **found** a cave with paintings.
2 People in the Middle East **have told** the story of Little Red Riding Hood for a thousand years.
3 New technologies **have brought** exciting new ways to tell stories.

B Which verb tense (present perfect or past simple) do we use to describe:

1 an event that started and finished at a specific time in the past? (We know exactly when it happened.)
2 something that started in the past and continues, or is still important, now?

C Learn and practise. Go to the Grammar Bank.

>> page 109 **GRAMMAR BANK**

PRONUNCIATION

5 A 🔊 2.05 | contracted *have* in the present perfect | Listen to four sentences with the present perfect. In which of the sentences is *have* contracted?

B Complete the sentences with your own ideas. Then read them aloud to a partner. Use contracted forms of *have* where appropriate.

I have never …   Have you ever … ?
What have you … today?   I have not seen …

SPEAKING

6 Move around the classroom. Ask your classmates questions and find a name to add to each activity in the table. Ask more questions and add extra information to the table.

A: Have you ever watched a really frightening horror film?
B: Yes, I have.
A: What did you think of it? Where did you see it? When did you … ?

Find someone who …	name	extra information
has watched a really frightening horror film.		
has been to the cinema recently.		
has seen every episode of a TV show.		
has read more than fifty books.		
has played a lot of different video games.		
has read or seen a play by William Shakespeare.		
has acted in a film, TV show or play.		
has met a famous writer, actor or YouTuber.		

The lives of stories: from cave paintings to video games

In December 2019, researchers in Indonesia found a cave with paintings on its walls. The paintings were 40,000 years old. The researchers realised that this was the earliest story ever told through art.

Storytelling is as old as language. Stories are everywhere and in every culture. India, China and Mexico all have their own version of the fairytale *Cinderella*. People in the Middle East have told the story of Little Red Riding Hood for a thousand years. Australian First Nation people tell stories about how the first people sang the world into existence.

Good stories last forever because they entertain us and teach us important life lessons. They show that there are good and bad people, dangers, problems and solutions. Stories often help us to see ourselves more clearly and to see how we can become better people.

Stories have always been important, but the ways we tell them have changed through time. Before the development of writing, people told their stories aloud. Then writing and books came along and changed all that. Now, with virtual reality and gaming technology, stories are more interactive than before. The players help to create the story. They choose names for their heroes, and decide where characters go, what they do and how they interact with other characters.

Video games and online media are a way for us to become storytellers. Video games are the world's most popular form of entertainment, bigger than films or TV shows, and their popularity grows every year. It seems that we all enjoy taking control and getting involved in stories, rather than just reading or watching them.

Humans are the storytelling animal. The things we love about stories don't change – an exciting plot, interesting characters, a great hero, humour in comedies, fear in horror films and maybe a happy ending. New technologies have brought exciting new ways to tell stories, and no doubt storytelling will continue to change and develop in the future.

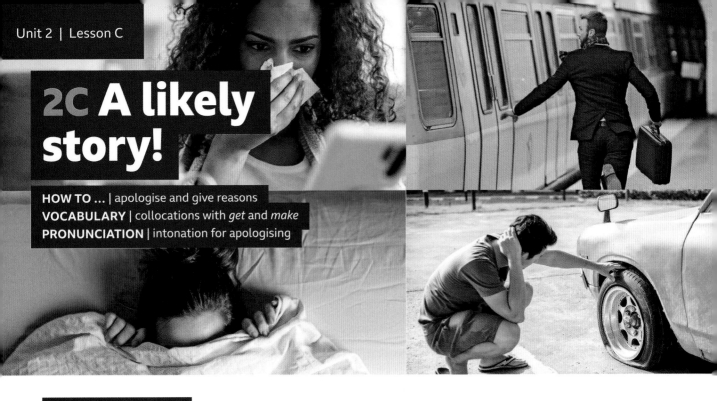

2C A likely story!

HOW TO ... | apologise and give reasons
VOCABULARY | collocations with *get* and *make*
PRONUNCIATION | intonation for apologising

VOCABULARY

collocations with *get* and *make*

1 A Work in pairs. Read the definition below. Which of the photos show good reasons for being late? Which show bad excuses?

> **excuse** (n) a reason given or invented to explain why you did something wrong

B Read these reasons people often give for being late or missing something. Which do you think are the most common? Which have you heard or used?

Sorry I'm late ...

> I got lost!

> I got off at the wrong bus stop!

> I had to make an urgent call.

> My little sister made a mess and I had to clean it up.

Sorry I missed the party ...

> I got the wrong day!

> I got held up at work.

> I made a mistake with the address.

> My partner made other plans and I didn't know until it was too late.

2 A Look again at the reasons in Ex 1B. Find collocations with *get* and *make*. Write the collocations next to their meanings.

get

1 to leave a bus or train ....
2 to not know where you are ....
3 to be delayed ....
4 to understand something wrongly ....

make

5 to do something wrong ....
6 to phone someone ....
7 to agree to do something at a certain time ....
8 to make something dirty or untidy ....

B Complete the text with the correct form of *get* or *make*.

That's a bad excuse!

Are you planning an excuse for not going to work? Then try to make it a good one. Here are some of the worst excuses we've ever heard.

'My dog's unwell.' Don't [1]........... the mistake of saying your pet is ill when everyone knows you don't have one.

'I fell asleep, so I didn't [2]........... off the bus.' No good when your boss knows that you drive to work.

'I thought it was Saturday today.' So, you [3]........... the wrong day? Do you want your colleagues to think you don't know what day it is?

'I fell over and broke my toe.' This is OK, but you need to [4]........... a plan to get back to work. You'll have to pretend you can't walk properly for a few weeks!

'First I [5]........... held up in a traffic jam, so I drove a different way, but then I [6]........... lost.' You've worked at the same place for five years, but can't find your way to work?

And finally, 'I spilled my breakfast and it [7]........... a mess on my shirt, and I don't have a clean one.' Do you want our advice? If you can't think of a good excuse, don't even [8]........... the call to the office!

C Work in pairs. Discuss the questions.

1 When was the last time you got lost?
2 Who usually makes a mess where you live?
3 When was the last time you got held up at work or somewhere else? What happened?
4 What plans have you made for the next few days?
5 Have you ever taken a train or bus and got off at the wrong place?
6 What was the last call you made?

How to ...
apologise and give reasons

3 A 🔊 **2.06 | Listen to six conversations. Match the conversations (1–6) with the problems (a–f).**

a a problem with a train
b a mistake with a class schedule
c a difficulty with technology 1
d a late flight
e a mistake with a package
f forgetting to charge a phone

B 🔊 **2.06 | Listen again. Complete the sentences from the conversations (1–6).**

1 Sorry to _____ you waiting!
2 I got the time wrong. Sorry _____ that.
3 The taxi driver _____ lost! I'll be there as soon as _____ .
4 It was our _____ . We sent the wrong one. There was a problem with the boxes – they look the same. I _____ .
5 Never _____ . You're here now.
6 My train got _____ .

C Complete the table with the phrases in the box.

> I got lost.   I'll call you back.
> It was our fault.   Never mind.
> Sorry about that.

saying sorry	Sorry I'm late./Sorry to keep you waiting. I apologise. 1 _____
giving a reason	There was a ... delay/problem with ... My train/flight was delayed/cancelled. I got the date/day/time/address wrong. The traffic was terrible. 2 _____
accepting responsibility	I made a mistake. 3 _____
taking action	I'll be there as soon as possible. 4 _____
responding and reassuring	Don't worry. No problem. It's/That's fine. 5 _____

D Learn and practise. Go to the Grammar Bank.

➡ page 110 **GRAMMAR BANK**

PRONUNCIATION

4 A 🔊 **2.07 | intonation for apologising | Listen to four apologies. Choose the correct answer to complete the sentence.**

When someone apologises, their voice _____
1 starts high and gets lower.
2 starts low and gets higher.

B 🔊 **2.07 | Practise saying the sentences in pairs. Then listen again to check your intonation.**

1 Sorry! I made a mistake.
2 I apologise. It was my fault.
3 Sorry I'm late. I got the time wrong.
4 I'm really sorry. There was a problem with my ticket.

5 A Choose the correct words to complete the conversations.

1 A: Sorry to keep you waiting. My flight was delayed.
   B: **That's OK. / I made a mistake.**
2 A: Sorry, this line's really bad. **Never mind. / I'll call you back.**
   B: No problem.
3 A: I'm really sorry! **I got lost / There was a problem** with my wifi.
   B: It's fine. Are you ready to start now?
4 A: I apologise. **I made a mistake / That's OK** with the address.
   B: That's fine.
5 A: Sorry! **I got / I apologise** the time wrong.
   B: Don't worry. I've just arrived, too.

B 🔊 **2.08 | Listen and check your answers.**

C Work in pairs. Practise the conversations in Ex 5A, but think of a different reason or excuse. Try to use a collocation with _get_ or _make_.

1 Sorry to keep you waiting. I got held up at college!

SPEAKING

6 Roleplay two situations. Student A: Read the situations below. Student B: Read the situations on page 148.

Student A
1 You missed a work meeting.
• Apologise.
• Accept responsibility and give a reason.
• Explain how you will take action.

2 You made a plan to have dinner with a friend at a restaurant. The friend is very late.
• Accept your friend's apology.
• Check they are OK.
• Ask if they still want to eat.

> **MEDIATION SKILL**
> **asking questions to deal with disagreements**
> solve a problem between work colleagues
>
> ➡ page 151 **MEDIATION BANK**

2D BBC Documentary
The story of a place

GRAMMAR | prepositions of time
SPEAKING | the story of a place
WRITING | a review of a place

PREVIEW

1 A Work in pairs. Look at the photos and discuss the questions.

1 Where do you think this is?

2 What do you think is special about this place?

B Read the programme information and answer the questions.

1 What is the Mediterranean well known for?

2 What is Simon Reeve trying to show us with the programme?

3 What town does he visit?

Mediterranean with Simon Reeve

Simon Reeves goes on an extraordinary journey around the Mediterranean, an area that attracts about a third of the world's tourism with its beautiful beaches and fascinating historical sights. Simon travels around the Mediterranean trying to uncover the everyday reality and the history behind what tourists see. In this programme Simon visits the town of Matera, in southern Italy, where he learns about the history of its famous caves.

VIEW

2 A ▶ Watch the BBC video clip. Number the topics in the order they are mentioned.

a modern tourism

b a celebration

c Matera in the past

B ▶ Complete the summary of the video with one or two words in each gap. Then watch again to check.

People lived in the caves in Matera until the ¹ _____ . The government moved people out of the caves and into ² _____ . Now, Matera is turning the caves into holiday homes and ³ _____ . Before, families shared the caves with ⁴ _____ . Many towns and villages in southern Italy have been depopulated as young people move away, but a local ⁵ _____ is a sign that Matera has a ⁶ _____ .

C Work in pairs. Discuss the questions.

1 Do you think the government did a good or bad thing by moving people out of the caves? Why?

2 Would you enjoy visiting Matera and staying in one of the caves? Why/Why not?

GRAMMAR

prepositions of time

3 A Complete the sentences about Matera using the prepositions *before*, *until* and *during*.

1 The old way of life continued in Matera _____ the Italian government moved people out of the caves.

2 _____ they moved into modern homes, families shared the caves with their animals.

3 The changes happened _____ the 1950s.

B Learn and practise. Go to the Grammar Bank.

▶▶ page 111 **GRAMMAR BANK**

SPEAKING

the story of a place

4 A Work in pairs. Discuss the questions. Do you know any places which have changed a lot, or are changing a lot at the moment? What is changing?

B You will hear someone talking about Barcelona in the past and present. What do you think he will say about the topics in the box?

> Olympic Games   football stadium   architecture
> historical centre   art/artists   food market
> tourists   live music events   accommodation

C 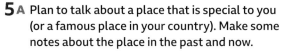 **2.09** | Listen and check your ideas.

D **2.09** | Listen again and tick the phrases that you hear.

KEY PHRASES

When I first visited … , it was …

… is well known/famous for its …

The city has changed a lot. Before … it was …

It has a wonderful atmosphere/a fantastic history/ great food/amazing art galleries …

The city has a lot to offer.

You can explore/enjoy/visit …

Nowadays, …

I really recommend it.

5 A Plan to talk about a place that is special to you (or a famous place in your country). Make some notes about the place in the past and now.

B Work in groups. Take turns to tell the story of your place. Use the Key phrases to help. Other students: listen and ask questions to learn more.

WRITING

a review of a place

6 A Read the review. How has Cornwall changed, according to the writer?

Cornwall: Then and now

I first went to Cornwall on a family holiday when I was a child. At that time, the villages were very small and the beaches were usually empty. Historically, the area was known for its fishing. I remember we used to spend all day on the beach and then walk into town in the evening to eat fish and chips. The towns and villages were quiet and only a few people were wandering around. Nowadays, Cornwall is one of the most popular tourist destinations in the UK, and it's becoming more popular every year. In the past, there were only a few campsites and one or two cheap hotels. Nowadays, the campsites are full and you have to book months in advance and the hotels are more expensive. Cornwall is still one of the most beautiful places to visit. It's well known for its beaches and surfing, and there are lots of places you can explore. I really recommend it for families or for anybody who enjoys exploring beautiful coastlines.

B Write a review of a place that you know. Write about:

- when you first went there.
- what it was like then.
- how it has changed.
- what it is like now.
- who you would recommend it for and why.

GRAMMAR

narrative tenses

1 Complete the story with the correct form of the verbs in brackets.

Tim ¹_____ (sit) at home when his friend, Angela, ²_____ (send) him a message. She ³_____ (wait) for him at a restaurant. Tim ⁴_____ (forget) they were planning to have dinner. He apologised and ⁵_____ (ask) Angela to wait. He quickly ⁶_____ (leave) the house and got on his bicycle. He ⁷_____ (cycle) about 1 km and then realised that he ⁸_____ (leave) his wallet at home. He went back to get it. He ⁹_____ (start) cycling again. It ¹⁰_____ (rain) and he couldn't see very well. He ¹¹_____ (not see) a red light. A car was driving towards him and he nearly ¹²_____ (fall) off his bike. A police officer stopped Tim and fined him for dangerous cycling. By the time Tim arrived at the restaurant, Angela ¹³_____ (eat) her meal and left!

past simple and present perfect

2 A Write sentences to say which things you have and haven't done. Use *I've …* , *I haven't …* and *I've never …* .

climb a mountain   go on a long journey
go skiing/surfing   go to university   play in a band
ride a horse   run a marathon   write a song/poem

I've never climbed a mountain.

B Choose three situations from Ex 2A. Tell your partner what happened.

prepositions of time

3 Correct one or two mistakes in each sentence.
1 We can't leave during six o'clock.
2 She has worked very hard at these last two months.
3 She'll meet us in eight o'clock at Saturday morning.
4 Marco Polo travelled to China on the 1200s.
5 Sam stayed with us on March and September.

VOCABULARY

4 A How would you feel in the situations (1–6)? Choose the best adjective(s) from the box for each situation.

amazed   annoyed   bored   calm   disappointed
embarrassed   excited   exhausted   frightened
nervous   proud   relaxed   surprised   worried

1 Your flight is delayed. **annoyed, bored**
2 You send a private email to all your colleagues.
3 A friend sends you some flowers unexpectedly.
4 You fail your exams.
5 You are enjoying a care-free holiday by the sea.
6 You have just finished running a marathon.

B Write some situations for the other adjectives in the box in Ex 4A.

amazed: A beautiful sunset when the whole sky goes red.

5 Complete the sentences by choosing from the words in brackets.

1 I'm going to the theatre tonight to see a really funny _____ . The _____ starts at 7.30.
(**comedy / ending / horror film / performance**)

2 If I'm really enjoying a book, especially if it's a _____ and I want to know what happens, I sometimes read the _____ before I've read the middle of the story.
(**adventure film / mystery / plot / ending**)

3 It's a great _____ with lots of exciting car chases, but the _____ is a bit boring, unfortunately.
(**western / action film / plot / fairytale**)

4 There aren't any TV _____ I enjoy watching at the moment. I'd like to watch an interesting _____ which teaches me about history, or something.
(**shows / animation / documentary / horror film**)

5 The book has got some wonderful _____ in it. I really like the _____ – he's great!
(**biopic / characters / fairytales / hero**)

6 I love watching _____ which tell us about a famous person's life. I can't watch _____ though. They terrify me and then I can't sleep!
(**biopics / animations / comedy / horror films**)

6 A Choose the correct option (A–C) to complete the text.

How to tell better stories

¹_____ a story about something that happened to you and found that by the end of the story, nobody ²_____ to you? They ³_____ their phones instead. Me, too. Here are a few things that I ⁴_____ to help me become a better ⁵_____ .

⁶_____ you start telling your story, you need to get the listener's interest. Use strong adjectives to introduce the story. Try things like, 'The most ⁷_____ thing just happened to me!'

Tell your story as if you were the ⁸_____ in a film. Make it dramatic. Use eye contact and hand gestures. Say things like, 'I was ⁹_____ of what was happening to me.'

Ask the listener if they can guess the ¹⁰_____ of the story. For example: 'I met Adam Sandler in the gym the other day. Guess what he said to me?'

1 A Did you tell	B Were you telling	C Have you ever told
2 A listens	B listened	C was listening
3 A were checking	B checked	C check
4 A have learnt	B had learnt	C was learning
5 A hero	B character	C storyteller
6 A Until	B During	C Before
7 A amazing	B amazed	C amazes
8 A plot	B hero	C performance
9 A terrifying	B terrified	C terrify
10 A heroes	B characters	C ending

B 🔊 **R2.01 | Listen and check your answers.**

questions 3

BBC

VLOGS

Q: What things are you curious about and why?

1 ▶ Watch the video. Note down the topics the people mention.

2 Which of the topics mentioned are you curious about? What other topics are you curious about?

GSE LEARNING OBJECTIVES

3A LISTENING | Understand a discussion about a quiz: knowledge; verbs and nouns

Talk about things that are important to you: question forms

Pronunciation: stressed words in questions

Write an email asking for information; use phrases for emails

3B READING | Read an article about making decisions: decisions

Talk about future plans and intentions: present continuous, *going to*, *might* and *will*

Pronunciation: weak forms of *are you* and *going to*

3C HOW TO … | make polite inquiries: facilities; places in a city

Pronunciation: polite intonation

3D BBC STREET INTERVIEWS | Understand people talking about what is important in their life

Talk about what is important to you: phrasal verbs

Write an online forum comment

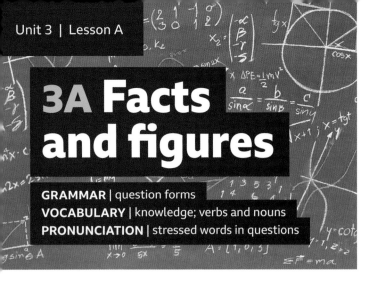

3A Facts and figures

GRAMMAR | question forms
VOCABULARY | knowledge; verbs and nouns
PRONUNCIATION | stressed words in questions

VOCABULARY

knowledge

1 Work in groups. Discuss the questions.

  1 Do you enjoy watching quiz shows? Are they popular in your country?

  2 What do you think you know a lot about? What don't you know much about?

2 A Read what two people say about things they know about. Which person is more like you? Why?

Marta: My **general knowledge** is fine, although I don't know much about sport! I read all the time and I have a good **memory**, so I remember what I've read about. At work, I need to understand **data** and I'm quite good with numbers. I love to do quizzes and **solve** problems, too. I think my **mind** works that way.

Jack: I'm studying for exams at the moment, so I have to learn a lot of facts. I **note down** new information, and I use my notes to **revise** for exams. With multiple-**choice** exams, I try to choose the best **option**, but if I don't know the answer, I just **guess**! Even if I get a good **score**, I forget everything immediately afterwards! And I'm terrible at quizzes!

B Match the words and phrases in bold in Ex 2A with the meanings (1–10).

  1 the part of you that thinks and understands things
    mind

  2 to write something to help you remember it

  3 to prepare for a test by studying books and notes

  4 your ability to remember things and not forget them

  5 a thing you can choose

  6 to find the correct answer to a problem

  7 to answer a question without knowing if you are right

  8 information on many different subjects

  9 the number of points you get during a game or test

  10 information, especially numbers or facts

C Choose six words and phrases in bold in Ex 2A. Write sentences about yourself. Compare with a partner.

  I always note down new English words.

D Learn and practise. Go to the Vocabulary Bank.

▶❙ page 138 **VOCABULARY BANK** verbs and nouns

LISTENING

3 A Work in pairs. Read the general knowledge quiz and choose the correct answers.

Quick quiz

1 Can fish live out of water?
(a) Yes. Some fish can breathe air and move on land.
(b) No. Out of water, all fish die after a few minutes.

2 Why do we have eyebrows?
(a) To warm our skin so our eyes don't freeze in winter.
(b) To protect our eyes, e.g. from dirt.

3 Why do we use the colour red in 'stop' signs?
(a) Because in the past only kings wore red clothes and other people stopped when the king was in the street.
(b) Because red means 'danger' and we can see it from far away.

4 Who wrote the Sherlock Holmes stories?
(a) Sir Arthur Conan Doyle (b) Roald Dahl

5 How many different materials does a smartphone contain?
(a) About 70, including the precious metals gold and silver.
(b) Over 150, most of them in tiny amounts.

6 Where was paper first invented?
(a) China (b) France

7 What did Tim Berners-Lee invent?
(a) Virtual reality (b) The World Wide Web

B 🔊 **3.01** | Listen to two friends discussing the quiz. Listen for the quiz answers.

C 🔊 **3.01** | Are the statements True (T) or False (F)? Listen again and check.

  1 The man thinks he will do well in the quiz.

  2 The woman gives extra information about fish that live out of water.

  3 The woman gives an example of how eyebrows protect our eyes.

  4 The man has never read a Sherlock Holmes book.

  5 The woman mentions four of the materials in smartphones.

  6 The man's final score is five out of seven.

D 🔊 **3.02** | Choose the correct words to complete the phrases. Listen and check. Why do the speakers use these phrases?

  1 By the **way / time**, there are about fifty types of …

  2 Moving **off / on** to the next one, …

  3 That **reminds / remembers** me: I think …

  4 This is completely **the topic / off-topic**, but …

GRAMMAR

question forms

4 A Read the examples (a–d) below and answer the questions (1–3).

    a What do you know a lot about?
    b Who wrote the Sherlock Holmes books?
    c Why do we have eyebrows?
    d What did Tim Berners-Lee invent?

    1 Which question ends in a preposition?
    2 Which three questions use an auxiliary verb? Which auxiliary verb is in the past?
    3 Which question does not use an auxiliary verb?

B Work with a partner. Look at the questions and answers in bold. Discuss the questions (1–3).

    A: **Who invented** the World Wide Web?
    B: **Tim Berners-Lee** invented the World Wide Web.

    A: **What did** Tim Berners-Lee **invent**?
    B: Tim Berners-Lee invented **the World Wide Web**.

    1 Which question asks about the subject of the sentence?
    2 Which asks about the object?
    3 Which one uses an auxiliary verb?

C Learn and practise. Go to the Grammar Bank.

 page 112 **GRAMMAR BANK**

PRONUNCIATION

5 A 🔊 **3.03** | **stressed words in questions** | Listen to the questions. Notice how we stress the important words (question words, main verbs, nouns and adjectives).

    1 Do you have a <u>good memory</u> for <u>names</u>?
    2 Did you <u>always revise</u> for <u>tests</u> at <u>school</u>?
    3 <u>Where</u> do you <u>study</u>?
    4 <u>What</u> do you <u>know</u> about <u>India</u>?

B Work in pairs. Underline the stressed words in the questions, then ask and answer them. Remember to stress the important words.

    1 When did people first land on the Moon?
    2 Who played the Black Panther in the 2018 film?
    3 Where is the Pink Palace?
    4 What object related to weather did Benjamin Franklin invent?

C 🔊 **3.04** | Listen and check. Did you get the answers right?

6 A Work in pairs. You are going to test your partner's general knowledge. Student A: Write questions from the prompts on page 148. Student B: Write questions from the prompts on page 146.

B Test your partner! The answers are on page 147 (A) and 149 (B). Who has the best general knowledge?

SPEAKING

7 A You are going to create a personal quiz. Write the name of one person, one object, one date and one place that is important to you.

My personal quiz

Person	
Object	
Date	
Place	

B You are going to find out information about your partner's answers. Read the Future Skills box and answer the question.

> ### FUTURE SKILLS
> #### Communication
> Listening carefully is an important part of communication. Asking follow-up questions is a good way to show that you are listening. If someone tells you, 'I met my partner in 2018,' what follow-up questions can you ask?

C Look at your partner's information. Prepare some questions to ask about each person or thing to find out why they are important to your partner.

D Ask your questions from Ex 7C. Listen to the answers and ask follow-up questions. Find out as much information as you can. You have two minutes.

When did you go to … ? How old is … ?
What did you do … ? Is this your … ?

E Tell the class something interesting about your partner.

WRITING

an email asking for information

8 A Work in pairs. Think of three situations where you write to someone or message them to ask for information.

B Look at these situations. Which ones require formal writing? Think of one question to ask in each situation.

> apply for a job   ask a friend where you're meeting
> ask a neighbour to feed your cat
> join a language course   rent a holiday home

9 A Read the two emails. What information do the writers want?

A

Dear Sir/Madam,

I am writing to express my interest in applying for a six-month internship at Leavis and Dunn. Before I formally apply, I would like to ask some questions.

In the advertisement, there is no mention of accommodation. Does Leavis and Dunn provide help with finding housing? If so, would this be shared housing? I would also like to know the type of work involved in the internship. Would I be working in the office or with clients?

Thank you for your attention and I hope to hear from you soon.

Yours faithfully,

Andrea Boesman

B

To: egavaskar1998@gmail.com
Subject: French class

Hi Liz,

Nice to chat the other day!

Can you send me some info about that French class you mentioned? What's the cost? Are the lessons in the teacher's home or in a public place (café, library, etc.)? Also, what time's the class? I'm working till 6 p.m. so need evening classes.

Thanks! Hope to see you soon.

Cat

B Work in pairs. Answer the questions.

1 Which email uses short sentences, and which uses longer ones?

2 Which one uses full forms of verbs (*I am*) and which uses contractions (*I'm*)?

3 Which one uses short forms of words, e.g. *info* (*information*)?

4 Which one uses full sentences, and which uses sentences with some words missing, (e.g. *Hope to …* instead of *I hope to …*)?

5 Which one uses polite phrases, and which uses informal ones?

6 Which one sounds more like spoken English?

7 Which email is formal and which is informal?

C Complete the table with phrases from the emails.

	formal	informal
greeting	1	Hi/Hello
request for information	Could you tell me … ? I 2 .... know …	Can you send me/ tell me … ?
thanking	Thank you for 3	Thanks!
sign off	4	All the best/Love/ See you soon.

10 Read the situations below. Choose one and write your email. Think about who you are writing to, and think about whether your email should be formal or informal.

> **Situation 1**
>
> You would like to have private English lessons. A friend gives you the email address of her Australian friend, who sometimes teaches English.
>
> Information you need:
> - teacher – available?
> - cost per hour?
> - materials?
> - at my house?

> **Situation 2**
>
> You are going to work in a different country for six weeks. You will contact your employer there.
>
> Information you need:
> - working hours?
> - dress code (What clothes you should wear)?
> - office for you?
> - anything else you should know?

3B Decisions

GRAMMAR | future plans and intentions
VOCABULARY | decisions
PRONUNCIATION | weak forms of *are you* and *going to*

READING

1 Work in pairs. Discuss the questions.

1 Are you good or bad at making decisions? What kinds of decisions do you find easy and difficult?

2 When you have an important decision to make, who do you discuss it with? Why?

When I have an important decision to make, I usually discuss it with my partner …

2 A You are going to read an article about making decisions. Read the title and the paragraph headings. What is the main message of the article?

a Life is full of decisions – either you are good at making them or you are not.

b There are different ways to arrive at the best decision.

c It is always a good idea to sleep before you make a big decision.

B Read the article. Then work in pairs and answer the questions.

1 What two types of decision does the article talk about?

2 Why is it important to reduce the number of decisions you make in a day?

3 What did Barack Obama do to help him make important decisions?

4 What is the problem with always choosing the easy option?

5 Is it always a good idea to consider the advantages and disadvantages? Why/Why not?

6 How does sleep help you to make a decision?

C Work in groups. Which ideas in the text do you agree with? Which ones seem like bad ideas? Why?

The art of making decisions

Our lives are full of **decisions.** There are small, day-to-day decisions like what clothes to wear or what to have for dinner, and bigger life-changing decisions that will affect our future, like where you **choose** to live, or what career you decide to have. If you find it hard to **make up your mind**, there are a few things that can help.

Focus on the big issues

Some scientists studying the brain have seen that all decisions – big or small – use the same amount of energy. We get tired when we make decisions all day and this makes it difficult to **focus on** the important choices we need to make, at home or at work. When you take away the smaller decisions, you allow your brain to focus on the bigger problems.

When Barack Obama was U.S. president, he chose to remove one decision from his daily life: what to wear. He always wore a blue or a grey suit with a white shirt. This 'uniform' allowed him to focus his energy on the more important decisions he needed to make. When you have a really important decision to make, don't waste energy on smaller decisions that aren't going to make a difference to your life.

Don't fear the consequences

When trying to reach a decision, we often **select** the easiest option, rather than the one which might be difficult or involve more effort. When you make an important choice, think of the option that will help you to develop as a person, rather than choosing the easy option and missing an opportunity.

Follow your gut instincts

For some decisions, you might **consider** all the **advantages and disadvantages**, but at other times a quick decision is best. Our brain makes quick judgements about people and situations all the time. We decide on a person's character within the first 100 milliseconds of seeing their face for the first time. After that, we don't usually change our mind. It's the same for other decisions, too. Sometimes it is more difficult to make a decision if you think too much, and following your gut instinct is the better **choice**.

Sleep on it

Sometimes it **makes sense** to stop thinking about the decision and wait for a while. In fact, if you're making a complex decision that requires you to consider different factors, research shows that allowing the brain to work on the problem while you're asleep often helps you decide on the best course of action.

VOCABULARY

decisions

3 A Look at the words and phrases from the article in the box below. Find:

1 two that mean to think about something.
2 three that mean *to decide*.
3 two that mean something you decide on.
4 one that means *to seem like a good idea*.
5 one that refers to the good and bad points something has.

> advantages and disadvantages   choice
> choose   consider   decisions   focus on
> make sense   make up your mind   select

B Choose the correct words to complete the comments on the article.

If I've got a ¹**decision / choose** to make, I list the ²**advantages and disadvantages / select** – it helps me to make the right ³**focus / choice**.

Anya Poland

In my job, people need answers quickly, so it's important to ⁴**select / make up your mind**. If I need to ⁵**choose / choice** between two options, I try to ⁶**focus / select** the one that will benefit most people.

Tom USA

When I have a big decision to make, I try not to think about it too much. I wait a few days, ⁷**choose / consider** all the options, and then do what I think ⁸**makes sense / makes up my mind**.

Jasmine UK

C Write your own comment like the ones in Ex 3B. Describe how you make decisions. Use at least three of the words and phrases in Ex 3A. Then compare with other students.

D Read the Future Skills box and do the activity.

FUTURE SKILLS

Leadership

When you make a decision in a group or team, it is important to listen to different ideas and opinions before you decide what to do.

Talk to a partner about a time when you listened to other people before you made a decision. How did their ideas and opinions help you?

GRAMMAR

future plans and intentions

4 A 🔊 **3.05** | Listen to two conversations about making decisions. What decision does each person need to make?

B 🔊 **3.05** | Listen again. Match the extracts (1–4) to the conversations.

1 I might get a job in a local restaurant.
2 Next week we're looking at a house in a village.
3 We'll see if we can find somewhere nice, then we'll make our decision.
4 They're going to travel around South America.

C Match the tenses and verb forms (a–d) with the examples in Ex 4B (1–4).

a present continuous to talk about a future arrangement
b *going to* for future plans
c *will* for a decision made at the time of speaking
d *might* for a plan which you are not sure about

D Learn and practise. Go to the Grammar Bank.

▶▶ page 113 **GRAMMAR BANK**

PRONUNCIATION

5 A 🔊 **3.06** | **weak forms of *are you* and *going to*** | Listen to the questions. Notice the weak sound /ə/ in *are you* /əjə/ and *going to* /gənə/.

1 What **are you** planning to do next year?
2 What are you **going to** do this summer?

B Make questions from the prompts.

1 What / doing / later?
2 What / cooking / dinner tonight?
3 Are / going / have / holiday soon?
4 What / going / do / after this lesson?
5 What / planning / do / next year?

C 🔊 **3.07** | Listen and check.

D Work in pairs. Ask and answer the questions in Ex 5B. Remember to use weak forms of *are you* and *going to*.

SPEAKING

talk about future plans and intentions

6A Prepare to talk for one minute about one or two of the topics below. Think about what you want to say and make notes.

Plans for this evening: What? Who? Where? Food? Entertainment?

Plans for the weekend: Sports? Activities? Social plans? Family?

Plans for your next holiday: Where? When? Why? How / travel? Places / visit?

Plans for the rest of the year: Career? Studies? Courses? Work? Marriage?

B Talk to other students about your plans and intentions. Ask questions to find out more information.

3C Can I ask you ... ?

HOW TO ... | make polite inquiries
VOCABULARY | facilities; places in a city
PRONUNCIATION | polite intonation

VOCABULARY

facilities

1 Work in pairs. Discuss the questions.

   1 Have you ever worked or studied abroad? Would you like to? Why/Why not?
   2 Where did you go, or where would you choose to go? Why?

2 A Read the webpage about Malta. Complete it with the words in the box.

> campus   employment office   gym
> halls of residence   language schools   library
> sports centre   study areas   theatres

B Read the webpage again. Are the statements True (T) or False (F)?

   1 Most people in Malta speak English.
   2 If you live in the EU, you don't need a visa.
   3 There is only one university on the island.
   4 It's very expensive to study in Malta.
   5 The weather is not very good.

C Work in pairs. What are the advantages of working or studying in Malta? Make a list.

D Would you consider a work or study trip to Malta? Why/Why not?

E Work in pairs. Make a list of other useful places and facilities in a town or city. Check your ideas in the Vocabulary Bank.

   bank, post office ...

   ▶ page 138 **VOCABULARY BANK** places in a city

Have you considered work and study abroad in Malta?

It can be a great way to improve your skills and experience, and perhaps even study the language while you're there. We answer your top five questions.

1 Can I register for an English course?
Ninety percent of the population of Malta speak English, so this a wonderful study or work abroad option for students who want to improve their English. You can register for a course at one of the many [1]_____ on the island.

2 What jobs can I do and do I need a work visa?
EU citizens can work and study in Malta, but people coming from outside the EU need to apply for a work permit from the [2]_____ . Many people find jobs in finance or tourism.

3 Is there a university?
There are several private universities in Malta. The University of Malta is the only public university, and is one of the oldest and most respected universities in the world. The university [3]_____ offers all the facilities you need. Lecture [4]_____ are located in beautiful, historical buildings. There are outside [5]_____ where students can study together, as well as the main [6]_____ , which has a huge selection of books.

4 How much does the accommodation cost?
You can stay in university [7]_____ or with home-stay families, where you will learn about Maltese culture. Living in Malta is not too expensive. In fact, Malta is one of the cheapest places to study in Europe.

5 What about leisure activities?
Malta is a fantastic place to practise water sports, with beautiful beaches and warm weather for much of the year. If you are studying at the University of Malta, the campus also has a [8]_____ with football pitches and a swimming pool, or you can join the university [9]_____ .

How to ...
make polite inquiries

3 A 🔊 **3.08 |** Listen to three conversations in which people make inquiries about working or studying in Malta. What information do they need? Write notes, then compare with a partner.

Conversation 1 _____

Conversation 2 _____

Conversation 3 _____

B 🔊 **3.08 |** Listen again. Are the statements True (T) or False (F)? Correct the false sentences.

Conversation 1

1 The caller is planning to work in Malta but not to study.

2 He doesn't need a work visa.

Conversation 2

3 You can walk from the accommodation to the campus in fifteen minutes.

4 There's a bus if you don't want to walk.

Conversation 3

5 Students at the university can use the swimming pool for free.

6 The gym is closed in the mornings.

4 A 🔊 **3.09 |** Complete the phrases to make inquiries. Then listen to check.

1 Could you _____ me which country you're planning to work in?

2 Can I _____ if you're going to register for an English course?

3 Can you _____ me where the university halls of residence are?

4 Do you _____ if there's a bus?

5 I'd _____ to know if the facilities are free.

6 Do you _____ what time the gym opens in the morning?

B The questions in Ex 4A are indirect questions. What do you notice about the word order? When do you think we use indirect questions?

C Choose the correct indirect question forms (a or b).

1 a Could you tell me where is the sports centre?
  b Could you tell me where the sports centre is?

2 a Do you know what time the library opens?
  b Do you know what time does the library open?

3 a I'd like to know if the accommodation is near the beach.
  b I'd like to know if is the accommodation near the beach.

4 a Can you tell me do I need a visa?
  b Can you tell me if I need a visa?

D Learn and practise. Go to the Grammar Bank.

▶▶ page 114 **GRAMMAR BANK**

E Rewrite the inquiries using indirect questions, to make them more polite. Use the prompts in brackets.

1 Where is the swimming pool? (Can / tell ... ?)
  Can you tell me where the swimming pool is?

2 What time does the accommodation office close? (I'd like / know ...)

3 What time does the bus leave? (Can / ask ... ?)

4 Is there free wifi? (I'd like ... / whether ...)

5 Can I use the gym? (Could you / if I ... ?)

6 Do I need a visa? (Do / know if ... ?)

7 Where is the university campus? (Can / tell ... ?)

8 How can I apply for a job? (I'd like / know how ...)

PRONUNCIATION

5 A 🔊 **3.10 | polite intonation |** Listen to two inquiries from Ex 4E. Notice how the intonation goes up and down a lot, to sound polite.

B 🔊 **3.11 |** Work in pairs. Practise making the inquiries in Ex 4E. Use intonation to sound polite. Then listen and check.

SPEAKING

6 Work in pairs. Roleplay situations 1 and 2. Student A: Read the instructions below. Student B: Go to page 147.

Student A:

1 You want some information about language courses at Ello Language School. Use indirect questions to make polite inquiries. Use the prompts to help you.

You are doing an intensive course.

- How many hours / study a day?
- miss lessons?
- receive / a certificate / end of the course?
- a study area / on campus?
- borrow books / library?
- free wifi?
- where / go shopping / near the school?

Can you tell me how many hours I will study a day?

2 You work at a sports centre. Your partner will make some inquiries. Use the information below to answer their questions.

- The sports centre is in the town square, opposite the theatre, next to the taxi rank.
- Anybody can use the sports centre facilities. You don't need to be a member.
- Prices for the gym: €10 per hour.
- There is a swimming pool open from 6 a.m.–8 p.m.
- Gym is open from 6 a.m.–10 p.m.

> **MEDIATION SKILL**
> **describing advantages and disadvantages**
> give a friend advice about where to study English
>
> ▶▶ page 152 **MEDIATION BANK**

Speak anywhere Go to the interactive speaking practice

What matters most?

Nikki

Devante

GRAMMAR | phrasal verbs
SPEAKING | a conversation about what's important to you
WRITING | an online forum comment

PREVIEW

1 Work in pairs. Talk about different people you know. Say which of the things in the box are important to them and why.

> creative activities   family   food
> free time   friends   music   sport
> travel   trends

A: My brother's an athlete, so sport is obviously very important to him.
B: Yes, and I suppose food is also important to him because an athlete has to eat well.

▶ BBC

Q1: What things are important in your life?

Q2: What things aren't important in your life?

VIEW

2 A ▶ Watch the video. Which of the ideas in the box in Ex 1 do the speakers mention?

B ▶ Watch the first part of the video again. Are the statements True (T) or False (F)?
  1 Lily is probably artistic.
  2 Lotte and Saffi socialise a lot with friends.
  3 Natalia sings to change her mood.
  4 Gerard has a job.

C ▶ Complete the things that the speakers say are or aren't important to them. Watch the second part of the video again and check.
  1 Lily: Other people's opinions are not very ....
  2 Lotte: I'm more interested .... current events.
  3 Mon Zer: I don't care .... new trends that much.
  4 Gerard: I'm not really .... brands at all.

D Work in pairs. Read what the speakers say. Do you agree with them? Do you have these things in your life now?
  1 'Making sure there's a good balance between my work and my personal life/my free time is important.'
  2 'Structure is really important to me.'

GRAMMAR

phrasal verbs

3 A Read the sentences from the video. Which words are phrasal verbs?
  1 Putting on a certain song can uplift you.
  2 [It's important to] look out for each other.

B Read the pairs of sentences. Are the a and b sentences both correct? What do you notice about the position of the object?
  1 a I put on a song.
    b I put a song on.
  2 a My friends and I look out for each other.
    b My friends and I look for each other out.

C Learn and practise. Go to the Grammar Bank.
  ▶▶ page 115 **GRAMMAR BANK**

Lotte | Saffi | Lily | Natalia | Gerard | Mon Zer

SPEAKING

a conversation about what's important to you

4A Work in pairs. Have a conversation.

1 Talk about three things or activities that are important to you. Why are they important? What part do they play in your life?

2 Talk about three things or activities that aren't important in your life.

3 Which things do you and your partner agree about?

B Read the Key phrases. Did you use any of these in your conversation? Complete four of the sentences in the box so they are true for you.

KEY PHRASES

The things that are important in my life are …
Spending time with … is important.
Spending time relaxing/socialising/working …
It's important to look after …
I'm not interested in … at all.
I don't care about … that much.
I'm not really into …

C Work with a new partner. Have a new conversation about the ideas in Ex 4A. Use the Key phrases to help.

WRITING

an online forum comment

5A Read a comment from an online forum. What is important to Alex and how frequently does he do the activity?

What's important in your life?

Alex, Maine, USA

The things that are important in my life are spending relaxed time at home and making delicious food. I'm very interested in cooking and I like to experiment with new dishes. I started cooking as a teenager and I still love it twenty years later. It's a very creative hobby and it's fun to try different types of food. I'm not really into shopping in big supermarkets, so I try to buy local ingredients from the farms and street markets near where I live. I cook at least once a day. Some dishes take two hours or more, but it's worth it!

B Write a comment about an activity that is important in your life. Write about:

- what the activity is.
- why you enjoy it and why it is important to you.
- when you first became interested in it.
- how much time you spend doing it.

GRAMMAR

question forms

1 A Correct the mistakes in the questions. One of the questions is correct.

1 When you started studying English?
2 Who did help you to learn English?
3 Did you to learn anything important at school?
4 Do you enjoy learning languages?
5 When you imagine the perfect career, what you think of?

B Choose four of the questions to ask your partner.

future plans and intentions

2 A Put the words into the correct order to make questions.

1 later / you / doing / are / what / today?
2 you / time / to / going / what / get / up / are / tomorrow?
3 you / this / doing / are / interesting / anything / weekend?
4 going / are / you / next / on / where / your / holiday?
5 planning / next / you / to / are / how / your / celebrate / birthday?

B Match the questions in Ex 2A with the answers (a–e).

a Yes! I'm going to see a film with my partner.
b Maybe to a small town by the sea.
c This year I'm going to invite my friends to a party!
d At about 6 a.m.
e After this lesson, I'm going to the library.

C 🔊 **R3.01** | Listen and check your answers.

phrasal verbs

3 Read the paragraph and look at the phrasal verbs in bold. Decide if the different word order (1–11) is correct.

A Day in the life of a writer

My alarm ¹**goes off at 4.00 a.m.** I ²**get up quickly** and get dressed. After a cup of coffee, I ³**put my coat on** and leave the house at 4.30. I ⁴**get on the 4.40 bus** and I'm in my office by 5.00. Most writers work from home, but I rent an office. I ⁵**switch on my computer** and begin work. Most of my day is spent writing and ⁶**looking up information**. I use the computer, but I also ⁷**write things down** on paper. Even if I ⁸**throw away the paper** at the end of the day, writing helps me to process the information. I don't like ⁹**sitting down all day** so I have regular breaks. I ¹⁰**go out at about 11.00** and have lunch in a restaurant. At 4.00 p.m., I ¹¹**shut down my computer** and take the bus home.

---

1 goes at 4.00 a.m. off **not correct**	6 looking information up
2 get quickly up	7 write down things
3 put on my coat	8 throw the paper away
4 get the 4.40 bus on	9 sitting all day down
5 switch my computer on	10 go at about 11.00 out
	11 shut my computer down

VOCABULARY

4 A Complete the advice with the words in the box.

> consider   knowledge   library   mind   note   revise

Tips for language students

1 .... down new words in a special notebook.
2 Join a .... that has lots of books and magazines in English, or read them online.
3 .... taking lessons from a private teacher.
4 .... grammar and vocabulary every day.
5 Watch videos in English, so you learn the language and improve your general ....
6 Train your .... to translate everything you hear and read into English.

B Work in pairs. Discuss the questions.

1 Are the ideas in Ex 4A good or bad advice? Why?
2 What other advice can you think of?

5 A Choose the correct options (A–C) to complete the text.

Online or face-to-face?

For schools and universities, online learning has many ¹........... . You don't need classrooms, study ²........... or dining facilities, and teachers can work from home. But what do students think of it? How many have tried online learning this year, and how many will ³........... next year?

'I love learning online,' says Jeanette Willis, a business student. I live quite a long way from the university ⁴........... , so online learning makes ⁵........... for me because I don't need to travel. I ⁶........... the same next year.'

'I hate it,' says Petrus Schwartz, an engineering student. 'I like studying with other people. They help me to ⁷........... on the tasks. Also, I always ⁸........... for exams with friends – that's how my ⁹........... works. Next year I'm definitely ¹⁰........... do face-to-face classes only.'

1 A problems	B sense	C advantages
2 A areas	B campus	C halls
3 A stick it with	B stick with	C stick with it
4 A stadium	B campus	C office
5 A sense	B meaning	C help
6 A do	B 'm doing	C will
7 A score	B consider	C focus
8 A revise	B note down	C solve
9 A data	B mind	C thought
10 A going to	B might	C will

B Work with other students. Discuss the question. Do you prefer learning online or face-to-face?

winners

4

VLOGS

Q: Have you ever won anything?

1 ▶ Watch the video. Note down the situations and activities the people mention. What unusual prizes do they mention?

2 Have you ever won anything? What was it? When? Where?

GSE LEARNING OBJECTIVES

4A LISTENING | Understand a podcast about success: success
Pronunciation: silent letters
Discuss your personal goals: modals for rules and advice
Write an email/letter giving advice; use phrases for giving advice

4B READING | Read about famous technology firsts: technology collocations; word building: suffixes
Pronunciation: *the*
Talk about social media and websites: articles

4C HOW TO ... | explain rules and procedures: sports and games
Pronunciation: *can* and *can't*

4D BBC PROGRAMME | Understand a TV programme about a car race in Nepal
Talk about a memorable journey: present perfect + superlative
Write a travel writing competition entry

4A Success

GRAMMAR | modals for rules and advice
VOCABULARY | success
PRONUNCIATION | silent letters

VOCABULARY

success

1 A Work in pairs. Do the questionnaire. Choose one answer for each question which reflects your ideas.

B Read the quiz results on page 147. Do you agree with what it says about you?

2 A Study the words in bold in the questionnaire. Then choose the correct words to complete the sentences.

1 She's a really **talented / success** dancer – she's so good!

2 He mostly works from home, so he needs to be **strict / talented** about when he starts work.

3 She's **giving up / doing well** at school and getting good grades.

4 He hates it when his team doesn't win. He's a **bad loser / failure**.

5 She's **giving up / working hard** so I'm sure she'll be successful.

6 The brothers are very **carry on / competitive**. They always want to win.

B Ask and answer the questions with a partner.

1 Are you stricter in some areas of your life than others? Can you give examples?

2 What things do you think you are most talented at?

3 Were you competitive when you were a child? Are you competitive now, at work or in your studies?

4 What successes are you proud of in your life so far?

How competitive are you?

Do you always try to win? Do the questionnaire to find out.

1 You can't do well and have **success** in life without:
A **working hard**.
B being **talented**, so you are naturally good at something.
C being lucky.

2 You're **doing well** in a game against a child. Do you
A stop trying and let them win?
B take it easy and see what happens?
C **carry on** playing and not stop until you win?

3 When I know that a task will be difficult,
A I try to forget about it and wait as long as possible before starting.
B I'm very **strict** with myself, so I start the task as soon as possible.
C I think about it and prepare carefully before I start.

4 Are you a **bad loser** who hates not winning? When you lose, do you
A try to understand what you did wrong and then try again?
B accept **failure**?
C get angry or sad?

5 Which of the following suits your philosophy of life?
A You win some, you lose some.
B The difference between winning and losing is not stopping or **giving up**.
C It's not winning or losing, it's how you play the game.

6 You won! Now what do you do?
A Party, party!
B Treat yourself to something nice.
C Nothing special. You won and that's good enough for you.

LISTENING

3 A Read the information about a podcast. Think of your own three rules for success, then compare with a partner.

Podcast: Rules for success

We all have dreams – to play international football, become a senior manager in a company or write a best-selling book. Only a few people achieve their dreams. What do these 'winners' share, and what can we learn from them? Are there rules we can all follow to achieve success?

B 🔊 **4.01** | Listen to the podcast. Number the main points in the order you hear them. Were any of your ideas mentioned?

a Work harder than other people.

b Be friendly to the people you meet.

c Decide what you want to achieve.　1

d Take action – don't wait before you start.

e Don't stop when you experience problems.

f Relax and enjoy time off work.

C 🔊 **4.01** | Are the statements True (T) or False (F)? Listen again and check.

1 Novak Djokovic decided he wanted to win Wimbledon when he was young.

2 He made himself a Wimbledon trophy out of wood and metal.

3 The speakers agree that when you have a plan, you should start immediately.

4 The actor Will Smith thinks he's successful because he worked while other people slept.

5 Walt Disney had a boss who believed in his talent.

6 The speakers agree that it's important to be nice to people if you want to be successful.

D Work in pairs. Do you agree with the points in Ex 3B? Why? Can you add any more points to the list?

GRAMMAR

modals for rules and advice

4 A Read the sentences (1–6) from the podcast. Match the words in bold with their meanings (a–d).

1 You **need to** set goals. You **have to** know what you want to achieve.

2 You **don't have to** be more talented than everyone else, but you have to make more effort.

3 You **must** work really hard.

4 You **mustn't** give up.

5 You **should** be nice to people.

6 You **needn't** work all the time.

a It's a good idea to do this. ....

b This isn't necessary. .... and ....

c It is necessary to do this. You have no choice. .... , ... and ....

d Don't do this. It isn't allowed or it isn't advised. ....

B What verb form follows the modals?

C Learn and practise. Go to the Grammar Bank.

▶▶ page 116 **GRAMMAR BANK**

PRONUNCIATION

5 A 🔊 **4.02** | **silent letters** | Listen to the sentences. Notice the pronunciation of *mustn't*, *should* and *shouldn't*. Do we pronounce the highlighted letters?

1 You mustn't give up.

2 You should be nice to people.

3 You shouldn't wait for the perfect moment.

B Work in pairs. Write three 'Rules for success' for one of the situations below. Use *need to*, *have to*, *should/shouldn't* and *must/mustn't*.

- run a marathon
- become a famous film star, actor or musician
- start a successful business
- be a professional sportsperson
- pass exams with good grades
- learn a language fluently
- be an online influencer

C Work in different pairs. Take turns to read out your sentences. Remember to pronounce *should/shouldn't* and *mustn't* correctly. Can your partner guess which situation your sentences refer to?

SPEAKING

6 A Work in a group. Read the situation and discuss the advice. Decide on the three best pieces of advice. Give your reasons.

A friend of yours has recently joined a new company. She is determined to be successful and have a senior job in ten years. Discuss the advice people have given her.

- work long hours
- have good ideas
- always arrive on time
- be nice to people
- look smart
- be a good listener
- help other people do their work
- make sure your boss notices your good work
- never take time off when you are ill
- relax and have fun

A: If she wants to do well, I think the best advice is that she should be nice to people. If you're nice to the people who you work with, they will want to keep working with you. And you will be successful. What do you think?

B: I'm not sure about that. You needn't be nice to everyone! I think that …

B Compare your ideas with another group. Do you agree or disagree?

C Work alone. What goals do you have for the next ten years? Think about goals in language learning, your career or life in general. Make some notes.

D Read the Future Skills box and do the task.

FUTURE SKILLS
Goal-setting

It is important to set goals and think about how you can achieve them.

Discuss your goals in pairs and think of things you need to do to achieve them.

WRITING

an email/letter giving advice

7 A Work in pairs. Discuss the questions.
1 What things do you ask friends for advice about?
2 What do people ask you for advice about?

B Look at the situations your friends need advice about. Work in pairs and think of two pieces of advice for each one.
- I'm going on a sports holiday and I need to get fit quickly.
- I'm moving to a new city in a few months. How can I make new friends?
- I'm fed up with my job. I hate working in an office. I need to change careers.

C Read the email. What's the problem and what's the advice?

Hi Sara,

Great to hear from you! I'm so pleased you're doing well.

You asked about changing careers. Well, I've got a few ideas. Firstly, **you need to** work out what it is you really want to do. What is it about your current job that you want to change? Are there any other jobs you'd rather do? **Try to think about** things you really enjoy doing, then see if there's a job related to that. I know you like being outside in nature. **Maybe you can** look for a job which involves that.

Next, do your research. **It's easy to** find out about different jobs by searching online, but **why not try** talking to people doing the job you're interested in? Then you'll find out what it's really like. **How about** doing some work experience? Or some voluntary work? This will help you to make the right decision.

Lastly, **make sure you** think carefully before making a big change. **You have to** be sure about your decision. Once you leave your job, there's no going back. **Don't** be afraid of change though. Take the first small step towards your new career, and then just keep going. I know you can do it!

I hope this is useful. If you want to talk about it, just get in touch. And good luck!

All the best,

Marilyn

D Work in pairs. Answer the questions.
1 Is the email formal or informal? How do you know?
2 How could you make the email more formal?
3 How many pieces of advice does Marilyn give her friend? What phrases does she use to order the information?

8 A Look at the phrases in bold for giving advice. Answer the questions.
1 Which phrases give strong advice? Which make suggestions?
2 What kind of word or verb form follows each phrase (infinitive/ -ing form/noun/adjective, etc.)?

B Choose one of the situations in Ex 7B. Think of three pieces of advice. Write the advice using the phrases in bold in the email.

C Write an informal email giving your advice from Ex 8B.

4B First!

GRAMMAR | articles
VOCABULARY | technology collocations; word building: suffixes
PRONUNCIATION | *the*

GRAMMAR

articles

1 A Work in groups. Look at the photos. What famous 'firsts' do you think the people achieved? Check your answers on page 146.

B Tell people in your group about another famous 'first' that you know of.

2 A Read the paragraph about another famous first. Why do some people believe Santos Dumont was 'the first'?

First to fly

Who made the first flight? [a] **Books** about the history of flight often say it was the Wright brothers, but some people believe it was [b] **an inventor** called Alberto Santos Dumont. So, did the first flight happen in [c] **a field** in North Carolina, USA, or in [d] **France**, where the Brazilian Santos Dumont lived? On December 17, 1903, Orville and Wilbur Wright succeeded in getting their plane into the air for twelve seconds. Three years later, on October 23, 1906, Santos Dumont also flew. [e] **The Brazilian**'s flight was watched by hundreds of people as well as experts from the Aéro-Club de France, an organisation dedicated to flying machines. This was very different to the Wright brothers' flight, which hardly anyone saw. For this reason, many people in Europe didn't believe that the Wright brothers had really flown. The puzzle of who made the first flight remains one of [f] **the biggest** questions in aeroplane history, and we may never know the answer.

B Look at the words in bold (a–f) in the paragraph. Match them with the rules (1–6).

We use *a/an*:

1 the first time something is mentioned (new information) c

2 with jobs ....

We use *the*:

3 when we know which person or thing we are talking about ....

4 with superlatives ....

We use no article:

5 when we talk generally about people and things ....

6 with most names of places ....

C Learn and practise. Go to the Grammar Bank.

▶▶ page 117 **GRAMMAR BANK**

PRONUNCIATION

3 A 🔊 **4.03** | *the* | Listen and write the articles and nouns that you hear.

B Answer the questions.

1 How is *the* usually pronounced? Is it /ðə/ or /ðiː/?

2 When *the* is followed by a vowel sound, how do we pronounce it?

C 🔊 **4.03** | Listen again and check.

D Say the phrases you wrote in Ex 3A. Focus on pronouncing *the* correctly.

READING

4A Do you know when different kinds of technology were first used? Work in pairs. Look at the questions about 'firsts' and choose the correct date.

When was the first … ?

1 webpage (1981 / 1991 / 2001)
2 video game (1958 / 1978 / 1998)
3 YouTube video (1995 / 2000 / 2005)
4 Instagram post (1990 / 2000 / 2010)
5 call made on a mobile phone (1973 / 1999 / 2010)
6 selfie (1839 / 1950 / 1989)
7 text message (1982 / 1992 / 2002)
8 Tweet (1996 / 2006 / 2016)

B Read the text to find the answers to Ex 4A. How many did you guess correctly?

C What content did the technologies in Ex 4A first show? Find the information in the text.

5A What extra information is in the text? Choose the correct option (a, b or c).

1 Martin Cooper's invention
  a became famous immediately.
  b was heavy and took a long time to charge.
  c was very expensive.

2 Robert Cornelius
  a sat still for a long time for the first selfie.
  b worked with Louis Daguerre to make the first camera.
  c took a picture of his family.

3 The first YouTube video and Instagram photo both involved
  a food.
  b animals.
  c family members.

4 Tim Berners-Lee and Jack Dorsey
  a invented the same piece of technology at the same time.
  b both used mobile phones to develop a new product.
  c included messages about their new invention when they first showed it to the world.

B Work with other students. Discuss the question. How have the inventions in the text changed the way we communicate, spend our free time and learn things?

Famous Tech Firsts

Frenchman Louis Daguerre invented the camera. But Robert Cornelius made changes to the invention and in 1839 tried an experiment using his own image. To **take the picture**, he sat still for fifteen minutes. The result was the very first selfie.

The first mobile phone call took place in 1973. Martin Cooper, an employee of the mobile phone company Motorola®, made it. And who did he call? His loved ones? His manager? No. He **made a call** to a competitor and explained that he'd won the race to invent the mobile phone. The invention weighed more than 1 kg and took ten hours to charge.

The first YouTube video appeared on 23 April, 2005. It was called 'meet me at the zoo' and it consisted of eighteen seconds of a boy talking about elephants! It didn't exactly **go viral**, but it did **launch a website** that has been incredibly popular ever since.

The first Instagram post was a photo of a dog next to a woman's foot. The photo was taken by the co-founder of Instagram, Kevin Systrom. The date was July 16, 2010, the place was a taco stand in Todos Santos, Mexico, and the foot belonged to Systrom's girlfriend. From these simple beginnings, Instagram became *the* place to **share videos** and photos.

1839
1958
1973
1991
1992
2005
2006
2010

William Higinbotham and Robert Dvorak created the world's first video game in 1958. It was a version of tennis. They developed the game to show to visitors at the Brookhaven National Laboratory, where they worked. Many years later, a similar game, called Pong, became famous. Now if you want a video game, you don't need to go to any lab – you just **download an app**.

The first webpage **went live** on 6 August, 1991. Tim Berners-Lee's invention showed how to **create webpages**! People read it to **find information** that, eventually, changed the world.

The first text message appeared on 3 December, 1992. Neil Papworth, working on SMS for Vodaphone, **sent the message** 'Merry Christmas'. The new development grew quickly: now about 5 billion people (65 percent of the world's population) send and **receive texts**.

The first tweet appeared at 12.50 p.m. PST on 21 March, 2006, sent by the co-founder of Twitter, Jack Dorsey. It read 'just setting up my twttr'. At the time, Twitter was still called Twttr. Since then, 1.3 billion people have **created accounts** on Twitter, and there have even been tweets sent by astronauts from space.

VOCABULARY

technology collocations

6A Look at the phrases in bold in the text. Complete the sentences (1–12) with the correct form of the phrases. Make any other changes necessary.

1 When we <u>launched a website</u> last year, we didn't expect so many people to visit it so quickly!

2 Some of her videos on YouTube have .... and been watched millions of times.

3 I .... to Jenny yesterday, but I don't think she's read it yet!

4 Excuse me, can I borrow your phone? I need to .... and it's urgent.

5 My new website .... tomorrow afternoon! Take a look!

6 The food looked amazing, so I .... on my phone. I'll send it to you.

7 I .... this morning saying I should call this number.

8 It's easy to .... on their website. You just use your email address and add a password.

9 I'm going to .... so I can sell my products online.

10 I use this website to .... about different subjects I'm interested in.

11 I .... with my friends on Instagram, and they do the same. I love watching them.

12 Why don't you .... onto your phone so you can keep track of your fitness goals?

B Work in groups. How can you use websites and apps to help you learn English? Read the Future Skills box and discuss the questions.

FUTURE SKILLS

Self-management

Apps and websites can be a great way to improve your learning.

Which websites and apps do you use to learn English? How often? How much time do you spend on them? Which are the most useful? Why?

C Look at the text again. What nouns are related to the verbs *invent*, *employ*, *compete* and *manage*?

invent – invention

D Learn and practise. Go to the Vocabulary Bank.

▶ page 139 **VOCABULARY BANK**
word building: suffixes

SPEAKING

7A Read questions 1–4 and think about your answers.

1 What social media do you use and for what reasons (personal, professional, etc.)?

2 Do you take pictures or make videos on your phone? What types of things? Do you post them on social media?

3 Can you remember the first or last time you did these things?

> commented on a webpage   downloaded an app
> found a great website   shared a video or photo

4 What are your favourite websites for the following activities? Why do you like them?

> getting news   online shopping
> planning holidays/travelling
> studying   watching videos

B Work in groups. Discuss your answers to the questions in Ex 7A. Do you have similar experiences?

C ⧉ Think of some important 'firsts' in your life (your first day at school or college, your first flight, your first home, etc.). Do you have a photo? Bring it to the next class to talk about.

4C Taking part

HOW TO ... | explain rules and procedures
VOCABULARY | sports and games
PRONUNCIATION | *can* and *can't*

VOCABULARY

sports and games

1 A Read the text. What does the writer want people to write comments about?

Is it a sport?

Can we call board games like chess a sport? If you are really good at computer games and take part in e-sports competitions, are you a sportsperson? Some people would call these activities games rather than sports, but not everyone agrees, and some organisations recognise them as sports. So, what makes a sport? First, it's an activity that requires physical skill and fitness. Secondly, it has a set of rules. And lastly, you can play it competitively, so there's a result, along with a winner and loser. Chess and e-sports certainly have rules and are competitive, and people who participate in high-level competitions would say that both activities require a lot of mental strength and, in the case of e-sports, physical skills, too. What do you think? And what about other activities such as bowling, dance and fishing? Are they sports, or just hobbies? Let us know in the comments.

B Work in pairs. Do you think the activities in the box are sports, games or hobbies? Why?

> backgammon   bowling   chess
> dance   e-sports   fishing   snooker

2 A Work in pairs. Match the questions (1–6) with the answers (a–f).

1 Do you **take part** in any sports? e
2 What **video games** do you play?
3 Are you a **fan** of any teams or players?
4 Does your favourite team usually win or **lose**?
5 Have you ever watched a rugby **match**?
6 Do you have any **board games** at home?

a No, I don't **support** anyone, but I watch football on TV occasionally.
b No, I don't understand the **rules** of that sport, or how you score points!
c Yes, we have a chess set, but I prefer **outdoor** sports and games.
d Lots! I spend at least two hours a day playing in front of a screen.
e Yes, I love **team sports** and I play basketball.
f We win, of course! We're the **champions**!

B Work in pairs. Look at the words and phrases in bold in Ex 2A. Then say sentences using them.

I support Manchester United.

C Work in pairs. Ask and answer the questions in Ex 2A.

How to ...
explain rules and procedures

3 A You are going to listen to a description of a game called floorball. First, look at the photo. What type of game is it? Can you guess the rules?

B 🔊 **4.04** | Listen and check your ideas.

C 🔊 **4.04** | Are the statements True (T) or False (F)? Listen again and check.
1 Floorball is an outdoor sport.
2 You can't score goals in floorball.
3 There are six players in each team.
4 All of the players use a stick.
5 The game starts with a 'face-off'.
6 A match takes one hour and twenty minutes.

D Complete the phrases in the table with the words in the box.

~~aim~~	by	can't	first	lasts

rules and procedures	
how to win	The goal is to …/The ¹aim of the game is to …
organisation and equipment	There are (six players). It is played on a field. It ² _____ one hour.
procedure	³ _____/To start with, Then/Next, … After that, …
rules	You score ⁴ _____ shooting (the ball into the goal). You can … You have to/must … You ⁵ _____/mustn't …

E Learn and practise. Go to the Grammar Bank.

▶▶ page 118 **GRAMMAR BANK**

PRONUNCIATION

4 A 🔊 **4.05** | *can and can't* | Listen to seven rules from a different sport. Which things can you do? Which can't you do?
1 score points can
2 catch the ball
3 play inside or outside
4 use a stick
5 hit the ball with any part of your body
6 hit the ball more than three times
7 hit the ball after it touches the net

B 🔊 **4.05** | Listen again and check. Then work in pairs and practise saying the sentences. Which has the longer vowel sound in connected speech: *can* or *can't*?

C Can you guess which sport it is?

D Work in pairs. What other sports vocabulary do you know? Choose two sports and brainstorm words for the equipment, the people, the places where you play and verbs connected to sports.

E Learn and practise. Go to the Vocabulary Bank.

▶▶ page 140 **VOCABULARY BANK** sport

SPEAKING

5 A Choose a game or sport that you know, or create your own game. It can be any type of game: board game, video game, outdoor sport, etc. Make notes using the ideas below.

Type of game   Where it's played   Number of players
How to win   Organisation and equipment   Rules   Procedure

B Read the Future Skills box and answer the questions about your notes in Ex 5A.

FUTURE SKILLS
Communication

When we explain rules and procedures, we should present the information in a clear sequence and with a clear structure, starting with more general information and then adding more details.

What words can help present the sequence? Which information is quite general and basic? Which information is more detailed and takes longer to describe?

C Present your sport or game to other students.

My sport is a mixture of climbing and basketball. You have to climb up to the basket to score a goal!

D Discuss all the games. Which have you played? Which would you like to try? Why?

MEDIATION SKILL
describing how something is similar or different to something else
help someone understand a game.

▶▶ page 153 **MEDIATION BANK**

4D **BBC** Entertainment

Top Gear: Nepal

GRAMMAR | present perfect + superlative
SPEAKING | talk about a memorable journey
WRITING | a travel writing competition entry

PREVIEW

1 A Work in pairs. Look at the photos and discuss the questions.

   1 Where do you think this is?

   2 What type of programme do you think this is?

B Read the programme information and check your ideas.

Top Gear

Top Gear is the BBC's international award-winning television series about cars. On the show, the three presenters compare and test-drive cars, and organise all kinds of crazy races. In some episodes, they travel to different parts of the world, choose a car each, and race to see who can reach a place first. In this episode, the presenters are in Kathmandu, the capital of Nepal. They are racing to get to a city called Lo Manthang, but it's a difficult drive with lots of traffic, mountains and rivers to cross!

VIEW

2 A ▶ Watch the BBC video clip. Number the events in the correct order.

The presenters …

   a leave the blue Renault 4 car by the side of the road.

   b drive out of Kathmandu.

   c arrive at 'the Forbidden City' of Lo Manthang.

   d camp for the night.

   e receive their instructions on a piece of paper. 1

   f drive along the side of a mountain.

   g drive across a river.

B ▶ Are the statements True (T) or False (F)? Watch again and check.

   1 The presenters find it easy to drive out of Kathmandu.

   2 Outside Kathmandu the roads are bumpy.

   3 One presenter asks for help because his car gets stuck in the water.

   4 One presenter says that driving on the mountain is frightening.

   5 They leave the blue car on the side of the road after ten days.

   6 The red car is 'the winner'.

C Work in pairs and discuss the questions.

   1 Do you think it was important who won the race? Why/Why not?

   2 Would you like to do a difficult trip like this one? Why/Why not?

GRAMMAR

present perfect + superlative

3 A Read the sentence from the programme. Then choose the correct words to complete the rule.

'This is the worst … I've ever seen!'

We can use the [1]**present perfect / past simple** + the [2]**comparative / superlative** form of an adjective to talk about an experience related to our whole life.

B Complete the sentences with between one and three words in each gap. Several answers may be possible.

   1 This is the best holiday .... ever had!

   2 It's the .... hotel I've ever stayed in.

   3 It's the longest journey I .... been on!

C Learn and practise. Go to the Grammar Bank.

   ▶▶ page 119 **GRAMMAR BANK**

SPEAKING

talk about a memorable journey

4 **A** ◀) **4.06** | Listen to someone talking about a memorable journey. Answer the questions.

1 Where did she go, and who with?
2 How did they travel?
3 What did they see?
4 Why did they have to stay in a town 'for a few days'?

B ◀) **4.06** | Listen again and tick the phrases that you hear.

KEY PHRASES

The most memorable journey I've ever been on was …
It was my first time …
It was one of the most amazing …
It was memorable because …
The journey took … days.
… is definitely the most interesting place I've been to.

C You are going to talk about an interesting or memorable journey. Think about your journey and answer the questions. Use the Key phrases to help.

1 Where were you going? Why?
2 Who were you with?
3 How long was the journey?
4 What did you see and do?
5 Why was it interesting or memorable?

D Work in groups. Take turns to tell other students about your journey. Use the Key phrases to help. Other students: listen and ask questions to learn more.

WRITING

a travel writing competition entry

5 **A** Read about a writing competition. What type of story are they looking for? What can you win?

Writing competition

Tell us about a difficult journey. Where were you going? Who with? What happened and why was it difficult? What happened in the end? We accept stories about all kinds of journeys: road trips, train trips, car journeys, hikes, flights, etc. The winner wins an all-expenses trip to a Caribbean island! Write 100-140 words and include as many interesting details as you can.

B Read an entry to the competition. What are Jamal's answers to the questions in the competition description?

Car trouble in the Big Easy

The most difficult car ride I've ever had was in my friend Ricky's 1959 Buick Roadmaster in New Orleans. Ricky and I were trying to find a jazz club. Neither of us knew the city, and these were the days before Google Maps. The only thing we knew was the name of the club, Fritzel's. We got lost several times. At one point, we turned a corner and there was a street party in front of us. We turned around again.

Two hours later, the car made a strange noise and stopped. We'd run out of gas. Ricky just laughed. We left the car by the side of the road and started walking. We never found that jazz club, but we did find a great restaurant which sold the best seafood sandwiches ever.

Jamal Washington Jr

C Write your competition entry. Answer the questions in Ex 5A, and invent two details about your experience. Add a title.

D Read other students' work. Can you guess which details were invented?

GRAMMAR

modals for rules and advice

1 A Choose the correct words to complete the tips.

Six tips for how to live a happier life

1 You **should / don't have to / mustn't** try to spend some time enjoying nature each day. It reduces stress.

2 Make sure you get enough exercise. You **mustn't / need to / don't need to** run a marathon, but a small amount of exercise will make you feel better.

3 Spend time with friends and family. You **must / mustn't / need to** spend too much time alone. People who have good social relationships live longer.

4 You **should / mustn't / needn't** get enough sleep. Most people **don't need to / need to / shouldn't** sleep for between six and eight hours.

5 Learn something new. Your brain needs to be challenged. You **have to / must / don't have to** be really talented, but learning a new skill can be fun.

6 You **have to / shouldn't / mustn't** laugh as much as possible. Humour can help you get you through difficult times.

B Work in pairs. Look at the advice in Ex 1A. Which things are important to do every day?

articles

2 A Complete the joke by adding articles where necessary.

[1]_____ police officer stops [2]_____ man driving [3]_____ car. He notices two penguins sitting on [4]_____ back seat of [5]_____ car. He asks [6]_____ driver, 'Hey, why have you got two penguins on [7]_____ back seat of your car?'

[8]_____ man says, 'I found them. I like [9]_____ animals, so I put them in my car. What should I do with them?'

The police officer says, 'Well, why don't you take them to the zoo?'

'Great idea!' says the man, and he drives away.

[10]_____ next day, [11]_____ man drives past [12]_____ same place. [13]_____ same police officer stops him again. He sees that [14]_____ penguins are still there. 'Hey,' he says to [15]_____ driver. 'You've still got [16]_____ penguins. I told you to take them to the zoo.'

'Yes, I took them to [17]_____ zoo yesterday and we had [18]_____ great time,' says [19]_____ driver. 'Today I'm taking them to [20]_____ beach.'

B 🔊 **R4.01** | Listen and check.

present perfect + superlative

3 Complete the sentences with the correct form of the words in brackets. Use the present perfect and a superlative.

1 It's the most interesting book I've ever read. (interesting / read)

2 That was _____ pizza we _____ ! (good / eat)

3 This is _____ hotel I _____ in! (bad / stay)

4 Venice is _____ city I _____ . (amazing / visit)

5 She's _____ person I _____ . (funny / meet)

VOCABULARY

4 A Complete the sentences with the words/phrases in the box.

> bad loser   carry on   giving up   strict   working hard

1 At the moment, I'm _____ to try and build up my new business.

2 I think I'd like to _____ with my studies.

3 I try to be very _____ about not working too much.

4 I get very angry when I don't win. I'm a _____ .

5 I'm thinking about _____ my job. I don't enjoy it.

B Change two of the sentences in Ex 4A so that they are true for you.

5 Match the sentence halves.

1 I worked on the website and created some new

2 I can't access the website. I think I need to download

3 I can't remember my password. I've created so many new

4 I told you I would be late. Didn't you receive all

5 Do you mind if we take

a webpages.

b a photo for social media?

c an app first.

d accounts recently.

e my texts?

6 A Choose the correct options (A–C) to complete the text.

Fascinating Nobel Prize winners

[1]_____ Cambridge University has produced ninety-six Nobel Prize winners over [2]_____ years. We take a look at two of them.

Ernest Rutherford was born in New Zealand in 1871 and is one of the best-known scientists who [3]_____ at Cambridge. He's known as the 'father of nuclear physics' for his [4]_____ around radioactivity. Under his [5]_____ the neutron was discovered by James Chadwick in 1932.

Dorothy Hodgkin won a Nobel Prize in chemistry. She was very [6]_____ about her studies and during her career she had a lot of [7]_____ ; she [8]_____ advanced techniques of X-ray crystallography, and she worked on the structure of penicillin and Vitamin B.

1 A A   **B** The   **C** –

2 A a   **B** the   **C** –

3 A ever studies   **B** has ever studied   **C** was ever studying

4 A introductions   **B** failures   **C** discoveries

5 A leadership   **B** leader   **C** leading

6 A working hard   **B** doing well   **C** strict

7 A creation   **B** success   **C** talent

8 A succeeded   **B** invented   **C** gave up

B 🔊 **R4.02** | Listen and check.

news

5

BBC

VLOGS

Q: How do you get your news?

1 ▶ Watch the video. Note down some of the sources for getting news the people mention.

2 How do you get your news? Do you use any of the sources the speakers mention?

GSE LEARNING OBJECTIVES

5A READING | Read an article about fake news: news and social media

Pronunciation: *wh-*

Talk about a news story: relative clauses

5B LISTENING | Understand a podcast about young people in the news: social issues; the environment

Pronunciation: silent letters

Plan a campaign: reported speech

Write an online comment in response to an article

5C HOW TO ... | give and respond to personal news: events and occasions

Pronunciation: intonation to exaggerate feelings

5D BBC STREET INTERVIEWS | Understand people talking about the news

Plan a news app: *will*, *might* and *be going to* for predictions

Write a webpage about a news app

5A Fake news

GRAMMAR | relative clauses
VOCABULARY | news and social media
PRONUNCIATION | *wh-*

READING

1 Work in pairs. Discuss the questions.

1 What was the last news story you discussed with someone? Where did you read or hear it?

2 How important is it to understand what is happening in your country, or the world?

3 How do you decide if something you see online is real or fake?

2 A Look at the photos above and discuss the questions.

1 Do you think they are real or fake? Why?

2 Imagine the photos are in a newspaper or magazine. What might the news stories be?

B Read the article. Answer the questions.

1 What jobs do the two people in the article do?

2 How are their jobs connected?

C Read the article again. Are the statements True (T) or False (F)?

1 Christopher Blair works for a traditional newspaper.

2 Blair always writes news stories about similar topics.

3 Maarten Schenk needs to work quickly to discover the real facts about a story.

4 Schenk is often unable to stop a fake news story from spreading.

5 Christopher Blair and Maarten Schenk are working against one another.

6 People who write fake news are not motivated by money.

7 Fact checkers are used by social media companies to reduce the amount of fake news.

D Work in pairs. Discuss the questions.

1 How do you think Christopher Blair and Maarten Schenk feel about their work?

2 In what ways can fake news be dangerous?

3 How do you think social media sites should deal with fake news?

4 Who should pay to find and change fake news?

5 Would you prefer to be a fake news writer or a fact checker? Why?

Real or fake?
The news that travels fast

Christopher Blair, who lives on the U.S. East Coast, is one of the world's most creative news writers. He isn't a **journalist** who writes articles for a newspaper. He writes news stories which are not true. He invents them and **publishes** them online. He writes about anything: politics, a famous athlete or someone who has been in the news recently. First, he writes a **headline** which will get attention. Then, he adds a few details and before long, he has written a **blog post**, which is about 200 words long. He **posts** his story **online**, sits back and watches the 'likes' and 'shares' begin. Sometimes he gets thousands of views in just minutes.

Maarten Schenk, who lives in a small town near Brussels, Belgium, works from home. He sits at his desk in front of three computer screens. On one of the screens, he suddenly notices a lot of activity. The USA is waking up, and there's a new story which is being shared by lots of people on Facebook and other social networks. Schenk is a man who likes to **find out** the truth. He does some fact-checking, goes to his website, and starts to type. His job is to tell the world that what he's seeing online – the story that's currently going viral about a U.S. politician – is completely invented. It's **fake news**.

Blair and Schenk are in a game of cat and mouse, and the mouse usually wins. Why? Because he's one step ahead. Fact checkers work day and night, but by the time they find the fake news, it's often too late. The story has already gone halfway around the world.

Why do Blair and other fake news writers do it? What motivates them? In some cases, their websites began as a joke. Then they realised they were writing **content** that people wanted to read. Sometimes the motivation is financial, other times political. Or maybe it's just the joy of creativity. Instead of publishing short stories and novels, which take years, they can put their work in front of the world in minutes.

What about Schenk and the fact checkers? Nowadays, they're often employed by social media sites, and their job is to find and spread the truth. It's an old-fashioned type of work: investigating, making phone calls, searching the internet. What motivates them is discovering the lie, and maybe the fact that their job is never finished. For every Maarten Schenk, there are dozens of Christopher Blairs producing stories like rabbits out of a hat.

VOCABULARY

news and social media

3 A Look at the words in bold in the article. Match them with the meanings (1–8).

1 makes a story available for other people to read, in print or online
2 someone who writes about the news for a newspaper, radio, TV, etc.
3 to discover information
4 uploads a story on the internet
5 the title of a story in the news, usually printed in large letters
6 news that is invented and not true
7 the main information in the news story
8 an article on someone's personal webpage

B Complete the sentences using the correct form of words and phrases from Ex 3A.

1 I sometimes .... my own ideas online on social media.
2 When I look at newspapers I never read a full article – I only read the ....
3 I think it's difficult to .... if a story is fake news.
4 I think it's important for .... who write for newspapers to check the facts.
5 I try to write a .... twice a week, sharing my thoughts and feelings.
6 I think it's pretty easy to spot .... This kind of story never contains facts and the writers are not well respected.

C Change the sentences in Ex 3B so they are true for you. Then compare your ideas with a partner.

I often read the headlines first, but then I choose two or three news stories to read in full.

D Work with other students. Read the Future Skills box and discuss the questions.

FUTURE SKILLS
Critical thinking

When you read news stories, it is important to think about whether they are true or fake. Before you share a news story, you should:

• look at the source and author of the article to see if you can trust them.
• read the whole article, not only the headline.
• check if the same news story is in other news sites that you trust
• check some of the facts in the article, e.g. the names of experts.

Do you use any of these strategies when you access the news? Which ones? What else do you do?

GRAMMAR

relative clauses

4 A Complete the sentences about the article with *who, which, when, where* or *whose*.

1 Christopher Blair is a journalist .... writes fake news.
2 He writes news stories .... are completely fake.
3 This is the room .... Maarten Schenk works.
4 He makes a note of the time .... a story is first shared on social media.
5 This is the politician .... story went viral.

B In which sentences can the relative pronoun be replaced by *that*?

C Learn and practise. Go to the Grammar Bank.

▶▶ **page 120 GRAMMAR BANK**

PRONUNCIATION

5 A 🔊 **5.01 | *wh-* |** Listen to two sentences. Notice how the sound *wh-* is pronounced in *who* and *when*. Which one is pronounced as /h/?

B 🔊 **5.02 |** Complete the table with the words in the box. Then listen and check.

~~when~~ where which ~~who~~ whose

/h/	/w/
who	when

C Complete the sentences with your own ideas. Then practise saying them.

1 I know someone who …
2 I'd like to go to a place where …
3 I remember a time when …
4 … is something which I enjoy doing.
5 I am someone whose …

6 Work in pairs. Student A: Go to page 148. Student B: Go to page 146. Guess the people and things.

SPEAKING

7 A Work in groups of three, Students A, B and C. Read your news story and prepare to retell it. Use the word web to make notes to help you. Plan two relative clauses you can include.

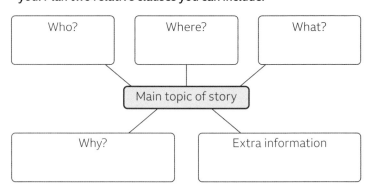

Who?	Where?	What?

Main topic of story

Why?	Extra information

BREAKING NEWS … Journalist Amy Ellis reports **A**

WHALE LANDS IN FARMER'S FIELD A 30,000 kg whale has landed in a farmer's field in Arkadelphia, 482 km off the coast of Louisiana. The whale, which was picked up by the powerful winds of Hurricane Delta, was 15 m long. Jerry O'Bourke, 97, had the surprise of his life when he discovered the whale outside the back of his house. O'Bourke, who has been a farmer all his life, says he has never seen such an incredible thing. Other animals that have been picked up by hurricanes include cats, frogs, dogs and cows.

WORLD NEWS DAILY REPORT **B**

SPIDER BITE! Three brothers from La Paz, Bolivia, were taken to hospital after being bitten by a black widow spider. The boys, who were aged eight, ten and twelve, let the spider bite them because they wanted to develop superpowers, like their favourite superhero. Soon afterwards they felt ill and had to be taken to hospital. Luckily the boys survived, and went home after spending a week in hospital.

LOCAL NEWS **C**

YOUR PIZZA DELIVERY! A man who lives in Belgium keeps receiving pizzas which he never orders. Every day for nearly ten years, deliveries of pizzas and other fast food arrive at his house, but he never orders them. Jean Van Landeghem says he waits in his house every day until he hears the delivery scooter on the street. One day, ten delivery drivers arrived in a single day, and one of them tried to deliver fourteen pizzas. The 65-year-old has reported the problem to the police.

B Tell your news story to the other people in your group. Try not to look at the text. Then work together in your groups.

This story is about three brothers who …

C Which story do you think is fake news? Why? Check the answer on page 146.

8 📲 Research a short news story or create a fake one. Then work in groups to tell your stories. Can other students guess if your story is true or fake?

5B Newsmakers

GRAMMAR | reported speech
VOCABULARY | social issues; the environment
PRONUNCIATION | silent letters

High **levels** of **pollution** found in cities

Scientists report that there is increasing pollution in many cities around the world. It is thought that the increasing number of cars in cities is to blame.

Town makes plan to **recycle** old car parts

A small town in New Zealand is taking old cars and using their parts to create works of art.

Schoolchildren remove **waste** from a beach to protect the **environment**

Over a hundred children spent the day collecting plastic, tin cans and paper cups from a beach in Cornwall, UK. Ten-year-old May Jones said, 'The natural world is our responsibility.'

Activists start a **campaign** against killing of elephants

Yesterday thousands of people walked through the streets of Nairobi, Kenya, calling for new laws to protect elephants.

Local company **donates** $10,000 to charity

A fishing company has given $10,000 to a group that works to save whales.

Teenagers **collect** coins for **charity**

Magda Kowalski, 14, and Jan Bartosz, 15, of Katowice raised over €2,500 for two charities, Children in Need and Food for the Poor, by asking for coins.

VOCABULARY

social issues; the environment

1 A Work in groups. Read the news stories. What do the words in bold mean? Use the context to help you.

Levels of pollution means the amount of dirt or unwanted objects in the environment.

B Choose the two correct words to complete each sentence.

1 Big companies should .... money to protect the ....

   (**level** / **donate** / **recycle** / **environment** / **waste**)

2 It's important that .... for social change.

   (**pollution** / **campaign** / **levels** / **activists** / **environment**)

3 I admire people who .... money or do other activities for ....

   (**pollution** / **activist** / **collect** / **waste** / **charity**)

4 There should be a law that makes people .... their ....

   (**charity** / **waste** / **campaign** / **levels** / **recycle**)

5 There are high .... of .... because we buy too many things we don't need, and then throw them away.

   (**campaign** / **recycle** / **levels** / **charity** / **pollution**)

C Work in groups. Do you agree with the opinions in Ex 1B? Give reasons and examples.

I agree that big companies often damage natural places, so they should pay to clean them again.

PRONUNCIATION

2 A | **silent letters** | Work in pairs. The words in the box each have a silent letter. Which letter do you think is silent?

> campaign   character   colleague   environment
> friend   mechanic   plumber   scientist

B 🔊 **5.03** | Listen and check.

C Write four sentences. In each sentence, use two words from Ex 2A. Read your sentences to a partner. Be careful with silent letters!

My friend is a scientist.

D Read the Future Skills box and discuss the questions.

> **FUTURE SKILLS**
> ### Self-management
>
> When you record new vocabulary, it is important to record the meaning and also extra information that will help you use the word in the future, e.g. the pronunciation.
>
> What information do you record when you note down new vocabulary? What other information would it be useful to record?

E Learn and practise. Go to the Vocabulary bank.

▶▶ page 141 **VOCABULARY BANK** the environment

Yash Gupta

Melati and Isabel Wijsen

LISTENING

3 A You are going to listen to a podcast called *Young people in the news*. First, look at the photos of the people. What can young people do to help others? Use the vocabulary in Ex 1A to help you.

B 🔊 **5.04** | Look at the photos above and listen to the podcast. Complete the table with the correct information.

name	from	the problem	their projects
Yash Gupta			
Melati and Isabel Wijsen			
Kelvin Doe			

C 🔊 **5.04** | Work in pairs. Answer the questions. Then listen again and check.

1 What happened to Yash when he was in High School?
2 What has his charity done so far?
3 How old were Melati and Isabel when they started their campaign?
4 What happened in 2019 because of their campaign?
5 How old was Kelvin when he started working with technology?
6 How does he find materials for his inventions?

4 A Work in groups. Discuss the questions.

1 What do you think of the young people and their ideas? Which of their projects do you like best? Why?
2 Do you know other examples of campaigns or young activists in the news?

B Read the Future Skills box and discuss the questions.

FUTURE SKILLS

Social responsibility

A lot of people enjoy taking part in projects to help their local community, like volunteering to coach sports or planting trees.

What community projects happen where you live? What projects are needed?

GRAMMAR

reported speech

5 A Read the pairs of sentences and answer the questions below (1–3).

1 a 'He is a genius.'
b His friends said that he was a genius.
2 a 'It has changed my life.'
b One child in Mexico told us that it had changed his life.
3 a 'Bali will ban single-use plastic bags.'
b The governor said that Bali would ban single-use plastic bags.

1 Look at the verb tenses in the 'a' sentences that people say and in the 'b' reported sentences. How do verb tenses change in reported speech?
2 Look at sentences 2a and 2b again. What other change happens in the reported speech?
3 Which verbs in the 'b' sentences report what the people said? Which one is followed by a pronoun?

B Learn and practise. Go to the Grammar Bank.

▶▶ page 121 **GRAMMAR BANK**

Kelvin Doe

SPEAKING

6 A Work in groups. What problems are there in your town or city? What changes could improve them? Discuss the ideas in the box or your own ideas.

> better public transport
> cleaning up waste   more recycling
> more restaurants
> providing public exercise areas
> reducing pollution

B You are going to start a campaign for one of your ideas in Ex 6A. In your groups, discuss the questions (1–3) and make notes about your campaign.

1 What is the issue and why did you choose it?

2 What is your goal? Who will help you achieve it?

3 How can you get your campaign into the news?

C Present your campaign to the class. As you listen, make notes on the other presentations.

D In your groups, discuss the other campaigns. Which idea do you think is the best? Why?

WRITING

an online comment

7 A Read part of an article on a local newspaper's website. Then read the comment from a reader. What problem is the article about? What do you think of the reader's suggestions?

> Our town is popular with tourists because of its beautiful weather and perfect beaches. People from all over Europe spend their summers here. **The problem is** that Bawlyn Beach has become polluted. In July and August, there are a lot of parties, and there aren't enough rubbish bins on the beach. **Unfortunately**, people leave a lot of plastic, cans and other rubbish. **This issue is** becoming more serious every year. What can we do?

Comments

> **One idea is to** organise groups of young people to do clean-up projects. **We could** organise a group of around fifteen young people to clean the beach on the first and third Saturdays of every month, May to September. **Another suggestion is to** ask the local government for more rubbish bins on the beach, so people won't drop as much rubbish there. **It would also be good to** start a recycling project, for example collecting plastic from the beach and sending it to a place where it can be used again.

 **Nellie Abberly**, Vice Principal, Castle School

B Look at the words and phrases in bold in the article and comment. Which introduce a problem? Which introduce a solution?

C Work in pairs. Read about another problem. What solutions can you suggest? Discuss the ideas in the box and your own ideas.

> a café for young people   a new sports facility
> a skatepark   a music studio

> The issue is that our town has very little for young people to do. Unfortunately, we have only one small park, where people walk their dogs, and the playgrounds are in bad condition for younger children. Many towns of a similar size have skateparks, football pitches, sports centres and other places where teenagers can relax safely in public. In our town, there's nowhere for students to go after school. What can we do?

D Write a comment offering a solution to the problem in Ex 7C. Use phrases for introducing solutions.

5C Good news

HOW TO ... | give and respond to personal news
VOCABULARY | events and occasions
PRONUNCIATION | intonation to exaggerate feelings

VOCABULARY

events and occasions

1 A Work in pairs. Answer the questions.

    1 Are you having a good week? Why/ Why not?

    2 Has anything exciting happened to you in the last week/month?

B Read the texts. What good things and bad things have happened to the people?

The best week ever! I can't believe it. I've just moved into a really nice house, and I passed my driving test. Work's going really well. I got promoted, so I'm now earning more money. My sister has had a baby, so now I'm an aunt, I've had a new haircut and everyone says it really suits me. I also posted a video online of me singing with my band and it got over 2,000 likes!

I'm having a terrible week! I failed my accountancy exams for the third time – I'm now worried I might lose my job. I broke my phone. I had an argument with a friend and now he isn't speaking to me. I bought a new pair of shoes and then realised they don't fit very well. And I've got my driving test tomorrow – I'll probably fail!

2 A Complete the table with the words in the box.

> break   celebrate   fail   get (x3)   graduate
> have (x2)   lose   move   pass   win

good news	bad news
.... your exams/driving test	...... your exams/driving test
.... a baby	.... your job
.... 2,000 likes	.... your phone/laptop
.... promoted/a new job	.... an argument
.... a competition/a match	
.... engaged/married	
.... your birthday	
.... from university	
.... house	

B Read what the people say. Guess their news.

  1 Filippo: It was going really well until I didn't stop at the roundabout and ended up in a flower bed!

  2 Eva: Lolita was born on Saturday. She weighs 3.5 kg.

  3 Dan: It's so annoying that I can't call anyone or see my messages!

  4 Natasha: The interview went really well and they've asked me to start on Monday!

  5 Emilio: I got angry because she always leaves the house in a mess. Now we're not speaking.

  6 Ana: We're having a party for my 40th. Would you like to come?

C Complete the questions with the correct words. Then ask and answer them in pairs.

  1 When was the last time you .... an argument with someone? What was it about?

  2 How did you .... your last birthday?

  3 Have you ever .... your phone or laptop? What happened?

  4 Why did you last .... house or flat?

  5 Have you ever .... a competition and got a prize?

How to ...

give and respond to personal news

3 **A** 🔊 **5.05** | Listen to six conversations. Match them with the pictures (A–F).

B Look at the pictures again. What happened in each situation? Was it good news or bad news?

4 **A** Complete the table with the words in the box.

> afraid   believe   news   pleased
> shame   sorry   what   wonderful

giving good news	Guess [1] .... ! I've got some amazing [2] .... I've got some good news to tell you. I'm really pleased to tell you …
giving bad news	Bad news, I'm [3] .... Unfortunately, … There's something I need to tell you.
giving good or bad news	You won't [4] .... this (but) … I've got something to tell you … You know … ? Well, …
responding to good news	Wow, that's amazing/fantastic/awesome! That's [5] .... news! I'm so [6] .... for you. I can't believe it. That's great! Well done! Congratulations! That *is* good news.
responding to bad news	That's terrible/awful. I'm really sorry. What a [7] .... I'm so [8] .... to hear that.

B 🔊 **5.05** | Listen again and check.

C Learn and practise. Go to the Grammar Bank.

▶▶ page 122 **GRAMMAR BANK**

PRONUNCIATION

5 **A** 🔊 **5.06** | **intonation to exaggerate feelings** | Listen and underline the stressed syllables in the phrases. Notice how the speakers use intonation to exaggerate their feelings.

Wow, that's amazing!	I'm so pleased for you.
That's awesome!	Oh no! That's awful.
Congratulations!	I'm really sorry.

B Choose the correct words to complete the rule.

When we respond to news, we can exaggerate our feelings by stressing the **vowel** / **consonant** sounds and making them **longer** / **shorter**.

C 🔊 **5.07** | Listen to six people giving news. Respond with a suitable response from Ex 4A. Then compare your response with the speakers.

SPEAKING

6 **A** Think of five pieces of good or bad news to tell other students. Use some of the situations from Ex 2A, or your own ideas. Think about how to introduce each one.

B Move around the classroom and speak to different students. Each time, tell them one piece of your news and respond to one piece of their news.

A: You won't believe this, but I got a promotion!
B: Really? That's amazing!

MEDIATION SKILL
agreeing to a change of plans
agree on a plan

▶▶ page 154 **MEDIATION BANK**

5D 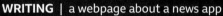 **BBC** Street Interviews

The future of news

GRAMMAR | *will*, *might* and *be going to* for predictions
SPEAKING | plan a news app
WRITING | a webpage about a news app

Rob

Matt

Ayesha

Devante

PREVIEW

1 Work in pairs. What types of news interest you the most? Which types are you not interested in?

I'm really interested in news about sport and culture. I'm not at all interested in news about business or politics.

BBC

Q1: What kind of news interests you the most?

Q2: How do you think news will change in the future?

VIEW

2 ▶ Watch the first part of the video. Tick the types of news that are mentioned.

celebrities   crime   culture   international news
local news   music   politics   sports   technology

3 A ▶ Watch the second part of the video. Make notes on some of the predictions that the speakers make about news in the future.

B ▶ Work in pairs. Choose the correct word to complete the summary for each speaker. Then watch part 2 again and check.

1 Isabelle: I think print media will **develop** / **disappear** over time.

2 Matt: There's too much **positivity** / **negativity** on the news.

3 Natalia: I think the **younger** / **older** generation will be more interested in the news.

4 Rob: Hopefully, people will stop getting their news from **traditional** / **social** media.

5 Devante: Hopefully, it'll be a bit more **interesting** / **selective**.

6 Ayesha: I definitely think that **celebrities** / **influencers** are going to be more prominent in the news.

7 Henry: I think the news will be **online** / **offline** a lot more.

C Work in pairs. Which statements in Ex 3B do you agree with?

Henry

Natalia

Isabelle

B B C

GRAMMAR

will, *might* and *be going to* for predictions

4 A Complete the sentences from the interviews with the words in the box.

> going to be   might be   will

1 I think print media _____ disappear.
2 I think it _____ hard then to distinguish real news from fake news.
3 I definitely think that celebrities are _____ more prominent.

B Learn and practise. Go to the Grammar Bank.

▶▶ page 123 **GRAMMAR BANK**

SPEAKING

plan a news app

5 A Work in groups. You are going to plan your own news app. Choose a topic from the box, or think of your own idea. Then discuss the questions (1–5).

> celebrity gossip   crime in your area   festivals
> funny news   good news   jobs   sport   the arts

1 What will your app be called?
2 What kinds of information will it include?
3 Who will use it?
4 Why will it be useful?
5 How will it be different to other news apps?

B Present your ideas to other groups and justify your decisions. Use the Key phrases to help.

> **KEY PHRASES**
>
> It will definitely have …
> It's going to …
> It probably won't have …
> Users will be able to …
> It might have …
> People will probably use it …

WRITING

a webpage about a news app

6 A Read about the Happy News app. Would you subscribe to this kind of news app? Why/Why not?

happy news

Have you had enough of reading about bad news every day?

Welcome to Happy News – a news app that brings you the best good news stories from around the world every day, delivered directly to your phone.

We will bring you wonderful stories about people from all around the world who are doing amazing things. Their stories will definitely bring a smile to your face.

We won't publish stories about disasters and political problems. We'll share stories of people turning a terrible situation into something better, stories about positive change.

Why?

We believe that by sharing these kinds of stories, instead of spending all our time thinking about all the bad things in the world, we might start to make the world a better place for everyone.

Click **here** to subscribe or follow us on social media. #happynews

By the way, we won't use advertising, but we will invite you to have a look at our #happynews shop where you will find all sorts of things to help make your day happier, from coffee cups and notebooks to happy artwork.

B Write a webpage to give people information about your news app. Include:

- a description of your news app.
- information about what it will include and won't include.
- why you think people should subscribe.

GRAMMAR
relative clauses

1 A Choose the correct words to complete the definitions.

1 a person **what** / **who** / **which** plays in the same team as you
2 the team **that** / **when** / **it** finishes top at the end of the season
3 the place **that** / **which** / **where** most of a university's buildings are located
4 someone **which** / **that** / **what** campaigns to create change in the world
5 the way people feel on a day **which** / **that** / **when** they have nothing to do
6 a process **when** / **which** / **who** involves taking old things and using them again
7 to give money to help other people at a time **who** / **that** / **when** they need it

B Match the definitions in Ex 1A with the words in the box.

> activist   bored   campus   champion
> donate   recycling   teammate

2 Work in pairs. Take turns to choose a person or thing in the box and give a definition. Your partner guesses the word that you defined.

> a famous book or film   a famous singer
> a person in the news   a person in the room
> a room in the building   a town or city
> an object in your bag   an object on the table

He's the actor who …   It's the room where …

reported speech

3 Read the direct speech, then complete the reported speech.

1 'I never buy newspapers.'
Jack said .... newspapers.
2 'I watched a really interesting programme about fake news.'
Jade told .... a really interesting programme about fake news.
3 'We aren't going to buy a new car.'
My parents said .... a new car.
4 'I'll help with the party.'
My sister told .... the party.

4 A Work in pairs. Take turns to ask and answer the questions (1–4). Make a note of your partner's answers.

1 What are your plans for your next holiday?
2 Where did you grow up? Is it different there now?
3 What do you usually do on a Saturday afternoon?
4 What are you going to do later?

B Work with another student. Report what you learnt about your first partner.

My partner said she was going on holiday to Fiji …

will, might and be going to for predictions

5 A Put the words in order to make sentences.

In the future:

1 a / different / job / probably / do / I / think / I'll
2 retrain / think / I / might / I
3 won't / move / I / probably / house
4 I / have / lots / of / to / think / I'm / children / going
5 leave / I / country / definitely / this / won't
6 I / play / learn / might / to / guitar / the

B Change the sentences so that they are true for you. Compare with a partner.

VOCABULARY

6 Work in pairs. Student A: Say a word or phrase from the box. Student B: Choose a second word or phrase and make a sentence using both. Then swap roles.

> activist   campaign   celebrate your birthday
> collect   environment   fail your exams   fake news
> get married   get promoted   graduate from university
> have a baby   have an argument   headline
> journalist   lose your job   pollution   post online

A: Fake news.
B: Journalists should not report fake news.

7 A Choose the correct options (A–C) to complete the text.

New magazine launch

WORLDCHANGE is a new monthly magazine ¹............ looks at issues related to the environment. The idea is to cover all the ²............ news in this field. Our journalists will ³............ out what's really going on and write detailed ⁴............ to educate the public. The focus of the magazine will be on issues like the recycling of ⁵............ and climate ⁶............ . In addition to the print magazine, our website will include daily blog posts. These ⁷............ about new ⁸............ to save the environment, and the work of ⁹............ like Greta Thunberg. Our managing editor, Laura Grundwig, said that the magazine ¹⁰............ be a torch that shone a light on the biggest issue of our times.

	A	B	C
1	what	it	that
2	strong	breaking	immediate
3	find	learn	decide
4	fake news	articles	headlines
5	waste	weather	charity
6	campaign	resources	change
7	will probably be	probably will	will be probably
8	charities	campaigns	disasters
9	activists	resources	issues
10	can	would	must

B 🔊 R5.01 | Listen and check your answers.

creators

6

VLOGS

Q: What creative things do you do or are you interested in?

1 ▶ Watch the video. Note down five different activities the people mention, then compare your notes in groups.

2 What creative things do you enjoy?

GSE LEARNING OBJECTIVES

6A READING | Read an article about two famous people in the arts: the arts; people, places, things

Pronunciation: *used to*

Talk about past hobbies: *used to*

6B LISTENING | Understand people talking about creativity in their lives: creativity: word building

Pronunciation: word stress in word families

Talk about ways to be more creative: comparatives and superlatives

Write a review

6C HOW TO ... | ask for and give opinions and reasons: extreme adjectives

Pronunciation: intonation for expressing opinions

6D BBC PROGRAMME | Understand a documentary about an artist

Talk about a creative genius: present perfect + *for, since* and *yet*

Write a nomination for an award

6A The two Pablos

GRAMMAR | *used to*
VOCABULARY | the arts; the arts: people, places, things
PRONUNCIATION | *used to*

One was possibly the greatest **painter** of the twentieth century, the other was one of the greatest **musicians** and **composers**. Both were called Pablo, both were from Spain, both produced incredible work, both spent years abroad and both died in 1973. In the **arts**, Pablo Picasso and Pablo Casals are world-famous. Picasso worked in many different **styles** and produced thousands of **works** of art about different **subjects**, and created some of the most famous **images** of the twentieth century. Casals was a great **performer**, whose **recordings** continue to influence musicians today. Both lived very long lives, but their work will live even longer.

VOCABULARY

the arts

1 A Do you recognise the men in the photos? What do you know about them? What can you guess?

B Read the introduction to an article to find out about them.

2 A Complete the meanings with the correct form of the words in bold in Ex 1B.

1 A .... is someone who is paid to play a musical instrument.
2 The .... are music, writing, art, literature, film, etc.
3 A .... is someone who plays music or acts in public.
4 A .... is something that is recorded so people can watch or listen again in the future.
5 A .... is a person who paints pictures.
6 The .... of a work of art is the way it looks.
7 Your .... are the things you are writing about, drawing or discussing.
8 A .... is someone who writes music.
9 Artists' .... are the things that they create (music, books, etc.).
10 An .... is any kind of picture.

B Work in pairs. Tell your partner about:
- a composer, musician or painter from your country.
- your favourite and least favourite of the arts.
- a style of music or painting that you like.
- a work of art, image or recording that you like.

C Learn and practise. Go to the Vocabulary Bank.

▶ page 141 **VOCABULARY BANK** the arts: people, places, things

READING

3 A Work in pairs. Student A: Read Text A. Student B: Read Text B. What is the main topic of your text? Choose the correct answer.

1 Pablo never achieved as much success as he wanted.
2 Pablo started young and never stopped working on his art.
3 Pablo changed after he became famous.

B Read your text again and answer the questions.

1 What does the text say about the artist's childhood, his father and how he started his career?
2 Why is the city of Paris mentioned?
3 What type of life was the artist living when he was twenty-three?
4 What were his work habits?
5 What was he still doing in his nineties?

C Use your answers in Ex 3B to tell your partner about the artist in your text.

D Work in pairs and discuss the questions.

1 In what ways were the two Pablos similar?
2 Do you know any other artists or performers who kept working when they were old?
3 Why do you think some people never want to stop working?

A Pablo Picasso
the 3 a.m. genius

Picasso's mother said that her son's first word was 'piz', a short form of 'lapiz', the Spanish word for a pencil. The boy's father was an artist, and the house was full of pencils, paint and paper. From the age of five, Picasso drew everything he saw. He used to draw at school, at home, in restaurants, even in bed. He painted his first painting when he was seven and kept it for the rest of his life. He produced nearly 50,000 works.

In 1904, Picasso moved from Spain to Paris. He was twenty-three years old and so poor that he had to burn some of his paintings to keep warm. He used to pay his bills by giving people drawings instead of money. It was in Paris that Picasso became a great artist. His fortunes changed and he became successful. When he was famous, he once refused to sign a drawing in a restaurant, saying he was buying a meal not the whole restaurant.

As his fame grew, he continued to produce more and more art. He used to arrive at his studio in the afternoon and often worked until 3 a.m. He painted in many different styles and used everything around him in his art. His studio was full of old furniture, newspapers, bus tickets, bottles, plates, boxes and guitars. He left these objects on chairs, tables and the floor until eventually they appeared in his works.

Picasso lived a long life. He worked for over seventy years, and was still painting in his nineties. By the time he died, aged ninety-one, many people believed he was the greatest artist in history.

B Pablo Casals
Ninety years of music

Pablo Casals was one of Spain's greatest musicians. His father was a music teacher and as a baby, Casals used to listen to his father playing the piano. By the age of six, Casals played the piano and the violin. One day, he saw someone performing on a cello. He immediately fell in love with the instrument, stopped playing the violin and the piano, and became a cello player.

For Casals, the cello was more than a hobby. From the age of thirteen, he used to start the day with a walk in nature. After this, he used to practise playing the same notes again and again, all before breakfast! One day, he was in a second-hand music store with his father when they found a sheet of cello music by Bach. They bought it and this changed Casals' life. He fell in love with Bach's music and later became famous for his performances of this composer's music.

When he was still a young man, Casals went to live in Paris. There, his fame as a musician and composer grew. He then travelled all over the world playing the cello. At the age of twenty-three, he even played for Queen Victoria in London. Sixty-two years later, when he was eighty-five, he played for President Kennedy in the White House.

Casals never stopped practising the cello, even as an old man. When he was in his nineties, an interviewer asked him why he still practised every day. Casals replied that it was because he thought he was getting better! By the time he died, aged ninety-six, Casals was loved all over the world and had influenced a generation of musicians.

GRAMMAR

used to

4 A Look at the verbs in bold in the sentences from the texts. Which describe a single event in the past? Which describe a regular habit in the past?

  1 He **used to draw** at school.
  2 He immediately **fell** in love with the instrument.
  3 He **used to listen** to his father playing the piano.
  4 He **painted** his first painting when he was seven.

B Learn and practise. Go to the Grammar Bank.

▶▶ page 124 **GRAMMAR BANK**

PRONUNCIATION

5 A 🔊 **6.01 | *used to* |** Listen to the sentences. Notice the pronunciation of *used to* and *didn't use to*. Do we pronounce the 'd' in *used to*?

  1 I used to collect toy cars when I was a child.
  2 We used to live in the countryside.
  3 I didn't use to like vegetables.
  4 I didn't use to like playing sports at school.

B Complete the sentences so they are true for you. Then say your sentences to a partner. Make sure you pronounce *used to* correctly.

  I used to enjoy …   I didn't use to like …
  I used to go …   I didn't use to spend much time …

SPEAKING

6 A You are going to talk about a hobby that you used to have. Match the sentences (1–4) with the photos (A–E).

  1 I used to skateboard when I was a child. I got quite good at it and could do jumps and tricks.
  2 When I was ten years old, I used to collect toy cars.
  3 I used to play tennis every day when I was younger. I stopped playing a few years ago.
  4 I used to spend hours drawing cartoon characters on my computer.
  5 I used to have a guitar lesson once a week when I was a child.

B Think about the hobby you used to have. Answer the questions and prepare what you will say.

  1 What was the hobby?
  2 When did you start?
  3 How long did you use to spend on it every week?
  4 Why did you enjoy it?
  5 How did you get better at it?
  6 Is the hobby still important to you now?

C Work with other students. Describe your hobby. Ask your classmates questions to find out more about their hobbies.

  A: I used to dance every day …
  B: What type of dance did you like the best? Who did you use to dance with?

6B Be creative

GRAMMAR | comparatives and superlatives
VOCABULARY | creativity: word building
PRONUNCIATION | word stress in word families

VOCABULARY

creativity: word building

1 A Work in groups. Do the paperclip challenge. You have one minute.

> ### The paperclip challenge
>
> Try this test to see how creative you are.
> Look at the paperclip. What do you think it
> could be used for? Write down as many ideas
> as possible. You have one minute.

B Look on page 147. Were any of the ideas the same as yours? Which group had the most creative ideas?

C Work in pairs. Answer the questions.

1 Do you think the activity in Ex 1A is a good way to measure how creative someone is? Why/Why not?
2 In what ways do you think you are creative?
3 How important is it to be creative in everyday life? Why?

2 A Read the text. Do you agree with what it says about creativity?

What is creativity?

When we think about **creativity**, we often think of the world's most **talented artists** – people like Frida Kahlo, Einstein or Mozart. But you don't have to have more **talent** than everyone else to **create** something new and exciting. All you need is a little **imagination** and a bit of free time. You might not be very **artistic**, or even interested in **art**, so your painting skills may not be brilliant, but maybe you're a **skilful** and **imaginative** cook and enjoy creating new and original recipes. Or you could be someone who has brilliant ideas for solving problems at work. Maybe you show your creativity in the clothes you wear, or perhaps you are keen on **photography** – maybe you use your **photographic** abilities to take pictures of your friends, then use your digital **skills** to change them and make interesting images. All of these are **creative** activities. And they are very important. When we look at the way that computers and technology are capable of doing many of the everyday jobs we used to do, it is easy to **imagine** that creativity is perhaps the most important skill for the future.

B Complete the table with the bold words in the text in Ex 2A.

verb	noun	adjective
X		talented
imagine		
	creativity	
X	art/	
photograph/ take a photograph	photo/	
X		skilful

PRONUNCIATION

3 A | **word stress in word families** |
Underline the stressed syllable in each word in Ex 2B. Is the stress on the same syllable in each word in a word family?

B 🔊 **6.02** | Listen and check. Practise saying the words.

C Work in pairs. Write three questions to ask your partner using the words in Ex 2B. Then ask and answer your questions.

In what ways are you talented?

D Read the Future Skills box and do the task.

> **FUTURE SKILLS**
> ### Creativity
>
> Creativity can be useful for language learning. Visualising new vocabulary, drawing pictures and creating interesting or unusual sentences or stories with new language are all ways that can help fix the language in your mind. Can you think of other creative ideas for language learning? With a partner, write a list of creative ways to learn English.

LISTENING

4 A 🔊 **6.03** | Listen to four people talking about creativity in their lives. Write the number of each idea next to the person who mentions it.

Roza, film-maker ....   Fabio, chef .... , ...

Joshua, designer ....   Meera, accountant .... , ...

1 I try to experience new situations.
2 I look for new ways to do things.
3 I use nature for inspiration.
4 I need to be creative when looking after my daughter.
5 I am inspired by what other people in my profession are doing.
6 I don't think creativity is important for my work.

B 🔊 **6.03** | Listen again and choose the correct option (a or b) for each question (1–6).

1 Roza believes that creativity
   a is important for everyone.
   b is especially important for writers and film-makers.
2 Roza thinks that
   a being creative makes it easier for her to talk to other people.
   b talking to people with different opinions helps her to be more creative.
3 Joshua thinks it is helpful to
   a use natural materials when you design things.
   b pay attention to the things that you see around you.
4 Fabio
   a tries to find ways to improve his business.
   b enjoys cooking when he has an audience.
5 Meera
   a doesn't enjoy her job because it isn't creative.
   b often does creative activities at home.
6 Meera plays with her daughter
   a creating new toys and games.
   b building computers and robots.

C Work in pairs. Read some of the ideas the people expressed. Which do you agree with? Why?

1 I enjoy talking to people who have different opinions to me.
2 I'm always learning from other people's ideas.
3 I'm not very interested in the arts, music or painting.

GRAMMAR

comparatives and superlatives

5 A Complete the sentences with the words and phrases in the box.

> as important as   harder   more carefully
> more interesting   most important
> my best   easier   the hardest

1 Creativity is the .... part of my job.
2 I think being creative is just .... these other things.
3 It forces you to think .... about your ideas.
4 I think it makes my films ....
5 It's .... for me to get ideas when I'm outside.
6 All of .... ideas come from nature.
7 That's .... thing about cooking.
8 I have to work .... when I'm at home than when I'm in the office!

B 🔊 **6.04** | Listen and check your answers. Then look at the words and phrases you added in Ex 5A. Which are adjectives and which are adverbs?

C Complete the rules for forming the comparatives and superlatives of adjectives and adverbs.

1 For short adjectives and adverbs, e.g. *fast*, *hard*:
   Comparatives: add ....
   Superlatives: add ....

2 For longer adjectives or adverbs ending in *-ly*, e.g. *quickly*
   Comparatives: use ....
   Superlatives: use ....

3 Some adjectives and adverbs are irregular, e.g. *good/well*, *better*, *the* ....

4 We can also use *(not) as* + ... + *as* to make comparisons.

D Learn and practise. Go to the Grammar Bank.

▶▶ page 125 **GRAMMAR BANK**

6 Work in pairs. What do you do differently now compared to five years ago? Use an idea from each box to make sentences.

> cook   meet friends   run   speak English
> take photographs   use social media   work

> accurate   careful   far   fluent
> good   hard   often   quick

I work harder now than five years ago, and I don't take photographs as often as I used to.

SPEAKING

7 A Work in pairs. Look at the tips to help you become more creative. Can you add two more?

13 ways to be more creative

1 Drink more coffee
2 Turn off your mobile phone
3 Travel somewhere new
4 Write lists
5 Change your routine
6 Sleep more
7 Spend more time outdoors
8 Be more sociable
9 Do some exercise
10 Organise your workspace
11 Stop trying to be perfect
12 Listen to music
13 Learn something new

B Work alone. Which of the tips:

1 might help you work or study better?
2 could help you to be more imaginative?
3 can you fit into your day the most easily?
4 might help you think about problems more clearly?

C Discuss your ideas in groups. Give reasons for your opinions. Which do you think are the best ideas?

WRITING

a review

8 A Work in pairs. Think about something creative that you have enjoyed recently. Use the ideas in the box or your own ideas. Discuss the questions below.

> album   art exhibition   book   film
> restaurant meal   video game

1 Why did you enjoy it?
2 In what ways was it original or creative?
3 Why was it better or worse than similar ones you have experienced before?

B Read the restaurant review below. Note down the positive and negative points.

9 A Read the comments that people have added to the review. Answer the questions (1–3).

> **SA** ✎ 2 reviews ⊙ GB   A day ago
>
> It was quite expensive. We won't go back there, **unless** it's a special occasion.

> **AD** ✎ 22 reviews ⊙ GB   A day ago
>
> **Although** a lot of the dishes are traditional, they all have something special.

> **KG** ✎ 12 reviews ⊙ GB   2 days ago
>
> **While** the staff are busy, they still find time to be friendly.

> **BH** ✎ 8 reviews ⊙ GB   3 days ago
>
> I would happily eat here again **because of** the wonderful food.

1 Which two linking words in bold do we use to connect ideas which contrast with each other?
2 Which do we use to talk about a cause or a reason for something?
3 Which do we use to suggest a condition?

B Read the review in Ex 8B again. Find and underline the linking words.

C Join each pair of sentences or ideas using the word(s) in brackets.

1 Don't buy this album! Or only buy it if you're already a fan of their music. (Don't / unless)

Don't buy this album unless you're already a fan of their music.

2 This game has very bad reviews. Nobody wants to buy it. (Nobody / because of)
3 The food was delicious. The service was poor. (Although)
4 The historical information was interesting. The plot was too slow. (While)

D Choose a restaurant, film, video game, book or music album. Write a short review.

 Paul ✎ 62 reviews ⊙ GB   A day ago

The best restaurant I've ever been to

Nannarella, in Rome, is probably the best restaurant I've ever been to. It's located near a busy square in Trastevere. In the evening, you can sit outside and listen to talented musicians playing while you eat.

The chef has created an imaginative menu, which is based on traditional Italian food, but with new, original ideas. We had a rosemary focaccia to start, followed by two different types of pasta. The carbonara and the lasagne were delicious, although it was a shame that we had to eat quite quickly because we were in a hurry. We finished with the tiramisu, which was the tastiest dessert I've ever eaten.

While it is busier than other restaurants, and there are a lot of tourists, the atmosphere was very friendly and relaxed. The staff made sure that we had everything we needed. If you come at lunchtime, make sure you book a table, unless you don't mind waiting. Also, it wasn't as expensive as similar restaurants in the area. I would recommend Nannarella to anybody visiting Rome because of both the food and the service. You'll remember the experience.

6C Why do you think that?

HOW TO ... | ask for and give opinions and reasons
VOCABULARY | extreme adjectives
PRONUNCIATION | intonation for expressing opinions

VOCABULARY

extreme adjectives

1 A Read the text. What are the benefits of public art? Why do some people dislike it?

B Discuss in pairs. Is there public art where you live? What do you think of it?

2 A Read the statements. What do you think each one is describing?

1 It's in the city centre and it's **huge**. I don't know if it's for offices or flats. **a building**
2 It was **fantastic**! The acting was really good.
3 It was really **outstanding**. All the flavours were amazing!
4 It's **terrible**. It takes up loads of memory on my phone!
5 The plot was **impossible** to understand, so I switched off. I won't watch the other episodes.
6 It's **tiny**! I could hardly see it on the gallery wall.
7 It's **essential** if you want to get fit. It tells you how much exercise you've done each day.
8 I think it looks **horrible**. No one would wear those colours together!
9 The curved walls are **fascinating** when the sun shines.

B Add the adjectives in bold in Ex 2A to the table, next to the adjectives with a similar meaning. Do extreme adjectives have a stronger or weaker meaning than normal adjectives?

adjectives	extreme adjectives
1 bad	terrible, ...
2 good	fantastic, ...
3 interesting	....
4 big	....
5 small	....
6 important	....
7 difficult	....

Public art – love it or hate it?

From the art we see painted on the walls of our cities to the huge sculptures we might find outside a museum, public art is everywhere. In the past, public art often meant statues of historical figures. These days, all kinds of fantastic art has moved outside art galleries, where it has more space and a bigger audience. Public art is for everyone. It's free and you don't need to buy a ticket. It can also help to create a city's identity. For example, Louise Bourgeois's *Maman*, a sculpture of a giant spider, outside the Guggenheim Museum, has become a symbol of Bilbao, Spain. Anthony Gormley's outstanding sculpture *The Angel of the North* is similarly popular with visitors to the north of England. However, not everybody likes public art. Some say it's a waste of money. Others think it's ugly. One example is graffiti. Some say it's art and others say it's vandalism. What do you think?

3 A Read the two statements (a and b). Then choose the correct words to complete the rules (1 and 2).

a We can say 'very bad'. We can't say 'very terrible'.
b We can say 'absolutely fantastic'. We can't say 'absolutely good'.

1 We use *very* with **normal / extreme** adjectives to make them stronger.
2 We use *absolutely* with **normal / extreme** adjectives to make them stronger.

B Work in pairs. Student A: Close the book. Student B: Make a sentence with *very* and a normal adjective. Student A: Reply with *absolutely* and an extreme adjective. Then change roles.

B: It was a very bad film.
A: Yes, it was absolutely terrible!

C Work in pairs. Discuss the photos in this lesson. Try to use extreme adjectives!

I think the sculpture is absolutely fantastic!

How to …

ask for and give opinions and reasons

4 A 🔊 **6.05** | Listen to three conversations. Answer the questions about each one.

1 What are the people discussing?

2 Do the speakers in each conversation have the same opinions or different opinions?

3 What do they agree in the end?

B 🔊 **6.05** | Complete the table with the phrases in the box. Listen again and check.

> For me, …   How about you?   I guess we all like different things.
> In my view, …   The reason is …   What makes you say that?

asking for an opinion	What do/did you think of … ? 1 ....
giving an opinion	I think … I would say … 2 .... 3 ....
asking for a reason	Why do you think that? 4 ....
giving a reason	It's because … 5 ....
agreeing to disagree	I suppose we're all different. I guess it's good we're not all the same. 6 ....

C Learn and practise. Go to the Grammar Bank.

▶▶ page 126 **GRAMMAR BANK**

PRONUNCIATION

5 A 🔊 **6.06** | **intonation for expressing opinions** | Listen to the opinions (1–3). Which word is stressed in each one?

1 For me, it has no meaning.

2 In my view, it's a really new and exciting design.

3 I think it's a fantastic app!

B 🔊 **6.06** | Listen again. Then practise saying the sentences.

SPEAKING

6 A Choose three categories in the box and make a list of your top 5 for each.

> apps   artists   bands or songs
> films or TV programmes   video games
> websites   YouTubers

My top 5 websites are BBC Sport, Wikipedia, …

B Read the Future Skills box and do the task.

FUTURE SKILLS
Critical thinking

When we give an opinion, we usually give reasons to support it. Think about your answers in Ex 6A. What reasons can you give to support them?

C Work in groups. Take turns to talk about your lists.

- Explain your opinions and ask for your partner's opinion.
- Ask for and give reasons for your opinions.
- If you have different opinions, agree to disagree.

MEDIATION SKILL
describing why something interests you

agree on a book to read for a book club

▶▶ page 155 **MEDIATION BANK**

6D B B C Documentary

An artist at work

GRAMMAR | present perfect + *for, since* and *yet*
SPEAKING | a creative genius
WRITING | a nomination for an award

PREVIEW

1 A Look at the photo of artist Yinka Shonibare below. What do you think is special or different about his work?

B Read the programme information and check your ideas.

B B C

What do artists do all day?

Yinka Shonibare is one of the UK's top contemporary artists. He became famous in the 1990s and since then he has produced a unique body of work, which is often colourful and humorous. He is influenced by his Nigerian origins and his work often uses colourful African fabrics. This film shows Yinka creating a figure called *Balloon Man*, and talking about his life and career.

VIEW

2 A ▶ Watch the BBC video clip. How does Yinka feel about his artwork when it is finished?

B ▶ Number the stages for creating one of Yinka's works in order. Then watch again to check your answers.

a Nigel Schofield takes some photos for the sculpture.
b The sculpture goes to a costume-maker who covers it in fabric.
c Yinka sketches his idea on paper. 1
d The finished sculpture goes to the gallery.
e They use the photos to make a realistic figure.
f Yinka checks the sculpture and suggests changes.

C Work in pairs and discuss the questions.

1 Do you like this kind of artwork? Why/Why not?
2 Do know of any other artists who have interesting work practices?
3 Are there any well-known art galleries where you live? Have you visited these or any others?
4 Do you ever buy art? What kind of art do you like?

GRAMMAR

present perfect + *for, since* and *yet*

3 A Complete the sentences from the programme with *for, since* and *yet*.

1 The art gallery has supported Yinka .... the start of his career.
2 Nigel Schofield has worked with Yinka .... more than ten years.
3 Yinka hasn't seen the finished sculpture ....

B Complete the rules with *for, since* and *yet*.

1 We use the present perfect with .... or .... to talk about something that started in the past and is still true now.
2 We use .... to refer back to a particular time in the past.
3 We use .... to refer to a period of time which started in the past.
4 We use .... with the present perfect to talk about 'at any time up to now'. We use it to emphasise that something hasn't happened, but we expect it to happen soon.

C Learn and practise. Go to the Grammar Bank.

▶▶ page 127 **GRAMMAR BANK**

SPEAKING

a creative genius

4 A 🔊 **6.07** | Listen to someone nominating a person for a creative genius award. Answer the questions.

1 Do you think Jake is creative? Why/Why not?
2 What kinds of things does he enjoy?

B 🔊 **6.07** | Listen again and tick the phrases that you hear.

> **KEY PHRASES**
>
> I'm going to nominate/tell you about …
> … is the most amazing …
> He has enjoyed … since …
> He is always drawing/cooking/looking for …
> He has also done a lot of …
> For the last few years, he has …
> He hasn't … yet, but …
> I think … deserves the award because/as …

C You are going to nominate someone for a creative genius award. Read the instructions and make notes about the person you have chosen.

- Talk about someone who is creative. It can be someone you know or someone famous, e.g. a singer, actor, sportsperson, etc.
- Talk about their abilities and give reasons why they should get the award. Use the Key phrases to help.

D Work with other students. Take turns to talk about the person you want to nominate. Use the Key phrases to help. Other students: Listen to the nominations and ask questions to learn more.

E Work together to decide who should win the award and why.

WRITING

a nomination for an award

5 A Read about the MacArthur prize. Do you think prizes like this are a good idea? Why?

> The MacArthur Fellowship offers creative individuals prize money to help them continue their creative work. The award can go to scientists, engineers, musicians, artists, journalists, etc. It can be anyone who is pushing the boundaries of creativity within their field in order to discover new things or new ways of doing things for the benefit of society.

B Your college or workplace is organising its own creative genius award. Read the nomination below. Do you think this person should win the award? Why/Why not?

To: admin@creativegenius.com
Subject: Creative genius award

I would like to propose my friend Marco Santini for the creative genius award because Marco is the most creative pasta chef I know. He can cook all different types of pasta dishes using whatever ingredients he has in the kitchen. Even when you think there is nothing left to eat, Marco can always surprise you with a delicious meal from nowhere. He has always made his own pasta since his grandmother taught him when he was a child. But nowadays, he's always inventing his own new recipes. He makes pasta of all different colours and shapes and when he shows you the dish, it looks like a work of art. It's always delicious, too! I think Marco deserves the award as he is definitely the most creative person I know.

C Write a nomination for the creative genius award. You can nominate someone you know, or you can nominate yourself!

GRAMMAR

used to

1 A Correct the mistakes in the sentences.

1 We used to going on holiday every year when we were kids.
2 I didn't used to like my physics teacher at school.
3 Did you use draw a lot when you were a child?
4 I use to play the piano, but I don't play now.
5 My best friend at school used live just across the road from me.
6 Have you use to have more free time than you do now?
7 I used spend a lot of time with my grandparents when I was younger.

B Use the ideas in Ex 1A to make four sentences that are true for you.

C Work in pairs. Compare your sentences. Then find three things that you both used to do as children, but you don't do now.

comparatives and superlatives

2 A Complete the sentences with the correct comparative or superlative form of the adjective or adverb in brackets.

1 I think walking is .... (good) than running for helping to give you creative ideas.
2 I love playing sport, but I'm always too busy. I'd love to be able to do this .... (regularly).
3 I feel .... (happy) in the countryside than in the city.
4 I think being able to cook is one of the .... (important) skills to have.
5 I love singing, but I'm not very good. I'm .... (talented) my sister.
6 I drove over 600 km to Scotland. It's .... (far) I have ever driven.

B Work in pairs. Discuss the questions.

1 What things would you like to do more regularly?
2 What are the most important skills in life?
3 What do you find are the best ways to relax?

present perfect + for, since and yet

3 A Complete the sentences by adding for, since or yet in the correct place.

1 My parents have been married forty years!
2 I've lived in this city ten years.
3 I haven't visited the USA, but I plan to.
4 I have worked in this job 2012.
5 I have played the guitar I was about fifteen years old.
6 I'd like to live somewhere different in the future, but I haven't decided where.

B Choose three of the sentences in Ex 3A and rewrite them so they are true for you. Then compare your sentences with a partner.

VOCABULARY

4 Complete the words in bold.

1 I'm not very **art**............ . I sometimes do **draw**............ of animals, though.
2 My brother is really good at **photogr**............ . He takes amazing photos!
3 My brother's greatest **sk**............ is cooking – his food is amazing!
4 It's just some flowers – it isn't a very original **sub**............ for a **paint**............ !
5 I love her architecture. It's so **imagin**............ .
6 I don't think I'm a very **creat**............ person. I don't have a lot of **tal**............ .
7 The football stadium is sometimes used as a **ven**............ for music concerts.
8 Pablo Picasso worked in many different **sty**............ .
9 I really enjoy the **wo**............ of Matisse and Cézanne.
10 My friend Fernando is an abstract **paint**............ who spends a lot of his time in his **stu**............ .

5 A Choose the correct options (A–C) to complete the text.

David Hockney – a life of colour

David Hockney is considered by many to be one of the most [1]............ artists. His work is very colourful and [2]............ . When Hockney was a young boy, he used to watch his father painting old bicycles. He knew immediately that he wanted to spend his life doing [3]............ . However, at school art was not considered a serious subject, and it was only taught to students who weren't very [4]............ in other areas. But Hockney was determined to study art. He spent a lot of time doing [5]............ with pencils and pens, in order to develop his [6]............ . At the age of sixteen, he decided to go to art school. He worked hard all his life, often spending days and nights in his [7]............ painting. He wrote a sign at the end of his bed which said, 'Get up and work immediately.' He worked in different [8]............ and using different media. Later in his career, he used technology, like iPads, to produce his [9]............ . His works have been enjoyed by art lovers [10]............ many years now, and they are shown in [11]............ around the world.

1 **A** creative	**B** creativity	**C** create
2 **A** imagine	**B** imaginative	**C** imagination
3 **A** art	**B** arts	**C** artist
4 **A** talent	**B** talents	**C** talented
5 **A** shows	**B** drawings	**C** recordings
6 **A** skills	**B** subjects	**C** works
7 **A** style	**B** studio	**C** architecture
8 **A** paintings	**B** styles	**C** designs
9 **A** shows	**B** venues	**C** images
10 **A** during	**B** since	**C** for
11 **A** art galleries	**B** shows	**C** photographers

B 🔊 **R6.01** | Listen and check your answers.

travel

7

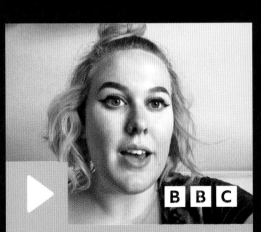

VLOGS

Q: Where do you feel happiest?

1 ▶ Watch the video. Note down the different places and activities the people mention.

2 Where do you feel happiest?

GSE **LEARNING OBJECTIVES**

7A **READING** | Read an article about responsible tourism: travel and tourism

Pronunciation: contractions

Talk about tourism: first and second conditionals

7B **LISTENING** | Understand someone talking about moving abroad: new experiences; the natural world

Pronunciation: emphasising quantity

Talk about new experiences

Write a description of an experience

7C **HOW TO ...** | make and respond to recommendations: describing places

Pronunciation: sounding enthusiastic

7D **BBC STREET INTERVIEWS** | Understand people talking about travelling

Talk about travelling: reflexive pronouns

Write an essay about why we travel

7A Good tourists

GRAMMAR | first and second conditionals
VOCABULARY | travel and tourism
PRONUNCIATION | contractions

READING

1 Work in pairs. Ask and answer the questions.

  1 How often do you go away on holiday?

  2 What type of holidays do you like? Why?

  3 Where is your next holiday going to be?

2 A Work in pairs and discuss the questions.

  1 Do you think tourism is generally a good or a bad thing? Why?

  2 Why do you think some people might not like tourists in their area?

B You are going to read an article about how to be a better tourist. Look at the headings (A–F), which have been removed from the article. What suggestions do you think the article will make for how 'responsible tourists' should behave?

  A See more than just the key sights

  B Try somewhere different

  C Say something!

  D Be respectful

  E Keep it clean

  F Time your trip carefully

C Read the article. Put the headings from Ex 2B in the correct places (1–6). Were your predictions from Ex 2B correct?

3 A Work in pairs. Answer the questions.

  According to the article, …

  1 what is the problem at Machu Picchu?

  2 in what way is the festival in Annecy different to the one in Venice?

  3 how can you avoid going to places that are very crowded?

  4 why is it important to find out about the local culture and customs? How can you do this?

  5 why should you try to learn a few words of the local language?

  6 what should tourists take from tourist destinations, and what should they leave behind?

B Work in groups. Discuss the questions.

  1 Do you agree with the ideas in the article?

  2 Do you follow any of these recommendations?

  3 Can you think of any other ideas to add?

Be a better tourist

There are **traffic jams** at Machu Picchu, in Peru, and more than 30 million tourists visit the city of Venice every year. We all love travelling, but we have to accept that people also live in the places we visit. To make their lives easier, here are some tips you can follow.

1 ....

Why go to the same place as everyone else? Instead of going to the most popular **festivals**, you could try alternative destinations. For example, instead of going to Venice to see its famous carnival, you could try Annecy, in France, where they recreate the magic of the Venetian carnival, but without the crowds. If people tried going somewhere different, the main tourist destinations wouldn't be so busy.

2 ....

If possible, travel **out of season**, so that popular places don't become too crowded. If you plan a **trip** to Prague, why not spend a week there rather than just two days? Use the time to really get to know the city. When you visit Amsterdam, you can use a special app that sends notifications to your phone if part of the city is busier than usual. This way you can help avoid making long **queues** at museums.

3 ....

If you go to Paris, you'll probably want to **go sightseeing**. Visit the Eiffel Tower and the Louvre, but don't just stop at the main **tourist attractions**. Travel to the edges of the city and see what you can discover there. You will have special memories of a city if you discover some local places for yourself.

4

Try to find out about the local **culture** of the place you're visiting. If you travel to somewhere new, you'll understand the culture better if you read a book about its history, or read a novel by a local author. Customs differ around the world and it's important to understand and respect local **customs** and **traditions**. Tourist organisations in some countries like Iceland and Japan offer advice to tourists on how to behave and what not to do. You need to watch your body language. Is it polite to shake hands when you meet someone for the first time, or should you bow your head? If you get these customs wrong, you can easily offend people.

5

Try to learn a few of the most common words or phrases. 'Hello,' 'excuse me,' 'thank you' and 'goodbye' are all essential. If you try to speak their language, people will appreciate your efforts.

6

Don't leave a mess wherever you go. From the beaches of Goa to the streets of London, plastic waste is a huge problem for the environment. If everyone took their litter home with them, tourist **destinations** would be a lot cleaner and more attractive. When you visit somewhere beautiful , remember the saying, 'Take only memories, leave only footprints.'

VOCABULARY

travel and tourism

4 A Complete the sentences with the correct form of the words and phrases in bold in the article.

1 It's a local _____ in Poland for people to throw water at each other on Śmigus-dyngus, or 'wet Monday'.

2 Family life is very important in Italian _____ .

3 You can usually find much better prices if you travel _____ when there are not so many tourists.

4 Chinese New Year is one of China's most important _____ . It's a time for family celebrations and most people have a week's holiday.

5 The USA, Spain and Japan are three of the most popular tourist _____ .

6 We're going for a short _____ to the Lake District this weekend.

7 Be careful if it's your birthday in Mexico. When you have a birthday cake, it's a _____ for someone to push your face into it.

8 I'd prefer not to _____ today. We saw all the main _____ yesterday and it was too busy for me. I hate standing in _____ with all those people.

9 The problem with driving to the beach at this time of day is that it's very busy and there are often _____ .

B Work in pairs and discuss the questions.

In your country,

1 what are the main tourist destinations?

2 what foods or traditions are part of your culture?

3 do you ever go sightseeing? What tourist attractions do you visit?

4 what celebrations and festivals are an important part of your culture?

5 are there any good places to visit for a weekend trip near where you live?

C Learn and practise. Go to the Vocabulary Bank.

▶▶ page 142 **VOCABULARY BANK**
travel and tourism

GRAMMAR

first and second conditionals

5 A Look at the sentences (a–d) from the article. Which sentences describe:

1 a possible situation in the future?

2 a situation that is hypothetical or not real?

a If you travel to somewhere new, you'll understand the culture better if you read a book about its history.

b If you try to speak their language, people will appreciate your efforts.

c If people tried going somewhere different, the main tourist destinations wouldn't be so busy.

d If everyone took their litter home with them, tourist destinations would be a lot cleaner and more attractive.

B Read the rules. Then decide if the sentences in Ex 5A are first conditional or second conditional.

1 We use the first conditional for real, possible situations in the future.

2 We use the second conditional to talk about a hypothetical situation in the future.

C Complete the rules with *present simple* or *past simple*.

1 We form the first conditional with *If/When* +............... + *will*.

2 We form the second conditional with *If/When* +............... + *would*.

D Learn and practise. Go to the Grammar Bank.

▶▶ page 128 **GRAMMAR BANK**

PRONUNCIATION

6 A 🔊 **7.01** | **contractions** | Listen and complete the sentences with the contracted form of *will* or *would*.

1 If you learn the language, you............... be able to communicate with people.

2 If you leave rubbish everywhere, somebody............... have to clear it up.

3 If the city charged a tourist tax, they............... reduce the number of tourists.

4 If we stayed in a small hotel, we............... help the local economy.

5 If the hotel gets a good review, it............... encourage more tourists to visit.

6 If tourists had more respect for local customs, it............... be better.

B How are *will* and *would* pronounced as contractions in speech?

C Complete the sentences so that they are true for you. Say the sentences out loud to your partner to compare your ideas. Remember to pronounce the contractions correctly.

• If I go on holiday next year, I'll …

• If I don't have much money next year, I'll …

• If I could go anywhere in the world, I'd …

• If I spoke more languages, I'd …

• Life would be easier if …

SPEAKING

7 A Work in groups. What are the biggest problems with tourism in your town, city or country? Make a list.

I think there are too many/too few tourists.

All the tourists come in the same month.

Tourists only visit the capital city.

B In your groups, look at your list of problems in Ex 7A. Think of a solution for each one and make notes.

Tourists only visit the capital city. – Advertise other places of interest.

C Discuss the questions in your groups.

1 What will happen if each of your suggestions is accepted?

2 How would tourism in your area change if all the changes you suggested were made?

If we advertise other places of interest, more tourists will visit them, so there won't be as many tourists in the capital.

If we made all these changes, the capital city would be less crowded and other places around the country would earn more money from tourism.

8 Read the Future Skills box and discuss the questions.

FUTURE SKILLS

Social responsibility

Good tourists are socially responsible. They respect local customs and try to make sure that their visit does not have a negative impact on the area.

What would you teach a tourist if they wanted to travel around your country? Think about the ideas below or your own ideas.

clothes   customs   greetings
important words
things to avoid saying and doing

7B Globetrotters

GRAMMAR | quantifiers
VOCABULARY | new experiences; the natural world
PRONUNCIATION | emphasising quantity

GRAMMAR

quantifiers

1 A Work in pairs. Guess the answers to the quiz questions.

Travel quiz

1 Which country is the most popular tourist destination?
  a South Africa   **b** France   **c** Brazil
2 Which age group travels the most? People born:
  a 1965–80   **b** 1981–96   **c** after 1996
3 People from which country travel the most (including inside their own country)?
  a Finland   **b** New Zealand   **c** Spain
4 People from which country spend the most on tourism each year?
  a Argentina   **b** the USA   **c** China

B Check your answers on page 146. How many did you guess correctly? Which answers are surprising?

2 A Read some online comments about travel. Which person is the most similar to you? Why?

Leah Uganda ☑6 👍3	I'd visited **hardly any** other countries until my twenties. Then I began to go on **a lot of** trips for work and now I've visited five continents.
Milena USA ☑1	I haven't been to many places outside my own state. I don't have much time to travel because I work and study.
Sunil UK ☑3	I went to plenty of different countries when I was younger. Now that I have a family I don't have enough money to travel. Flights and hotels cost too much money.
Miyako Japan ☑28 👍12	I went on a few trips when I was a teenager, and fell in love with travelling. Now, whenever I have a bit of money, I spend it on travel.
Kerry Australia ☑9 👍8	Lots of people my age travel abroad. We want to see the world while we're young. That's why I'm travelling now.

B Find the words and phrases in the comments that refer to amounts or quantity. The first two have been highlighted.

C Work in pairs. Complete the rules with the quantifiers in the box. Use the sentences in Ex 2A to help you.

> a bit   a few   a lot of   enough   ~~hardly any~~   lots of
> ~~many~~   many   ~~much~~   plenty of   too much

1 We use **many** , **much** , ..., and .... to refer to a large number or amount.
2 We use **hardly any** , ... and .... to refer to a small number or amount.
3 We use *a few* and .... only with countable nouns.
4 We use .... to mean 'the right amount'.
5 We use *too many* and .... to mean 'more than we want'.

D Learn and practise. Go to the Grammar Bank.

▶▶ page 129 **GRAMMAR BANK**

PRONUNCIATION

3 A 🔊 **7.02** | **emphasising quantity** | Listen to four conversations. Write the final word of each one.

1 A: Were there lots of people?
  B: There were hardly ....
2 A: Did you see any wild animals?
  B: We saw a ....
3 A: Are there any free seats?
  B: There are ....
4 A: Did you eat enough?
  B: I ate too ....!

B 🔊 **7.02** | Sometimes we stress quantifiers if we want to emphasise a large or small amount. Listen again. Which words are stressed in the answers in Ex 3A?

C Read the questions and prepare your answers.

1 Do you travel a lot or not very much?
2 How many countries have you visited?
3 How many city breaks have you been on?
4 What was the last city or country you visited? How much time did you spend there? Was it enough time, too much or too little? Why?

D Work in pairs. Ask and answer the questions in Ex 3C. Stress the quantifiers.

LISTENING

4A Work in pairs. You are going to listen to part of an audiobook by an Englishman who moved to Brazil. Discuss the questions.

1 What problems might the man have moving to a new country?

2 What might he like about his new life?

B 🔊 **7.03** | Listen and check your ideas.

C 🔊 **7.03** | Listen again and answer the questions (1–8). Work in pairs. Compare your answers.

1 What two types of transport did the man use to get to his new home in Brazil?

2 What was new and different for him when he arrived?

3 What noises does he mention?

4 How does he describe the coffee in the cafés?

5 What two things does the town have, although it has no cinema, theatre or library?

6 Which people does he become friends with?

7 What does 'living by the sea' mean, in his opinion?

8 How do you think the man feels about his new life in Brazil?

D Work in groups. Discuss the questions.

1 Would you like to move to a new country? If so, where would you go and what would you do?

2 What are the advantages and disadvantages of moving to another country?

VOCABULARY

new experiences

5A Read the extracts from the audiobook. Choose the correct meanings for the words in bold.

1 In those first weeks, everything was **surprising** to me.

a I found it normal.

b It was different to what I thought.

2 It was **strange** to see a mango tree in my garden.

a It was normal.　　　　b It wasn't normal.

3 A shop sold lots of fruits I'd **never heard of**.

a I knew them before.

b I didn't know them before.

4 It was strange to **realise** this heat was normal for a Brazilian summer.

a I understood it for the first time.

b I didn't understand it.

5 I **explored** the town.

a I left the town.

b I walked around the town to find out about it.

6 I **came across** a few cafés.

a I found them by chance.

b I asked for directions to them.

7 They didn't seem to **notice** the stranger.

a They didn't see or hear him.

b They didn't like him.

8 They didn't notice the stranger with the **funny** accent.

a normal　　　　　b not normal

9 They **accepted** me.

a They weren't friendly to me.

b They let me become part of their group.

10 I'd **expected** to be lonely.

a I believed this would happen.

b I felt sad when this happened.

B Think of an idea for each category below.

• a place you enjoyed exploring

• a place you came across by chance

• something you expect to do tomorrow

• something you hadn't heard of until recently

• something that you noticed for the first time recently

• something surprising that you learnt recently

C Work in pairs. Tell your partner your ideas from Ex 5B.

D Read the sentences from the audiobook. Which words describe places in the natural world?

I walked along the coast every morning.

Those dogs on the beach were my friends.

E What other words do you know for places in the natural world?

F Learn and practise. Go to the Vocabulary Bank.

▶▶ page 143 **VOCABULARY BANK** the natural world

SPEAKING

6 A Work in pairs. Which of these new experiences have you had?

> first flight   first time away from home
> going to a new school or university
> moving to a new city
> spending time in a wild place (jungle, rainforest)   starting a new job
> visiting a new country

B Choose a new experience to talk about. Use one of the ideas from Ex 6A or your own idea. Think about the questions below and prepare to tell other students.

  1 What was surprising or strange about the experience?

  2 How did you feel at first?

  3 What did you enjoy about it and what did you find difficult?

  4 What interesting things did you notice?

  5 What did you learn from the experience?

In my first month living in Ankara, I had hardly any friends so I felt a bit lonely …

I explored the city and came across some interesting buildings.

C Work in groups. Take turns to talk about your experiences. Ask questions to learn more about other students' experiences.

WRITING

a description of an experience

7 A Zeinab is writing to her friend to describe a cycling trip. Read the email. Which ideas in the box does she mention?

> food   interesting places to visit   local customs
> meeting people   new ways of doing things
> problems   the landscape   the weather
> what she expected before the trip

Hi Geoff,

I've just got back from my trip to Santiago de Compostela. Three of us cycled in the north of Spain for two weeks and it was amazing. We met lots of people from many different countries and everyone was really friendly.

We enjoyed exploring. We were excited to come across beautiful little towns that we'd never heard of. Many of them had wonderful restaurants and squares, and some had castles and tiny museums. We learnt about the different cultures and customs of that part of Spain. I found the history very interesting.

I'd expected the cycling to be really difficult, but it wasn't too bad. There were hardly any days when I felt too tired to keep going, and the landscape was never boring. We went over hills, through valleys and next to streams and rivers. When we weren't cycling, we tried plenty of the local dishes, which were delicious! Anyway, I'll tell you more when I see you.

Best wishes,

Zeinab

B Find examples of the following phrases that Zeinab uses to describe her feelings and reactions.

  1 *It was* + adjective It was amazing.

  2 *I/We enjoyed* + *-ing*

  3 *I was/We were* + adjective + *to* (do something)

  4 *I found* … + adjective

  5 *I'd expected* … , *but* …

C What adjectives does Zeinab use to describe:

  1 the people?

  2 the towns?

  3 the restaurants?

  4 the history of the place?

  5 the food?

D Plan an email to a friend with a description of a recent experience.

  1 Choose an experience of when you travelled somewhere or did something new.

  2 Read the list of things in Ex 7A. Which will you write about?

  3 Think about how you can use the phrases in Ex 7B to describe your feelings and reactions.

E Write your email.

7C You must see ... !

HOW TO ... | make and respond to recommendations
VOCABULARY | describing places
PRONUNCIATION | sounding enthusiastic

VOCABULARY

describing places

1 Work in pairs. Discuss the questions.

  1 What's the biggest city you have ever visited?

  2 What did you like and not like about it?

  3 What do you know about Shanghai?

2 A Read a travel guide for Shanghai. Match the places mentioned with the photos (A–C).

  B Work in pairs. Look at the words in bold in the travel guide. Discuss places you know using these adjectives.

  The streets in the centre of town are narrow.

  C Choose the correct words to complete the sentences.

  1 This **ancient / modern** bridge is over 800 years old.

  2 The streets are so **narrow / wide** you can't drive down them.

  3 I love sitting in the park – it's so quiet and **famous / peaceful**.

  4 There are some old **wooden / modern** benches where you can sit and watch people walk past.

  5 The buildings are all grey. I prefer cities where the buildings are more **ancient / colourful**.

  6 So many people visit the city – it's become **traditional / famous** for its beautiful views.

  D Work in pairs. Ask and answer the questions.

  1 What historical attractions are there where you live?

  2 Are peaceful green spaces important to you in a city? Why/Why not?

  3 Do you enjoy seeing modern or traditional architecture?

Top things to do in Shanghai

Shanghai is China's largest and richest city. It's worth a visit to experience this vibrant, exciting and **modern** city. Here are the top three things you should do in Shanghai.

1 Travel to the top of the **famous** Shanghai Tower, based in Shanghai's financial district. From the top of this huge tower you can see fantastic views of the city. This is a great place to enjoy a meal in one of many restaurants.

2 Walk along the Bund and appreciate the many different **historical** buildings. Enjoy the view of Shanghai's famous skyline as you look out across the 500m **wide** Huangpu River, which splits the city in two. The Bund is also one of the best places to go shopping!

3 Enjoy the green space and **peaceful** surroundings at Yu Garden, in the old Chinese neighbourhood. Relax as you walk through these beautiful, **ancient** gardens (built in 1577), cross the **narrow**, **wooden** bridges and enjoy looking at the **traditional**, **colourful** buildings. Next door to the Yu Garden is a market where you can drink tea, try some delicious local snacks and buy some souvenirs for your friends.

If you want more information about our fantastic Shanghai tours, visit the website or call to speak to one of our expert guides.

How to ...
make and respond to recommendations

3A 🔊 **7.04** | Listen to the conversation and answer the questions.
1 Why is Mark calling?
2 Has Mark been to Shanghai before?
3 Who is Mark travelling with?
4 What things/places does Sam recommend?

B Check your answers with a partner.

C Match two of the descriptions (a–j) with each place (1–5).
1 Shanghai Maglev Train   4 Tianzifang
2 Shanghai Tower   5 Yu Gardens
3 The Bund

a It's a beautiful green space.
b It's exciting because it's so fast.
c It's the tourist shopping area in the old French district.
d You can enjoy it even if you don't go inside.
e It's a lovely place to walk in the evening and see the skyline.
f It takes seven minutes to get into the centre.
g It's a great place to buy souvenirs and to drink tea.
h It's very relaxing to walk around and take photos.
i It's a great place to see views of the city.
j You can eat at one of the fantastic restaurants while you're there.

D 🔊 **7.04** | Listen again and check.

4A Complete the phrases Sam uses to make recommendations with the words in the box.

> best   can   definitely   great   have to   leave   must   sure

making recommendations

There are a few things you absolutely ¹_____ see/do …
You ²_____ visit/try/see …
You should ³_____ visit …
Make ⁴_____ you …
… is one of the ⁵_____ things to do …
It's a lovely/⁶_____ place to …
You ⁷_____ … eat/see/walk …
Don't ⁸_____ without … visiting/seeing …

B 🔊 **7.05** | Listen and check.

C Complete Mark's responses with the words in the box.

> exciting   great   idea   sounds   that

responding to recommendations

¹_____, thanks.	That ⁴_____ good.
OK, that's a good ²_____.	⁵_____ sounds interesting.
Oh wow! How ³_____!	

D 🔊 **7.06** | Listen and check.

E Learn and practise. Go to the Grammar Bank.

▶▶ page 130 **GRAMMAR BANK**

PRONUNCIATION

5A 🔊 **7.07** | **sounding enthusiastic** | Listen to three sentences which are each spoken twice. Which version (a or b) sounds more enthusiastic? Why?

B Read the Future Skills box and discuss the question.

FUTURE SKILLS
Communication

Communication is about more than what you say. You can communicate feelings such as enthusiasm through your intonation, facial expression and gestures.

What kind of intonation, facial expression and gestures do you think you can use to show that you are enthusiastic?

C Complete the sentences below with places in your town, city or country. Then tell a partner. Add emphasis to sound enthusiastic.
1 You absolutely have to see …
2 You must visit …
3 You should definitely visit …

SPEAKING

6A Work alone. Think about a place that you know well and answer the questions. Use vocabulary from Ex 2B and phrases from Ex 4A.
1 Where is the place?
2 How would you describe it?
3 What would you recommend that people visit there? Why?
4 What activities would you recommend? Why?

B Work in pairs. Take turns to tell your partner about your place and make recommendations. Respond to your partner's recommendations.

MEDIATION SKILL
selecting relevant information

tell someone useful information

▶▶ page 156 **MEDIATION BANK**

7D   BBC Street Interviews

Go solo?

GRAMMAR | reflexive pronouns
SPEAKING | a discussion about travel
WRITING | an essay about why we travel

Nikki

Anabel

Will

Osaid

PREVIEW

1 Work in groups and discuss the questions.
   1 Do you like travelling?
   2 Have you travelled a lot?
   3 Where would you like to go next?

Q1: What's the most amazing place you've ever visited?

Q2: Do you prefer travelling by yourself or with other people?

VIEW

2A ▶ Watch the first part of the video. Number the places in the order the speakers mention them.

Iceland	Budapest	Mount Kilimanjaro
London	India 1	Syria
New Zealand		

B In the second part of the video, eight speakers are asked whether they prefer travelling by themselves or with other people. How do you think they will answer this question?

C ▶ Watch the video and check your ideas.

3A Read the reasons people give for liking a place. What do the words in bold mean?
   1 It's such a fantastic, big, **diverse** country.
   2 The **scenery** was amazing.
   3 There's such a **wide variety** of food to try.
   4 It just feels so **lively**.

B ▶ Look at the sentences in Ex 3A again. What places are the speakers talking about? Watch the first part of the video again to check.

C ▶ Choose the correct words to complete what the speakers say. Watch the second part of the video again and check.
   1 Molly: I prefer my own **family / company**.
   2 Dan: It can get a bit **lively / lonely** on your own.
   3 Nikki: Just go **on your own / alone**, I'd say.
   4 Osaid: … the experience is **shared / better** with my friends or family.
   5 Anabel: You can share the memory with them, rather than just **alone / yourself**.

D Work in groups. Have you been to any of the places mentioned in Ex 2A? Which would you like to visit? Why?

Molly

Dan

Lumi

B B C

Lotte

Saffi

GRAMMAR

reflexive pronouns

4 A Read the sentences from the video. Which two-word phrases mean 'alone'?

  1 Do you prefer travelling by yourself?
  2 I prefer going by myself.
  3 I like the freedom of travelling by myself.

B Match the sentence halves.

  1 My brother likes travelling by   **a** yourself.
  2 Ana prefers walking by   **b** himself.
  3 You always go by   **c** herself.

C Learn and practise. Go to the Grammar Bank.

  ▶▶ page 131 **GRAMMAR BANK**

SPEAKING

a discussion about travel

5 A Think about questions 1–4 and plan your answers. Use the Key phrases to help.

  1 Is it better to travel by yourself or with others? Why?
  2 What kinds of things do you like to do when you go to a new city or country?
  3 What makes some places special?
  4 What can we learn from travelling?

> **KEY PHRASES**
>
> I like travelling by myself because …
> Travelling with other people can be …
> What makes some places special is …
> Special places often have …
> One thing we can learn from travelling is …
> Another thing …

B Work in groups. Discuss the questions in Ex 5A.

WRITING

an essay about why we travel

6 A Read the essay. What reasons does the author give for travelling?

Why travel?

Travel writers, tour guides and flight crews make their living from travel. For the rest of us, if we're lucky, travel enriches our lives.

The main reason to travel is that it can open our minds. We see new sights, meet new people and learn new languages (or at least a few words). Things we always thought were 'normal' aren't necessarily normal in other cultures. This applies to customs, architecture, food, even driving. It means that when we get home, we see things with 'fresh eyes'.

Sometimes, people get stuck in a routine, doing the same things every day. When we travel, that routine often changes and sometimes we change, too. We escape from everyday life and we learn about ourselves.

For many people, travelling provides the most exciting experiences life can offer. If we keep our eyes and ears open, it can change our lives.

B Choose one of the questions you discussed in Ex 5A. Write an essay discussing the question you chose.

  • Think of a title for your essay.
  • Plan what each paragraph will contain before you write.
  • Include your own opinions and reasons.
  • End with a clear conclusion.

GRAMMAR
first and second conditionals

1 A Match 1–5 with a–e and write first conditional sentences using *you*.

1 go to bed early every night,
2 don't exercise,
3 argue with your manager,
4 travel a lot,
5 only study for ten minutes a day,

a won't pass your exams.
b open your mind.
c feel better in the morning.
d won't get fit.
e have problems at work.

1c If you go to bed early every night, you'll feel better in the morning.

B Think of other ways to finish 1–5 in Ex 1A. Compare your ideas with a partner.

2 Work in pairs. Student A: Use an *if* clause with prompts from box A. Start with *If I*. Student B: Respond by making *would* clauses using the prompts from box B.

A

> be / rich   give up / coffee   have / more / energy
> have / more / hours in the day   not have / a TV

B

> dance / all night   give / money / charity
> not sleep / so badly   not / waste / so much time
> work / more

A: If I had more hours in the day …
B: I would work more.

quantifiers

3 Choose the correct words to complete the conversation.

A: Let's have a house-warming party!
B: Definitely. How ¹**much / many** people should we invite?
A: Forty? Or is that ²**too / plenty** many?
B: Forty!? I think twenty is ³**much / enough**.
A: OK. Can we have a barbecue?
B: Sure. But we'll need to buy ⁴**a lot / much** of food for twenty people.
A: True. Let me make a list. So, we'll need burgers. And maybe a ⁵**lot / few** chicken legs?
B: ⁶**Lots / Many** of chicken legs. I love them!
A: What about vegetables for a salad? There are hardly ⁷**many / any** in the house.
B: Sure. And ⁸**plenty of / a bit of** drinks. And bread.
A: How ⁹**many / much** bread?
B: Twenty buns for the burgers. And we'll need a ¹⁰**few / bit** of cheese for the burgers, too.
A: OK. Let's go!

reflexive pronouns

4 Complete the sentences with the correct reflexive pronouns. Add *by* where necessary.

1 She walked up to the teacher and introduced _____ .
2 I always go to the cinema with other people. I don't like going _____ .
3 The cake was lovely, Sarah. Did you make it _____ ?
4 It was a great party! We really enjoyed _____ !
5 I was worried I might fall and hurt _____ .
6 Everyone else went out, so Dan spent the afternoon _____ .

VOCABULARY

5 Work in pairs. Think of travel advice using the words in the box.

> check-in   culture   destination   exchange rate
> expect   luggage   monument   nightlife
> notice   peaceful   resort   trip

Don't take too much luggage.

6 A Choose the correct options (A–C) to complete the text.

The best job in the world?

Travel writer. It sounds perfect. A magazine pays you to go to beautiful ¹_____ . You learn local ²_____ . You visit tourist ³_____ and come ⁴_____ amazing things you'd never expected to see. You write about your experiences, and you become rich and famous.

That's the dream. Unfortunately, there isn't ⁵_____ chance of it coming true. Firstly, ⁶_____ any travel writers make ⁷_____ money to live on. Secondly, editors have ⁸_____ of writers sending them stories. What makes your story different? If you don't have anything special to say, you ⁹_____ be just another tourist with a laptop.

Finally, you have to know your market. Make ¹⁰_____ you read the magazines you want to write for. How long are the articles? What's the style? If you ¹¹_____ your research, you'll have a better chance of getting published.

1 A trips	B souvenirs	C destinations
2 A festivals	B customs	C monuments
3 A breaks	B tours	C attractions
4 A across	B on	C up
5 A plenty	B a bit	C much
6 A hardly	B not	C a few
7 A many	B enough	C too much
8 A plenty	B all	C lot
9 A would	B can	C will
10 A always	B sure	C that
11 A will do	B do	C did

B 🔊 **R7.01** | Listen and check your answers.

know-how 8

B B C

VLOGS

Q: Are you good or bad at fixing things?

1 ▶ Watch the video. Note down the things the people talk about fixing. Compare in pairs.

2 Are you good at fixing things? What things can you fix?

GSE LEARNING OBJECTIVES

8A LISTENING | Understand people talking about their skills: practical abilities; abilities: phrasal verbs

Talk about your skills and abilities: *can, could, be able to*

Pronunciation: weak forms of *can, could* and *be able to*

Write an anecdote about learning a skill

8B READING | Read about video: video collocations; technology 1

Pronunciation: emphasising important information

Make a short video or plan an online video channel: active and passive

8C HOW TO … | describe a problem and make recommendations: technical problems; technology 2

Pronunciation: contrastive stress

8D BBC PROGRAMME | Understand a TV programme about a gifted language learner

Talk about the best ways to learn a language: *-ing* form

Write a forum comment about language learning

8A Doers and dreamers

GRAMMAR | *can, could, be able to*
VOCABULARY | practical abilities; abilities: phrasal verbs
PRONUNCIATION | weak forms of *can, could* and *be able to*

VOCABULARY

practical abilities

1 A Write down seven practical skills that people do with their hands.

putting up a shelf, throwing and catching a ball

B Add three skills to your list that you would like to do or be better at.

I'd like to bake good cakes.

C Work in pairs. Share your ideas from Ex 1A and Ex 1B. Ask follow-up questions about skills your partner would like to do better.

Do you play the guitar now? How often?

2 A Read the text about about Grégoire Kengen. How does he use his practical skills?

B Do you agree that Grégoire is 'living the dream'? Would you like to live a similar life? Why/Why not?

C Work in pairs. Look at the verbs in bold in the text. Then answer the questions.

1 repair / replace: Which verb do we use when we buy something new because the old one doesn't work?

2 upload / put up: Which verb do we only use when talking about the internet?

3 arrange / calculate: Which verb do we often use with numbers?

4 design / install: Which verb do we only use with technology?

5 turn (something) **into** (something else): Is it possible to turn a hobby into a job?

6 solve a problem: If you solve a problem, does it disappear?

D Work in pairs. Each choose three of the actions in the box. Tell your partner when you last did each one. Ask questions to find out more.

arrange a meeting   calculate the price of something
design something   put something up on the wall
repair/replace something   solve a problem
upload something

A: Last week, I put a picture up on my bedroom wall.
B: What was the picture of?

E Learn and practise. Go to the Vocabulary Bank.

▶▶ page 144 **VOCABULARY BANK**
abilities: phrasal verbs

Living the dream

Grégoire Kengen is a film-maker and photographer from Belgium. Grégoire travels around in his van (named Henri!), films his experiences and **uploads** the videos to YouTube. His YouTube channel, gregsway, has over 200,000 subscribers.

One reason why Grégoire is popular is that he's very practical and creative. For example, he turned his van into a mobile studio, added new parts and **installed** electricity. His van was made in 1990, and he sometimes has to **repair** things that go wrong or **replace** old parts. He always finds a way!

In 2017, Grégoire started a new project. He and a friend built a tiny house mainly from wood. With the help of an architect, he **designed** it and **calculated** what size it should be and what materials he needed. He then built it next to a forest. As the house is far from civilisation, they had to **solve** a few problems such as how to get water and electricity to it. They **arranged** access to running water, **put up** shelves and added a power supply. Now they rent the house to guests.

Grégoire started fixing things as a hobby, but he was able to **turn** his hobby **into** a job and a way of life. For this reason, some say he's really living the dream! What do you think?

LISTENING

3 A 🔊 **8.01** | Listen to four people talking about how they use their practical skills. Which of the people do you need if:

a you have a problem with your laptop?
Speaker ......

b you want to celebrate with friends?
Speaker ......

c you want something special to wear?
Speaker ......

d something is broken in your house?
Speaker ......

B Work in pairs. Are the sentences true (T) or false (F)?

Speaker 1, Ahmed

1 He drew an elephant very well while he was at the zoo.

2 Now he has his own fashion business.

Speaker 2, Candace

3 She learnt her skills when she moved to a new place.

4 She has a company that fixes problems in buildings.

Speaker 3, Dan

5 His friends always asked him to arrange parties for them.

6 He says he likes his job because it makes a lot of money.

Speaker 4, Maxine

7 She first built a computer when she was ten years old.

8 She loves designing video games.

C 🔊 **8.01** | Listen again and check.

GRAMMAR

can, could, be able to

4 A Read what the four speakers said about their abilities. Which refer to abilities in the present? Which are about the past?

1 I could draw quite well.

2 I was able to use my skills to design clothes.

3 I can fix a roof.

4 I'm able to install a washing machine.

5 I can't play video games.

6 I couldn't do any of that a few years ago.

B Learn and practise. Go to the Grammar Bank.

▶▶ page 132 **GRAMMAR BANK**

PRONUNCIATION

5 A 🔊 **8.02** | **weak forms of *can*, *could* and *be able to*** | Read and listen to the dialogues. Are the words in bold pronounced with a strong vowel sound or with a weak vowel sound? What pattern do you notice?

1 A: **Can** you put up a shelf?
B: Yes, I **can**.

2 A: **Could** you swim when you were six?
B: Yes, I **could**.

3 A: **Were** you able to speak English as a child?
B: Yes, I **was**.

4 A: **Could** you play an instrument when you were a child?
B: No, I **couldn't**.

5 A: **Were** you able to relax last weekend?
B: No, I **wasn't**.

B Work in pairs. Take turns to ask the questions in Ex 5A. Give your own answers.

SPEAKING

6 A You are going to ask and answer questions about your abilities. Read the questions and plan your answers. Make notes.

1 What abilities did you have when you were young?
2 What abilities and skills do you have now?
3 Do you have any special memories of learning these skills?
4 How have your abilities helped you? Have they been useful in your work or personal life?

B Work in pairs. Take turns to ask your partner about their abilities. Use the questions in Ex 6A and ask more questions to find out more information.

A: What abilities did you have when you were young?
B: I was able to play chess really well.
A: Did you enjoy playing chess?

WRITING

an anecdote about learning a skill

7 A You are going to write about a hobby or skill that you learnt. First, read Marta's text. What skill did she learn?

I could swim almost **before I could** walk. My parents were keen surfers and we lived next to the beach. We spent all day every day in the water. I was able to surf **when I was five** and I got my first surfboard **at the age of six**.

My friends and I surfed a lot, but none of us had any money, which meant we couldn't replace our old boards with new ones. So when I was twelve, I learnt how to repair surfboards. **At first**, my mother helped me. She showed me what to do and what tools to use. **After a few months**, I could do it alone. I worked on all my friends' old boards.

These days, I don't surf very often, although I go to the beach at weekends. **I can still** repair old surfboards and sometimes the young surfers bring their broken boards to me because I'm the only one who's able to fix them!

Marta Freire Alves

B Work in pairs. Discuss the questions.

1 Why did Marta learn how to repair surfboards?
2 When did she learn, and who helped her learn?
3 How does she use her skill now?

8 A Notice the words and phrases in bold in the text. What do they give information about? Choose the correct answer.

1 They describe how the writer was feeling.
2 They describe a sequence from past to present.

B Work in pairs. Answer the questions about the phrases in Ex 8A.

1 Which two phrases tell us the writer's exact age at that moment?
2 Which phrase tells us how much time has passed?
3 Which two phrases refer to the present?
4 Which two phrases refer to a particular time in the past?

C Make a list of skills that you have learnt and how you use them now.

Cooking – I can now invite friends to my flat for dinner.

D Write about a hobby or skill that you learnt. Use the paragraph plan and questions below to help you. Use words and phrases to describe the sequence.

Paragraph 1: What was the background? Why did you want to learn the skill? What could/couldn't you do before you learnt this skill?

Paragraph 2: Who helped you learn? How long did it take before you were able to do it well?

Paragraph 3: Do you still use this skill? How? At work or at home? As a hobby?

8B Video everywhere

GRAMMAR | active and passive
VOCABULARY | video collocations; technology 1
PRONUNCIATION | emphasising important information

A

B

VOCABULARY

video collocations

1 A Work in pairs. Match the types of video (1–6) with the pictures of videos (A–F).

1 fitness video
2 video game
3 'How to …' or instructional video
4 music video
5 funny animal video
6 promotional video

C

B 🔊 **8.03** | Listen to three people talking about videos. What types of video from Ex 1A do they talk about? What other types of video do they mention?

C Work in pairs. Discuss the questions. Use the ideas in the box to help you.

1 How do you use video in your life? 2 What kinds of video do you watch?

> at home   at work   for education   for entertainment   for leisure/hobbies

2 A Complete the collocations in bold with the words in the box.

> clip   comment   edit   like   make   podcast   share

1 A **video** .... is a short piece from a longer video.
2 If you .... **a video**, you send it to other people on social media, so they can watch it, too.
3 When you .... **a video**, you make it shorter and only keep the best parts.
4 If you find a video online and enjoy watching it, then you might .... **the video** or even .... **on** it.
5 A lot of people .... **videos** to use for marketing and to increase sales.
6 A **video** .... is often called a vlog.

D

B Write questions to ask a partner using the collocations in Ex 2A.

Do you ever comment on videos online?

C Work in pairs. Ask and answer your questions from Ex 2B. Ask more questions to find out more.

A: Do you make your own videos?
B: Yes, sometimes.
A: What sort of videos are they?

E

D Check your knowledge of technology vocabulary. Complete the sentences. Then check your answers in the Vocabulary Bank.

1 The first thing I do in the morning is .... my computer on.
2 I watch 'how to' videos when I need to .... an update.
3 I can't watch films on my phone because it .... out of charge too quickly.

E Learn and practise. Go to the Vocabulary Bank.

▶▶ page 144 **VOCABULARY BANK** technology 1

F

READING

3 A Work in pairs and discuss. Look at the headings in the article. In what ways does video influence these aspects of our lives?

B Read the article. Does it mention any of your ideas from Ex 3A?

C Complete the article by matching the missing sentences (A–G) with the gaps (1–6). There is one extra sentence that you do not need.

A Video also helps news travel fast.

B In this new media age, the screen has become our number one way of communicating.

C Video appeals to the emotions and helps us to feel present in a moment, as if we were there.

D Lots of people also watch videos for enjoyment.

E It is now easier than ever to make your own videos.

F As well as helping us learn facts or skills, it seems videos can also help us *want* to learn.

G Visual information is processed 60,000 times faster in the brain than other information.

4 A Match the words in bold in the article with the meanings below.

1 to take in new facts or details

2 to concentrate on one thing without getting distracted

3 the person who films themselves for a video channel

4 someone who watches a video

5 attractive or interesting to people

6 to be in touch with other people and communicate with them

7 to make someone else change the way they think about something

B Work in pairs. Choose two of the types of video from the article and discuss your experience of using them.

Watch, like, share

[1] __B__ Video is everywhere. We watch, like, share and make videos more than ever before. Every minute, hundreds of hours of video are uploaded to YouTube. And every year, more and more videos are shared online. Video has changed how we entertain ourselves, how we communicate, how we share information and how we learn.

Learning

[2] _____ This means that we **absorb information** more quickly from videos than from reading texts. Videos are naturally **appealing**, because our brains are programmed to notice movement, so we pay attention more easily. And it seems we remember information we watch in videos for longer, too. For all these reasons, video is being used more and more in formal education, but it's also a great way to learn new skills. People watch instructional 'how to …' videos to do all kinds of things: improve their cooking skills, learn new languages, learn musical instruments or do their make-up. 'With me' videos are popular, too, where people film themselves doing everyday tasks like cleaning, cooking and shopping. [3] _____ 'Study with me' videos show people silently studying. It might seem surprising, but when students watch these videos, they feel more motivated to **stay focused** on their own studies.

Communication

[4] _____ This is one reason why teenagers in particular often like using video as a way to communicate. Many love sharing and commenting on videos of themselves spending time with friends or sharing an exciting holiday experience. It helps them to **feel connected**. In 2019, 10 billion videos were watched every day on Snapchat.

[5] _____ In the past, journalists were sent somewhere to report on a news event, and they often arrived after the event had happened. These days, anybody with a phone can film what's happening and share it on social media. But we have to be careful. Videos can be a powerful way to **influence** people, so we should check that we know where the video comes from. Sometimes we think we're just watching a funny animal video that's gone viral, when in fact it could be someone trying to sell us something.

Entertainment

[6] _____ All the traditional forms of entertainment such as films, comedy shows, music, etc. are available online. But there are some newer trends, too, where people film themselves and others watch for fun. One of these trends is Mukbang videos. Mukbang (pronounced 'mook-bong') originated in South Korea, where it translates as 'eating broadcast' The **host** is filmed eating a large meal while chatting to the **viewer**. The videos have been so popular that many Mukbang hosts have become famous.

GRAMMAR

active and passive

5 A Look at the passive verb forms in bold in the sentences (a–c) from the article. Answer the questions (1–3).

a Every minute, hundreds of hours of video **are uploaded** to YouTube.

b Every year, more and more videos **are shared** online.

c In the past, journalists **were sent** somewhere to report on a news event.

1 Do we know who watched or shares the videos?

2 Do we know who sent the journalists?

3 Is it important to know the information in questions 1 and 2?

B Look at the active verb in bold in the sentence from the article. Answer the questions.

When students **watch** these videos, they feel more motivated.

1 Do we know who watches the videos?

2 Is it important who watches the videos?

C Look at the sentences in Ex 5A and Ex 5B again. How do we form the passive?

D Learn and practise. Go to the Grammar Bank.

 page 133 **GRAMMAR BANK**

PRONUNCIATION

6 A 🔊 8.04 | **emphasising important information** | We usually stress the important information in a sentence. This is often the subject of the verb in both active and passive sentences, and any additional important information. Listen to the sentences and notice how the words in bold are stressed.

1 These kinds of **videos** are watched every day. (*Videos* is the important information.)

2 A lot of **teenagers** watch these kinds of videos. (*Teenagers* is the important information.)

B Look at the pairs of sentences. Which words do you think are important and emphasised?

1 a The camera was sold for 200 euros.
  b Alfie sold his camera for 200 euros.

2 a The video was shared more than 6 million times.
  b People shared the video more than 6 million times.

3 a The students are given homework every day.
  b The teachers give the students homework every day.

4 a The clip was uploaded to YouTube.
  b Jenna uploaded the clip to YouTube.

C 🔊 8.05 | Listen and check. Then practise saying the sentences, emphasising the important information.

SPEAKING

7 A Work in groups. You are going to make a short video or plan your own video channel. Read the two tasks and choose which one you are going to do.

Task A: Make a short video

1 Choose from the following suggestions or use your own ideas:

- a promotional video – for a new product or event you want to promote.
- an instructional 'how to …' video, e.g. 'How to … make the perfect cup of coffee.'

2 Plan your video.

3 Film your video using a mobile phone.

4 Edit your video to add sounds, music, subtitles, etc.

Task B: Plan your own video channel

1 Decide what the channel will be called and what kind of videos it will show.

2 Plan who will be your target audience.

3 Plan how you will advertise your video channel.

4 Decide how it will make money.

B In your groups, read the Future Skills box and then complete Task A or B in Ex 7A.

FUTURE SKILLS
Creativity

When you are doing creative tasks, it is important to spend time thinking of imaginative ideas to help you create something good.

What imaginative ideas can you think of for Tasks A and B? Think about the visuals, the words and the sound.

C Give a short talk to the class about your video or video channel. If you have made a video, show it to the class. As you listen to other students, note down things you like about each video or video channel. Which is the best?

8C Help!

HOW TO ... | describe a problem and make recommendations
VOCABULARY | technical problems; technology 2
PRONUNCIATION | contrastive stress

VOCABULARY

technical problems

1 A Look at the photo. How is the person feeling? What do you think has happened?

B Read the text. Do you think you suffer from Computer Stress Syndrome? How do you feel when you have problems with technology?

Do you suffer from Computer Stress Syndrome?

It could be the one thing that stresses us out more than anything else in our work life – technical problems. Your phone **isn't working** and you can't download any apps. You finish writing an essay or a report and then realise you've just deleted the files by mistake, and lost everything. Or maybe the photocopier is **out of order** just when you need to copy an important document. Your computer keeps **crashing** in the middle of a meeting or you can't open a **file** or **attachment** on your laptop. Perhaps you've forgotten your **password**, or you have a slow internet **connection**. On top of all this, you find the printer is **broken**. You call the technical department but after waiting for twenty minutes to speak to a real person, you **get cut off**. All these technical problems contribute to 'Computer Stress Syndrome', something many of us suffer from. When the technology works, it's great. When it fails, it's a nightmare.

2 A Work in pairs. Complete the sentences about some more technical problems with the correct form of the words in bold in Ex 1B.

1 The heating is .... We need to fix it because the house is really cold!
2 My phone .... I can't download any apps.
3 I sent the email, but I forgot to send the file as an ....
4 My laptop sometimes .... when I download large files. It just switches off.
5 I was using the internet, but then I suddenly lost the wifi ....
6 You can't use your account until you log in and create a new ....
7 We only managed to talk for a few minutes before we ....
8 The lift was out of .... , so I had to use the stairs.

B Complete the collocations with words from Ex 1B.

1 open/download/attach a .... or an ....
2 create/change/forget a ....
3 lose the/have a slow internet ....

C Work in pairs. Which of the problems in Ex 2A have happened to you? Can you remember what you did to solve them?

D Learn and practise. Go to the Vocabulary Bank.

▶▶ page 145 **VOCABULARY BANK** technology 2

How to ...
describe a problem and make recommendations

3A 🔊 **8.06** | Listen to three conversations in which someone describes a problem. What is the problem and solution in each one?

B Complete the phrases in the table with the words in the box.

> broken need keeps problem time tried working works

describing a problem	There's a ¹............ with ... The ... isn't working. I can't ... It won't ... It ²............ (crashing). When/Every ³............ I ... , it ... I think it's ⁴............ .
making a recommendation	Have you ⁵............ + *-ing* ... ? Try + *-ing* ... Have you checked ... ? Maybe you ⁶............ to ... It sometimes ⁷............ if you ...
solving the problem	Yes, I'll try that. Yes, that works. Yes, it's ⁸............ now.

C 🔊 **8.07** | Listen and check.

D Learn and practise. Go to the Grammar Bank.

⏩ page 134 **GRAMMAR BANK**

PRONUNCIATION

4A 🔊 **8.08** | **contrastive stress** | Listen to the extracts from two of the conversations. Which words are stressed in each one?

1 A: Is there a problem with your presentation?
   B: No. My presentation's fine, but there's a problem with the internet connection.

2 A: Problem with your laptop?
   B: No, it isn't my laptop, it's the printer.

B Why do the speakers stress these words? Choose the correct answer.

1 They are correcting a mistake which the other person made.
2 These words are the most difficult to pronounce.

C Work in pairs. Student A: Choose one sentence to read to Student B. Don't say which sentence. Make sure you stress the correct word! Student B: Guess which sentence. Repeat the activity, then change roles.

1 No, I put the laptop on the table yesterday. (not the desktop computer!)
2 No, I put the laptop on the table yesterday. (not on the floor!)
3 No, I put the laptop on the table yesterday. (not today!)

SPEAKING

5A Work in pairs. Student A: Read the instructions below. Student B: Turn to page 147. Then roleplay the two situations.

Student A

1 You need to check some information urgently on your phone, but you don't have a wifi connection. You can see there are other networks available, but you don't know the passwords.
- Explain the problem to Student B.
- Respond to their recommendations.
- See if you can solve the problem together.

2 Listen to Student B's problem.
- Ask questions to find out more information.
- Make recommendations.
- Try to solve the problem together.

B Work in pairs. Choose more situations in which someone has a problem. You can use situations from Ex 2A or your own ideas. Have conversations in which one person describes the problem and the other makes recommendations. Try to solve the problems.

MEDIATION SKILL
using headings, bullet points and simple sentences
make instructions easier to understand

⏩ page 157 **MEDIATION BANK**

8D BBC Documentary

A gifted learner

GRAMMAR | *-ing* form
SPEAKING | the best ways to learn a language
WRITING | a forum comment about language learning

PREVIEW

1A Work with other students. Discuss the questions.

1 Do you think it is easy to learn another language? Why/Why not?

2 What do you find most difficult about learning languages?

3 Is it easier to learn when you are younger or older? Why?

4 Who is the most talented language learner you know? How many languages do they speak and how did they learn them?

B Read the programme information. Then look at the photo. What special talent do you think the girl might have?

Inside the Human Body

Inside the Human Body is a BBC science programme. In each episode, the presenter Michael Mosley looks at how a different part of the body works. In this episode, he explores the human brain and, in particular, our ability to learn languages.

VIEW

2A ▶ Watch the BBC video clip. When did Wendy start learning languages? How many can she speak now?

B ▶ Match the numbers in the box with the descriptions (a–e). Then watch again to check your answers.

> 4   over 1,000   over 7,000   over 10,000   60

a the number of languages humans have invented
b the number of new words we pick up every year as we grow
c the number of words we have in our vocabulary as teenagers
d the number of languages Wendy could speak aged two
e the number of minutes Wendy spends each week talking to her teachers

C Work in groups. Discuss the questions.

1 Why do you think Wendy is so good at learning languages?
2 Do you know any children who can speak more than one language?
3 Should all young children be encouraged to learn more than one language? Why?

GRAMMAR

-ing form

3A Read the sentences from the video. What are the first and second verbs in each sentence? What is the form of the second verb?

1 I started learning them.
2 She spends an hour every week talking to different people.

B With some verbs, when we put two verbs together, the second one is in the *-ing* form. Make sentences with the verbs in the box and another verb.

> hate   imagine   like   practise   recommend   remember   suggest

I like learning languages.

C Learn and practise. Go to the Grammar Bank.

▶▶ page 135 **GRAMMAR BANK**

B B C

SPEAKING

the best ways to learn a language

4 A 🔊 **8.09** | Listen to a woman talking about learning Arabic. How is she learning it?

B 🔊 **8.09** | Listen again and tick the Key phrases that you hear.

> **KEY PHRASES**
>
> I started learning … two years ago.
> I have lessons once a week.
> I spend an hour a day studying.
> I practise listening …
> It's good to learn from …
> I also like watching …
> It takes a long time to …

C Work in groups. Discuss different ways of learning a language. What are the best ways? Use the ideas in the box to help you, and give examples from your own experience.

> joining a class   listening to podcasts or radio
> listening to songs   living in a place
> reading   taking one-to-one lessons
> using language-learning apps
> watching films or TV programmes
> working from a grammar book

WRITING

a forum comment about language learning

5 A Read the forum comment and the responses. What is Sandra asking for, and why? What do Divya and Jun Lee recommend?

Language learning forum

> I'm moving to France for work next year. Does anyone have any tips for learning a new language quickly?
> **Sandra** ✎ 2 reviews ⊚ GB   A day ago

> Personally, I enjoy studying with other people more than by myself, so I recommend going to a class and using a grammar book. You need to know the basics, which you can get from a book, but you also have to practise speaking the language.
> **Divya** ✎ 16 reviews ⊚ PK   A day ago

> Try listening to songs in French. That's a really fun way to learn. I remember listening to my favourite British bands years ago, which is how I learnt English!
> **Jun Lee** ✎ 22 reviews ⊚ SG   A day ago

B Write a response to Sandra's comment. Include at least five tips for learning languages.

C Read other students' comments. Which of their ideas would you like to try?

GRAMMAR

can, could, be able to

1 A Choose the correct words to complete the sentences.

1 I **can't to / am able / can** type fast.
2 When I first heard English, I **can't / wasn't able / couldn't** understand anything.
3 Even when I'm stressed, I'm usually **able to / can / able** sleep.
4 I recently had a problem, but I **am able to / was able to / could** solve it.
5 I **'m not able to / couldn't / wasn't able to** do the job of my dreams (not yet anyway).
6 Last weekend I didn't have to work so I **was able to / could to / can** relax a little.

B Tick the sentences in Ex 1A that are true for you. Discuss your answers with other students.

I can type quite fast because I practise a lot.

active and passive

2 A Complete the sentences in Ex 1A with the correct active or passive form of the verb in brackets.

1 The hashtag symbol (#) has another name: it .... (call) an octothorpe.
2 The English language .... (speak) as a second language by nearly 2 billion people worldwide. But only 350 million people .... (speak) English as a first language.
3 The first soft drink that .... into space was a cola drink. (take)
4 The speed of a computer mouse .... (measure) in 'Mickeys'. A British scientist first .... (invent) the device in 1946, but it .... (not call) a 'mouse' until 1965.
5 Mosquitoes .... (attract) to people who have just eaten bananas.
6 The first T-model cars that .... (produce) by Ford .... (paint) different colours (grey, green, blue and red), not just black.

B Discuss the facts in Ex 2A with a partner. Which do you think are the most interesting or surprising?

3 A Rewrite the questions using passive verbs.

1 Does somebody usually cook dinner for you?

Is dinner usually cooked for you?

2 Has anyone ever advised you to change jobs?
3 Has a professional photographer ever photographed you?
4 Did your journey to school/work yesterday annoy you?
5 Has your family ever taken you on a holiday abroad?
6 Have you cleaned your bedroom recently?
7 Did the last book you read interest you?
8 Does somebody usually iron your clothes for you?

B Work in pairs. Ask and answer the questions.

-ing form

4 Find and correct five mistakes in the text.

I remember try to learn Latin at school. It was incredibly boring. We practised to reading texts aloud and changing verbs into different tenses. Everyone hated doing this. Even now, years later, I can't stand translate! We all knew that Latin was a dead language, but the teacher kept to tell us it was really important. He liked to explain that Latin was the root of many other languages, like French and Spanish. When I went to live in Italy, I began to understand what he meant. I could understand a lot of words in Italian because I understood Latin. Now I'd recommend to learn Latin at school!

VOCABULARY

5 A Complete the sentences with the words and phrases in the box.

arranged   calculate   installed   repaired
replace   put up   solve   upload

1 Have you ever .... something you own?
2 Do you know how to .... a video to YouTube?
3 When was the last time you .... a new program on your computer?
4 Have you ever .... pictures on the walls of your house?
5 Can you .... how much you spend on coffee each month?
6 Have you .... anything with your friends for this evening?
7 How often do you .... your phone with a newer model?
8 When was the last time you had to .... a problem?

B Work in pairs. Ask and answer the questions.

6A Match the sentence halves.

1 I never comment
2 I usually watch short
3 I often listen to
4 I wouldn't make
5 I often share
6 I always edit my

a online posts carefully before I share them.
b on videos online.
c clips of shows these days, not full programmes.
d podcasts when I'm on the bus or train.
e a video because I don't like to see myself on screen.
f photos of my dinner with friends.

B Which of the sentences are true for you? Tell your partner and give reasons.

I never comment on videos online. I don't like the idea of sharing my personal data with strangers.

7A Complete the conversations with one word in each gap.

1 A: The printer isn't working. Again.
B: Yes, it's been .... of order all week.

2 A: I waited for hours to speak to someone and then they .... me off.
B: I'd be furious!

3 A: Have you downloaded the files?
B: Not yet. I have a really slow internet .... right now.

4 A: Did you order those trainers?
B: No, I've .... my password for the account.

B Work in pairs and discuss. Which of the problems in Ex 7A are the most annoying?

8A Replace the words in bold with phrasal verbs from the box.

> come up with   get on well with   look after
> pick up   take up   work out

1 I don't **take care of** my things, so they often break or I lose them. ....
2 I find it easy to **learn** languages **quickly**. ....
3 I **have a good relationship with** my boss. ....
4 I don't like writing stories because it's difficult for me to **think of** ideas. ....
5 It takes me a long time to **solve** maths problems. ....
6 I don't want to **start playing** golf. It's really boring and expensive. ....

B Work with a partner. Guess if the sentences in Ex 8A are true for your partner. Use the phrasal verbs from the box.

I don't think sentence 1 is true. I think you look after your things – you are always tidy.

9A Choose the correct options (A–C) to complete the text.

How YouTube changed my life

When I posted my first videos on YouTube, I never thought I would ¹............. make so many friends. I was studying in London, I ²............. speak English very well and I didn't know very many people. I had a lot of free time, so I spent a few afternoons ³............. some short videos and uploading them to YouTube. I tried a few different types of video. I started with ⁴............. videos about how do well at the video games I was playing. In the first few weeks, hundreds of people ⁵............. and ⁶............. on the videos. Lots of ⁷............. also ⁸............. the videos with their friends. At first, I had a few hundred followers, but after six months I had thousands. It was amazing. I had to learn how to make my videos better, by ⁹............. them and adding music. Now, I'm doing a course in video ¹⁰............. design.

1 A able to	**B** be able to	**C** can
2 A wasn't able	**B** can't	**C** couldn't
3 A to make	**B** making	**C** made
4 A instructional	**B** funny animal	**C** fitness
5 A commented	**B** made	**C** liked
6 A edited	**B** commented	**C** downloaded
7 A viewers	**B** likes	**C** comments
8 A installed	**B** shared	**C** designed
9 A editing	**B** arranging	**C** repairing
10 A music	**B** game	**C** television

B Work in pairs and discuss the questions. Do you know anyone who uploads videos online? What sorts of videos do they post? Do they have a lot of followers?

1A present simple and present continuous; state verbs; adverbs of frequency

REFERENCE ◀◀ page 9

Present simple

We use the present simple to talk about something that is always or generally true, or for habits or routines (things that happen regularly).

Present continuous

We use the present continuous to talk about an activity happening right now, at the time of speaking.

We also use the present continuous to talk about a temporary activity happening around now.

He**'s studying** philosophy at university.

We often use these words and phrases with the present continuous: *now, at the moment, currently, this month.*

He**'s living** with his grandmother at the moment.

We also use the present continuous for future arrangements (see page 113).

We form the present continuous with the correct form of the verb *be* + the *-ing* form of the verb.

+	I**'m watching** a film at the moment.
-	He **isn't talking** to me.
?	**Are** you **living** with your parents at the moment?

State verbs

Some verbs are not usually used with continuous tenses. They describe thoughts, feelings, sense and perceptions. They are called 'state verbs'.

Common state verbs are: *be, believe, belong, feel, forget, hate, hear, imagine, know, like, love, matter, mean, need, prefer, realise, remember, seem, suppose, understand.*

Adverbs of frequency

Adverbs of frequency tell us how often something happens. We often use adverbs of frequency with the present simple.

The most common adverbs of frequency are: *always, often, usually, sometimes, occasionally, rarely, never.*

We also use expressions of frequency to talk about how often something happens, e.g. *every day/year, twice a week, hardly ever, once in a while.*

I **hardly ever** talk to him.

We usually put adverbs of frequency **before** the main verb, or **after** the verb *be*

I **often study** in the evenings.

I**'m not usually** late.

Adverbs of frequency can go at the beginning, in the middle or at the end of a sentence.

Occasionally, I see my aunt.

I **occasionally** see my aunt.

I see my aunt **occasionally**.

Always and *never* do not normally go at the beginning or end of sentences.

Expressions of frequency usually go at the beginning or the end of the sentence.

Once in a while he sends flowers.

We work together **every day**.

PRACTICE

1 Complete the sentences with the present simple or present continuous form of the verbs in brackets.

1 _____ you _____ with your parents at the moment? (live)

2 _____ your partner _____ how to cook? (know)

3 What song _____ you _____ to? I've never heard it before. (listen)

4 How often _____ you _____ your family? (see)

5 This month I _____ to finish this new project. (try)

6 When we go to Rome, we usually _____ with my sister. (stay)

2 Add the expressions of frequency on the line according to how often you think they happen.

| every day   every weekend   from time to time |
| hardly ever   once a month   once in a while |
| twice a year |

never _____ always

3 Complete the sentences. Choose the correct place (a or b) for the adverb or expression of frequency.

1 (a) _____ our manager deals (b) _____ with problems. It's her job. (usually)

2 I (a) _____ get up early (b) _____ and go for a run. (every day)

3 She's a close friend but (a) _____ we (b) _____ see each other – maybe only once a year. (rarely)

4 I (a) _____ clean the house at the weekend (b) _____ . I hate it when it's a mess. (always)

5 (a) _____ I (b) _____ speak to my manager – maybe once a month. (once in a while)

6 (a) _____ I (b) _____ work late at night because I get too tired and I can't concentrate. (never)

7 We go (a) _____ out for a meal together (b) _____ . (occasionally)

8 I (a) _____ wish I worked part-time because I'd love to spend (b) _____ more time with my family. (sometimes)

1D modifiers

REFERENCE ◀◀ page 16

We use modifiers to talk about how much, or how little, something is true.

quite, quite a/an …

Quite has a meaning which is less strong than *very*.

That's **quite interesting**. (but not very interesting)

That's **quite** an expensive hobby.

That's **quite** a lot of money.

We use:

quite + adjective

It's **quite difficult** to find a job at the moment.

quite *a/an* + adjective + noun

That's **quite a** difficult language to learn.

She's **quite an** easy-going person.

We can use other modifiers (*relatively*, *fairly*, *pretty*, *reasonably*, etc.) with adjectives, instead of *quite*, with a similar meaning.

This area is **relatively cheap** to live in.

He is **fairly happy** with his lifestyle.

My life is **pretty good** at the moment.

a bit more/a lot more

We use *a bit (more/less)* for a small amount more or less.
We use *a lot (more/less)* for a large amount more or less.

I'd like to travel **a bit more**.

She'd like to be **a bit more** healthy.

He'd like to see his friends **a lot more**.

She'd like to spend **a lot less**.

PRACTICE

1 Choose the correct word(s) to complete the sentences.

1 I think I have **quite** / **quite an** / **pretty** interesting job.
2 My lifestyle is **quite** / **a lot** / **reasonable** busy.
3 I live **a lot** / **more** / **fairly** near to my work.
4 I would say I'm **pretty** / **relative** / **fair** happy at the moment.
5 I would like to go out with friends **quite more** / **a bit more** / **bit**.
6 She reduced her hours at work so now she works **a bit more** / **a lot more** / **a bit less**.
7 He wants to travel **relatively** / **a bit more** / **fairly** and see the country.
8 For the lifestyle I would like, I need to earn **fairly** / **a lot more** / **a bit** money.

2 Put the words in brackets in the correct place in the sentences.

1 I live in a small flat. (quite)
2 We have a comfortable life. (relatively)
3 I work more these days. (a lot)
4 My new car was expensive. (quite)
5 It's cheap to live in an area like this. (reasonably)
6 I have an easy job at the moment. (quite)
7 My life is boring most of the time! (pretty)
8 I'd like to exercise more. (a bit)

3 Complete the sentences with the phrases in the box.

> a bit more healthily   a bit more productive
> a bit more time   fairly healthy   pretty bored
> quite a creative   quite an alternative
> work a bit less

1 I'm _____ person – I love to paint and write my own music.
2 I think I live _____ lifestyle because I don't have a traditional job.
3 I wish I could be _____ with my days. I'm always wasting time.
4 I think I'm _____ at the moment. I eat well and exercise every day.
5 I'd really like to apply for a part-time job so that I could _____ .
6 I'd like to have a more exciting job – I'm _____ with my work at the moment.
7 We should really try to eat _____ because we eat too many takeaways.
8 I spend a lot of time looking after my family, so it would be nice to have _____ to myself.

4 Use the prompts to make sentences.

1 I'm / quite / positive / person.

2 We'd like / have / bit / more / time with our grandchildren.

3 We / had / quite / nice / time / at the beach.

4 I / need / start / spending / lot / less / money.

5 This / is / quite / useful / app.

6 Raisa / would like / be / bit / more / easy-going.

GRAMMAR BANK

2A narrative tenses

REFERENCE ◀◀ page 21

Past simple

We use the past simple for states and actions in the past. We often specify the time when they happened.

I **left** university in 2015.

He **didn't know** the way to Sam's house.

How **did you meet** Harry?

Past continuous

We use the past continuous to give the background information for a story. We use the past simple to talk about the main events.

I **was walking** through the park.

The birds **were singing**.

Children **were playing** football.

Often the past continuous action is interrupted by another action (in the past simple) in the same sentence.

I **was reading** a book when the phone **rang**.

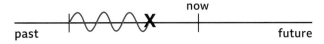

I **was listening** to music when the internet **crashed**.

We often use *while* and *as* to talk about two actions which were happening at the same time.

They were closing the café **as** we were finishing our coffee.

For more information on state and action verbs see section 1A, page 104.

Past perfect

We form the past perfect with *had* + past participle.

+	I **had finished** my work.
-	They **hadn't visited** for a long time.
?	**Had** you **been** there before?

We use the past perfect to make it clear that an action happened earlier in the past, before another action. We use the past perfect for the earlier past action.

I **didn't have** any money because I **had lost** my wallet.

When it is already clear which past action came first, we can use the past simple for both actions.

He **had lived** in Dublin for five years before he **moved** to Cork.

He **lived** in Dublin for five years before he **moved** to Cork.

We often use the past perfect after thinking verbs like *discover, find out, realise, remember, think,* etc.

When I got to work, I **realised I'd left** my laptop at home.

PRACTICE

1 Choose the correct word(s) to complete the sentences.

1 Fabio **was cycling / cycled** to work when he **fell / had fallen** off his bike.

2 I couldn't walk properly because I **had damaged / was damaging** my knee the previous day.

3 Jack was very surprised when he saw that I **painted / had painted** the living room pink!

4 I couldn't get into my flat because I **had forgotten / was forgetting** my keys.

5 I **had never been / was never going** to Egypt before, so I was really excited to see the Pyramids.

6 Our train was cancelled, so we **were waiting / had waited** for the next one to arrive.

7 I **looked / was looking** through some old photographs and I **found / was finding** this one of you at university.

8 When I got to the airport, I realised **I left / I'd left** my passport at home.

9 He **was going / had gone** so fast down the ski slope that he crashed into the restaurant.

10 We **were sitting / had sat** on the balcony and enjoying the view of the lake.

2 Complete the text with the verbs in the box.

> arrived   came off   felt   got onto   had rained
> was running   was wearing   was working

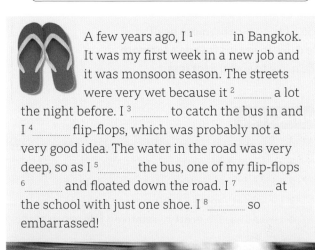

A few years ago, I ¹_____ in Bangkok. It was my first week in a new job and it was monsoon season. The streets were very wet because it ²_____ a lot the night before. I ³_____ to catch the bus in and I ⁴_____ flip-flops, which was probably not a very good idea. The water in the road was very deep, so as I ⁵_____ the bus, one of my flip-flops ⁶_____ and floated down the road. I ⁷_____ at the school with just one shoe. I ⁸_____ so embarrassed!

2B past simple and present perfect

REFERENCE ◀ page 24

Present perfect

We form the present perfect with *have/has* + past participle.

+	I**'ve been** to Poland a few times.
-	He **hasn't worked** here before.
?	**Have** you **bought** a new car?

We use the present perfect for general experiences in the past when it isn't important or isn't known exactly when these things happened.

I**'ve been** to Paris.

I **haven't seen** that film.

We often use the present perfect with *ever* and *never*.

Have you **ever** been to New York?

I've **never** met your brother.

We also use the present perfect when a past action is relevant in the present.

I can't play tennis today. I**'ve hurt** my leg.

We can also use the present perfect if we are talking about a period of time that is unfinished.

I**'ve run** six miles today. (Today is unfinished so I can run more.)

Past simple

We use the past simple for actions that happened at a specific time in the past.

I **went** to Sweden in 2019.

I **ate** a hamburger yesterday.

Notice the difference between the past simple and present perfect.

I **went** to London last year. (a specific time in the past)

I**'ve been** to London. (It isn't known when this happened.)

I **ran** five kilometres this morning. (a time in the past)

I**'ve run** five kilometres today. (an unfinished period of time)

Conversations about general experiences often begin with the present perfect and continue in the past simple as the speaker adds details.

A: I**'ve been** to Colombia.

B: Really? Where did you go?

A: I **went** to Medellín.

PRACTICE

1 Complete the conversations with the correct past simple or present perfect form of the verbs in brackets.

1 A: She ¹_____ her first book in 2018. (publish)

   B: ²_____ anything else since then? (she / write)

   A: Yes, she ³_____ me her second book a few months ago. (send)

2 A: My partner ⁴_____ in a play last year. (act)

   B: Really? Which one?

   A: I can't remember. He ⁵_____ in so many, I never remember the names. (be)

3 A: I do most sports, but I ⁶_____ tennis. I'd love to learn. (never / play)

   B: I can teach you. I ⁷_____ all my life! (play)

4 A: ⁸_____ Warsaw? (you / ever / visit)

   B: Yes, many times. The last time I ⁹_____ was in 2019. (go)

   A: Really?! I ¹⁰_____ there in 2019, too. (be)

2 Complete the text with the correct past simple or present perfect form of the verbs in brackets.

Bookworms together

I ¹<u>'ve known</u> (know) my best friend Natasha for over twenty years. We ²_____ (become) close friends at school because of a shared love of stories. When I was young, I ³_____ (be) extremely shy. I spent most of my time reading. That's how I ⁴_____ (meet) Natasha – in the school library. We ⁵_____ (discover) that we both loved books and films. Since those days we ⁶_____ (go) to the cinema together hundreds of times. Also, we ⁷_____ (share) hundreds of books: if she reads something she likes, she gives it to me to read, and I do the same. In all these years we ⁸_____ (not disagree) once!

GRAMMAR BANK

2C How to ... apologise and give reasons

REFERENCE ◀◀ page 27

We use these phrases to apologise and accept the apology.

apologise	accept the apology
Sorry I'm late.	Don't worry.
Sorry to keep you waiting.	No problem.
I'm really sorry.	It's/That's fine.
I apologise.	It's/That's OK.
Sorry about that.	Never mind.

We use these phrases to give a reason and accept responsibility.

give a reason	accept responsibility
There was a (delay/problem with …)	**I made a mistake.**
My (train) **was delayed.**	**It was** (my/our) **fault.**
My (train/flight) **got cancelled.**	
I got the (date/time) **wrong.**	
The (traffic/journey) **was terrible.**	
I got lost.	

We use these phrases to say we will take action.

take action
I'll be there as soon as possible.
I'll call you back.

PRACTICE

1 Match the sentence halves.

1 Sorry I'm		**a** that.
2 Sorry to keep		**b** date wrong.
3 Sorry about		**c** lost.
4 Don't		**d** you waiting.
5 Never		**e** worry.
6 I got the		**f** soon as possible.
7 My flight		**g** mind.
8 I got		**h** late.
9 It was my		**i** fault.
10 I'll be there as		**j** was delayed.

2 Complete the words in the conversations.

1 A: John?

B: Yes.

A: It's Mary here. Sorry to keep you ¹w_____!
My train was ²d_____ by thirty minutes.

B: Oh, that's OK.

A: I'm just walking past the museum now. I'll be there as soon as ³p_____ .

B: ⁴N_____ problem. See you soon.

2 A: I missed your party yesterday! I'm sorry.

B: Don't ⁵w_____ . Is everything OK?

A: Yes. I ⁶g_____ the date wrong. I thought the party was next week. It was my ⁷f_____ .

B: Oh no! Well, never ⁸m_____ . You can come to the next one.

3 A: ⁹S_____ I'm late! The traffic ¹⁰w_____ terrible.

B: ¹¹T_____ OK. Have a seat.

A: There was a delay on Main Street, so I took a different route, but then I ¹²g_____lost!

B: Oh, no! Well, you're here now.

3 Complete the conversations with the phrases in the box.

> I'll be there as soon as possible
> I made a mistake with the time   It was my fault
> Never mind   Sorry to keep you waiting
> The traffic was terrible

1 A: ¹_____ . My train was cancelled. I had to wait for the next one.

B: That's OK. I've only just arrived, too. ²_____ . The journey took me over an hour.

2 A: Sorry I'm late. I got lost. ³_____ . I forgot to note down your address.

B: ⁴_____ .You're here now.

3 A: I've just seen that this morning's meeting starts at 10 a.m. ⁵_____ . I thought it started at 11 a.m. and I'm out meeting a customer. ⁶_____ . I might be late though.

B: Don't worry. I'll let you know if you miss anything.

2D prepositions of time

REFERENCE ◀ page 28

We use prepositions of time to specify exactly when something happens.

before/after/during/until/between

We use *before/after* + a specific time or event.

We need to be there **before** 7 p.m.

After breakfast, she left for school.

We use *during* to talk about something that happens within a period of time.

During the 2010s a lot of people left the country.

We talked about it **during** lunch.

We use *until/till* to talk about something which happens up to a certain time and then stops.

She worked there **until** 2004. (Then she changed jobs.)

We'll wait **till** 6 p.m.

We use *between* to talk about a time that starts at a certain point and finishes at a certain point.

They lived in New York **between** 2005 and 2008.

They're leaving **between** 3 p.m. and 4 p.m.

in/at/on

We use *in* + months/years/decades/centuries/seasons.

We're going on holiday **in** August.

In 2020 I changed my career.

In the 1990s, there was a lot of investment.

In the twenty-first century, this type of work has become important.

We spend a lot of time on the beach **in** the summer.

We also use *in* + a period of time, to show when something will happen.

I'll see you **in** ten minutes.

The conference finishes **in** three hours.

We use *at* + a specific time.

We need to be there **at** 5 o'clock.

The film starts **at** 8.30 p.m.

We also use *at* + certain words such as *weekend* and *night*.

Let's go there **at** the weekend.

I wouldn't go there **at** night.

We use *on* + dates/days.

I'll see you **on** Wednesday afternoon.

My birthday is **on** 12 July.

They celebrate **on** New Year's Day.

We play football **on** Saturdays.

PRACTICE

1 Choose the correct words to complete the sentences.

1 They always travel to the Mediterranean **during** / **at** / **on** the summer holidays.

2 I lived there **at** / **on** / **until** 2020 and then I moved.

3 That sounds great. We'll see you **in** / **at** / **until** the weekend.

4 He visited Japan **at** / **on** / **in** February.

5 The ancient Olympic Games began **in** / **at** / **on** 776 BCE.

6 The best time to visit is **until** / **between** / **at** May and July.

7 **Before** / **Until** / **During** we start the meeting, let's make sure everyone is here.

8 I'll see you **on** / **at** / **in** a couple of weeks.

9 We weren't allowed to leave the country **until** / **between** / **during** the law changed.

10 We're planning a trip to see the Grand Canyon **in** / **at** / **on** my birthday.

2 Complete the sentences with prepositions.

1 .... 2021 I travelled to Mexico to research my book.

2 A lot of businesses have closed down .... these difficult times.

3 We'll postpone the trip .... we receive our new passports.

4 I saw Helena .... the weekend and she says 'hello'.

5 I'm hoping to move to New York .... a few weeks.

6 Greece attracted more than 31 million visitors .... 2019.

7 We usually celebrate with a big meal and fireworks .... New Year's Eve.

8 They lived in Portugal .... 2008 and 2011.

3 Complete the email with prepositions.

Hi Jess, ➦

How was your day? Mine was great. As you know, I usually stay in bed ¹............... Saturday mornings, but this morning I got up ²............... 5 a.m. and drove to the beach so I could go surfing with Allie. The last time I did it was ³............... 2020. We surfed for hours, ⁴............... we were too hungry to carry on! ⁵............... breakfast at a nearby café, we drove to some shops so I could get some clothes for my holiday ⁶............... July. I got home sometime ⁷............... 5 and 6 p.m. with very painful feet!

Anyway, I hope you had a good day. I'm really happy that you're coming to see me ⁸............... two months. I can't wait!

Mona x

3A question forms

REFERENCE ◀◀ page 33

Word order in questions

Notice the word order in questions.

question word	auxiliary verb	subject	verb
Where	do	you	live?
What	did	he	want?
When	are	they	coming?
Where	have	you	been?

Subject questions

When we ask about the subject of a verb, we don't use an auxiliary verb.

Who invited you to the party? John invited me. (We are asking about the subject.)

Who did you invite to the party? I invited all my friends. (We are asking about the object.)

Notice the word order in subject questions.

question word	verb	object
Who	wants	a drink?
What	happened?	–
Who	ate	the sandwich?

Compare subject and object questions.

Object question: **What did he write?**

Subject question: **Who wrote it?**

Questions with prepositions

When we use a verb + preposition such as *look for, write about, listen to,* etc., we usually keep the verb and preposition together. The preposition usually comes at the end of the question.

What did you **talk about**? Who are you **looking for**? What music do you **listen to**?

Yes/No questions

Yes/No questions don't use a question word. The answer to the question is *Yes* or *No*.

auxiliary verb	subject	verb	object
Does	he	work?	
Did	you	know?	
Have	they	arrived?	
Did	you	enjoy	the film?
Are	they	watching	the game?

PRACTICE

1 Put the words in brackets in the correct places to make questions.

1 the competition? (won / who)

....

2 were you thinking? (what / about)

....

3 to the old theatre? (happened / what)

....

4 Where your great-grandparents come? (from / did)

....

5 your parents here? (live / did)

....

6 she here for a long time? (worked / has)

....

7 is all that noise? (who / making)

....

8 house you looking for? (are / which)

....

2 Write questions for the underlined answers.

1 Where .... ?
I live <u>in Madrid</u>.

2 .... the game?
<u>Nick</u> won the game.

3 .... meat?
<u>No</u>, he doesn't eat meat.

4 .... doing?
They are <u>sleeping</u>.

5 What .... ?
I'm writing about <u>my first holiday</u>.

6 .... home?
We got home <u>yesterday</u>.

7 .... the chocolate?
<u>We</u> ate the chocolate.

8 .... the film?
<u>Yes</u>, we liked the film.

3B future plans and intentions

REFERENCE ◀◀ page 36

be going to + infinitive

+	I'm going to start university next year.
-	She isn't going to move to Paris.
?	What are you going to do?

We use *be going to* when we have already decided on a future plan or intention.

She's going to buy a house. (NOT ~~She will buy a house.~~)

Present continuous: *be* + verb + *-ing* form

+	I'm starting my course in September.
-	We aren't going away for very long.
?	What time are you leaving in the morning?

We use the present continuous to talk about future plans and arrangements that have already been made. We usually specify a future time such as *next week*, *on Friday*, etc. unless it's obvious that we're talking about the future.

We're flying to Greece on Friday. (We've already bought the tickets.)

She's staying in a hotel near the airport. (The hotel is already booked.)

We often use the present continuous instead of *be going to* when the main verb is *go* or *come*. Both forms are possible.

Instead of: We're going to go to Spain.

we say: We're going to Spain.

Instead of: I'm going to come and see you later.

we say: I'm coming to see you later.

In many cases both the present continuous or *be going to* are possible, with only a small difference in meaning.

I'm playing basketball on Saturday. (It is arranged.)

I'm going to play basketball on Saturday. (This is my plan.)

will

+	We'll meet you at the station.
-	We won't see you tomorrow.
?	Will you want a taxi?

We use *will* + infinitive without *to* when there is no plan or fixed arrangement but we make the decision at the time of speaking.

I'm tired. I think I'll go to bed.

might

| + | I might go out later. |
| - | We might not go on holiday this year. |

We use *might* + infinitive without *to* to talk about plans, when we are unsure what the plan is.

I might see you at the restaurant this evening. (But I'm not sure. I might decide not to go.)

We do not usually use *might* in question forms. It is considered to be old fashioned and formal.

Do you think you might see Maria later?

NOT ~~Might you see Maria later?~~

PRACTICE

1 Complete the conversations with the words in brackets in the correct form. Sometimes two options are possible.

1 A: What are you doing/going to do later? (do)

B: I 'm having dinner with my family. (have)

2 A: _____ you _____ to the match on Sunday? (come)

B: Yes, I _____ you there. (see)

3 A: A few of us _____ out for a meal later. Do you want to join us? (go)

B: Thanks, but I'm very tired. I think I _____ at home. (stay)

4 A: I'm _____ my boss later. (meet) I'm _____ him for more money. (ask)

B: Good luck!

5 A: My cousin _____ married in September. (get)

B: How lovely! Are they _____ a big celebration? (have)

6 A: I _____ from home tomorrow. (work)

B: That's fine. We _____ you if there are any problems. (call)

2 Choose the correct option (a, b or c).

1 He's _____ study biology at university.

a going

b not going

c going to

2 _____ to open a new shop here?

a Are they planning

b Will they plan

c They planning

3 We _____ have a holiday this year. We don't have enough money.

a 're not go

b aren't going

c aren't going to

4 _____ this afternoon?

a Are you going to work

b Are you work

c Will you working

5 I'm really hungry. I think I _____ stop for some lunch.

a 'll

b 'm going

c might to

6 They _____ their exams next week.

a will to do

b going to do

c are doing

3C How to … make polite inquiries

REFERENCE ◀◀ page 39

We use indirect questions when we want to make inquiries or polite requests.

Could you tell me if I have to pay for the swimming pool?

Could you explain how I get a work permit?

I'd like to know when the next train leaves.

I'd like to know how this works.

Do you know whether I can pay by credit card?

Do you know where the halls of residence are?

Can I ask if you know the way to the museum?

Can you tell me what time the gym closes?

We use a different word order when we ask indirect questions. The word order is the same as for statements.

Can you tell me **what time the train leaves**?

NOT ~~Can you tell me what time does the train leave?~~

Do you know **when the shops open**?

NOT ~~Do you know when do the shops open?~~

I'd like to know **where the bus stops.**

NOT ~~I'd like to know where does the bus stop.~~

PRACTICE

1 Find the mistakes and correct them. Two of the sentences are correct.

1 Could you tell to me if this is the way to the employment office?

2 Can I ask if you know what time the gallery opens?

3 I'd like to know if do I need my student card to study on campus.

4 Do you know whether is the cinema open?

5 Can you telling me where the nearest petrol station is?

6 I'd like know what time the flight arrives.

7 Do you know how to get to the shopping mall?

8 Could you if tell whether I need a visa?

2 Put the words in brackets in the correct order to complete the questions.

1 A: (you / know / I / where / do / find / can) the tourist information office?

B: Yes, it's just over there.

2 A: (to / like / I'd / know) about some good places to visit in the city.

B: OK, I can give you some recommendations.

3 A: (you / tell / is / me / far / how / it / could) to the airport from here?

B: It's about twenty kilometres.

4 A: (you / tell / is / can / market / me / the / where)?

B: Yes, there's a big market in the next street.

5 A: (me / you / could / tell / the way) to the station?

B: I'm going there now. You can come with me.

6 A: (know / you / whether / can / do / I) use these facilities?

B: Yes, are you a student here?

3 Complete the indirect questions. Use the direct questions in brackets to help you.

1 A: Excuse me, could you tell [1]............................? (What time is the next train to Seville?)

B: Sure. It leaves in thirty minutes.

A: Do you know [2]............................? (Is it a direct train?)

B: It is. It takes two hours and twenty minutes.

A: Great. I'd like to know [3]............................. (How much is a ticket?)

B: Let me look. Right, it's €61.50.

A: OK thanks. I'd like two tickets then, please.

2 A: Hello. I'm here for the college open day.

B: Could you tell [4]............................, please? (What is your name, please?)

A: Yes, it's Melissa Walker.

B: OK Melissa. I have your name here. Can I ask [5]............................? (Is it your first time at the college?)

A: Yes, it is. I'm thinking of applying for a course here next year.

B: Lovely. Do you know [6]............................? (Which course do you want to do?)

A: Yes, I'd like to be a chef.

B: Great! Right, so someone will be here in about ten minutes to show you and other people around. Just wait here for now.

A: OK. Can you tell [7]............................? (Are there any toilets near here?)

B: Yes, they're just over there on the right.

A: And do you know [8]............................? (How long does the tour take?)

B: It'll be about an hour.

3D phrasal verbs

REFERENCE ◀◀ page 40

A phrasal verb is a combination of a verb and a particle (a preposition or an adverb). The combination has a new meaning that is usually different from the meaning of the verb alone.

I **get up** at 6.15. (get out of bed)

My car **broke down**. (stopped working)

Some phrasal verbs don't take an object.

I **go out** at night.

My alarm **goes off** at 7 a.m.

The plane **takes off** in ten minutes.

Other phrasal verbs take an object.

I put on **my hat**.

I look after **my dog**.

With some phrasal verbs, we cannot separate the verb and the particle.

I **look after** my children.

NOT I look my children after.

We **got on** the bus.

NOT We got the bus on.

Other examples of phrasal verbs that behave in this way are: *look after someone, come across something* (= find), *stick with something* (= continue doing it), *log onto (a computer), break into (a house)*.

With other phrasal verbs, we can separate the verb and the particle.

I **put on** my coat.

I **put** my coat **on**.

Put away your toys!

Put your toys **away**!

We **picked up** our rubbish.

We **picked** our rubbish **up**.

I'll **take off** my jacket.

I'll **take** my jacket **off**.

Other examples of phrasal verbs that behave in this way are: *throw away (rubbish), switch on (the TV), write down (information), shut down (a computer), look up (a word), try on (clothes)*.

If the object is a pronoun (e.g. *it*), the pronoun always comes before the particle.

I'll **throw it** away.

NOT I'll throw away it.

She picked **it** up.

NOT She picked up it.

PRACTICE

1 Rewrite the sentences. Use the phrasal verb in brackets in the correct form.

1 He didn't put my number on paper. (write down)
He ....

2 Rosa lifted the pen. (pick up)
Rosa ....

3 I'll tell him to leave. (go away)
I ....

4 My alarm didn't make any noise. (go off)
My alarm ....

5 They are caring for that dog. (look after)
They ....

6 Juan Pablo turned off his computer. (shut down)
Juan Pablo ....

7 I'm finding the word in the dictionary. (look up)
I'm ....

8 We put the old clothes in the rubbish bin yesterday. (throw away)
We ....

2 Look at the phrasal verbs in Ex 1 again. Which ones can have the particle in two positions?

1 He didn't write my number down. OR He didn't write down my number.

3 Correct the mistakes in the sentences. Two sentences are correct.

1 Can you help me put on all these toys in the cupboard?

2 I heard a new English word yesterday, but I forgot to write down it.

3 I don't like trying clothes on in shops.

4 We've just come some old photos across.

5 My alarm goes at 6 a.m. off every day.

6 You buy a ticket from the driver when you get up the bus.

7 I'm enjoying my Spanish lessons, so I'm going to stick with them.

8 Mrs Garcia has asked me to take her cat and look it after while she's away.

9 Their plane will take on in thirty minutes.

10 I saw some money on the floor so I picked up it.

4A modals for rules and advice

REFERENCE ◀◀ page 45

We can use modals to talk about rules and to give advice.

have to/need to/must

We use *have to/need to/must* when we talk about rules and things that are necessary. You have no choice, or it's a very strong suggestion.

You **must** talk to your manager about the problem.

We **have to** pay tax on the money we earn.

I **need to** get up early to catch my flight tomorrow.

In the positive form we often use *have to*, *need to* and *must* with the same meaning.

In the negative form, *don't have to/needn't* (or *don't need to*) and *mustn't* have different meanings. We use *don't have to*, *needn't* and *don't need to* when something is not necessary, but you can do it if you want.

You **don't have to** finish that report today. Tomorrow will be fine.

You **needn't** worry too much about that.

You **don't need to** bring a laptop.

We use *mustn't* when something is not allowed.

You **mustn't** use your mobile phone when you're on the plane. (It is not allowed and it's dangerous.)

We use *must* to talk about present or future situations. For past situations, we use *had to*.

We **must** leave soon, before it gets dark. (present/future)

We **had to** leave early yesterday morning. (past)

should/shouldn't

We use *should/shouldn't* when we are giving advice. We use *should* to talk about things that are a good idea, and *shouldn't* to talk about things that are not a good idea.

You **should** come to work in smart clothes.

You **shouldn't** arrive late to meetings.

Should I wear a tie?

Notice that *must* and *should* are followed by the infinitive without *to*.

We **must get** there on time.

NOT ~~We must to get there on time.~~

You **should ask** Helen for some advice.

NOT ~~You should to ask Helen for some advice.~~

PRACTICE

1 Match the sentence halves.

1 I really look forward to the weekend because I
2 I must try
3 You don't
4 I really think Clarissa should
5 You mustn't give
6 You don't have
7 Can I call you later? I need to
8 Should we

a need to wait for me, I'll see you later.
b to put on your webcam if you don't want to.
c don't have to get up early for work.
d ask for a pay rise. She deserves it.
e wait until everyone arrives?
f to visit Frank while he is in hospital.
g ask you a few questions.
h your phone number to any of the clients.

2 Choose the correct word(s) to complete the text.

5 Steps for fitness success

- Make sure you get some exercise every day. You [1]**don't have to / need to** go running if that's not your style, but you [2]**should / don't have** try to do at least an hour of moderate exercise.

- You [3]**should to / need to** eat healthily. You [4]**mustn't / should** try to plan your meals so that you don't get too hungry. You [5]**mustn't / don't have to** eat lots of sweet snacks. Try eating fruit or vegetables instead.

- Keep track of how many calories you eat. You [6]**shouldn't / have to** eat more calories than you will use in the day.

- Make sure you get enough sleep. You [7]**don't need to / should** go to bed early every day, but most of us need six to eight hours of sleep a night.

- Try to stay motivated. If you want to make changes in your life, you [8]**must / don't have to** stay positive.

4B articles

REFERENCE page 47

We usually use articles in front of nouns, for various purposes.

Use *a/an* (indefinite article):

*   the first time something is mentioned.
    I saw **a** mouse in the kitchen.
*   before a singular noun when the speaker doesn't know which one.
    She's watching **a** film.
*   with jobs.
    I'm **a** doctor. He's **an** artist.

Use *the* (definite article):

*   when there is only one of something.
    I see **the** Sun.
*   when the speaker knows which one, e.g. it has been mentioned before.
    I got on a plane. **The** plane (that I was talking about) was huge!
*   with seas, oceans, rivers and country names that are plural or use extra words like *Kingdom*.
    the River Danube, **the** Pacific Ocean, **the** United Kingdom
*   before the names of some areas.
    the south of France, **the** coast of Italy
*   with superlatives.
    Ali was **the** greatest boxer.
*   with some defining expressions.
    the first, **the** only
*   in some phrases with prepositions.
    in **the** morning, at **the** end, by **the** next day
*   with dates in spoken English.
    the fifth of June

Use no article (zero article):

*   to talk generally about things or people.
    Elephants are bigger than lions.
*   with most names of towns, cities and countries.
    I live in Paris.
*   before plural nouns.
    I bought six bottles of water.
*   in some phrases with prepositions.
    on Monday, at work, for lunch, on foot
*   with sports.
    I like tennis. He plays football.

PRACTICE

1 Choose the correct alternatives.

1 My parents are both **the** / – doctors.
2 We live on **a** / **the** west coast of France.
3 My son's been **a** / **the** plumber for about five years.
4 That bike's blue but **a** / **the** one I had was red.
5 I was at **the** / – work when you called yesterday.
6 It's common that **a** / – homes are bigger here than in the city.
7 Yuri Gagarin was **a** / **the** first man in space.
8 I grew up in – / **the** Delhi.
9 I've just bought **a** / **the** new pair of trainers.
10 Do you think that it's usual for **the** / – people to work too hard these days?

2 Correct the mistakes in the sentences.

1 I have mobile phone.
2 I think YouTube is best platform for video sharing.
3 Are you ready to go? Flight leaves at 6 p.m.
4 I saw a doctor about my pain. Fortunately, a doctor said it was nothing serious.
5 Bobby's girlfriend is engineer.
6 The women live longer than men.
7 We went to a party, but there weren't the many people there.
8 We looked up and saw an aeroplane in sky.
9 I work as cleaner in an office.
10 My wife and I have lived in USA for several years.

3 Complete the text by adding *a, an, the* or – (no article).

My first YouTube video

¹.......... first time I was on YouTube I was eight years old and living in ².......... Wales. I had ³.......... new dog and I wanted to make a video of her playing with me and ⁴.......... friend. I borrowed my mother's phone and started filming. Unfortunately, ⁵.......... dogs don't always understand the plans of eight-year-olds! She lay on ⁶.......... floor and closed her eyes. I gave her ⁷.......... old toy to play with. She ignored it. We jumped around and sang. She didn't move ⁸.......... inch. Eventually, I lay on the floor next to her while my friend held ⁹.......... phone. Suddenly, the dog bit me on ¹⁰.......... nose and ran off. I screamed. My friend thought this was really funny and posted it on YouTube.

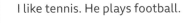

4C How to ... explain rules and procedures

REFERENCE ◀◀ page 51

We use these phrases to explain the rules and procedures of a sport or game.

explain the aim or goal

The goal is to ...
The aim is to ...

talk about the organisation of a game

There are (six players/ten groups/five stages).
It is played (on a court/in a sports hall/on grass/outdoors).
It is made of .../It consists of ...
It lasts (10 minutes/all day/one hour).
It takes (three days/two hours).

talk about the procedure

First/To start ...
Then/Next ...
After that ...

talk about rules

You score/succeed by (shooting the ball into the goal/doing ...)
You can ...
You have to/must ...
You can't/mustn't ...

PRACTICE

1 Match the sentence halves. Which game is it?

1 The aim of the
2 There are eleven
3 The game is played
4 The game lasts
5 To start
6 After
7 You score by
8 You mustn't

a on grass usually.
b the game, you kick the ball.
c push other players.
d kicking or heading the ball into a goal.
e game is to score goals.
f that, another player kicks it.
g ninety minutes.
h players on each team.

2 Choose the correct words to complete the sentences.

1 The **score** / **time** / **aim** of this game is to win points.
2 The game is **play** / **played** / **for play** outdoors.
3 **For** / **To** / **At** start the game, you throw a coin.
4 This board game **makes** / **has** / **lasts** about an hour.
5 To take part, you **have** / **must** / **can't** to be under sixteen years old.
6 You win the match **by** / **for** / **in** scoring more points than the other team.
7 You **score** / **mustn't** / **haven't** kick the other players.
8 First, you swim. **Then** / **On** / **After** that, you run.
9 You score **at** / **by** / **for** using all your cards before other players.
10 The game **consists** / **has** / **made** of a board and some cards.

3 Correct the mistakes in the sentences.

1 The game is play on a board.
2 The goal are to get from one end of the board to the other.
3 There is two to three players.
4 The game usually lasts an hour to play.
5 At start, pick up a card and read the number.
6 Then, you must to move forward that number.
7 After then, read the instructions on the square.
8 You can't to answer the question on the square.
9 You not can move forward without a correct answer.
10 You succeed for getting to the end of the board first.

4 Complete the description with the phrases in the box.

> First   is played   lasts   must   succeed by
> The aim   Then   There are   You can   you can't

How to play Chinese Chess

Chinese Chess ¹............ on a wooden board. ²............ two players and each player has sixteen pieces. ³............ , you take out the board and place the pieces on the board. ⁴............ , you choose a player to start. On your turn you ⁵............ move one piece, then it's your opponent's turn. Each piece can make certain moves according to the symbol written on it. ⁶............ capture your opponent's pieces by moving onto a space where your opponent's piece is placed. When one of your pieces is captured, it is removed from the game and ⁷............ use it again. You ⁸............ capturing your opponent's pieces. ⁹............ of the game is to get your opponent's general in a place where it has no option but to be captured in the next move. The game usually ¹⁰............ between twenty minutes and several hours.

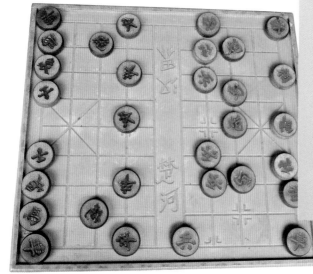

4D present perfect + superlative

REFERENCE ◀◀ page 52

We use the present perfect with a superlative adjective to show that something is the best/worst/greatest, etc. experience of our whole life until now.

It's **the most amazing** holiday I**'ve had**.

It's **the best** film I**'ve seen**.

It's **the biggest** company I**'ve worked** for.

He's **the strongest** man I**'ve met**.

We often add *ever* to the present perfect structure. This emphasises that we are talking about our whole life. *Ever* goes between *have* and the past participle.

It's the nicest trip I've **ever** been on.

That's the most beautiful car I've **ever** seen.

It's the worst restaurant I've **ever** been to.

PRACTICE

1 Match the sentence halves.

1 This is the slowest car
2 Claire is the most unusual person
3 I think that was the worst meal
4 This is the most expensive hotel
5 Those are the kindest words
6 I think I'm the coldest
7 That's the most interesting question
8 This is the saddest book

a I've ever stayed in.
b I've ever cooked.
c I've read.
d I've ever driven.
e I've ever been.
f anyone has said to me.
g you've asked me.
h I've ever met.

2 Correct the mistakes in the sentences. Two sentences are correct.

1 It's the most of memorable journey I've ever been on.
2 This is the biggest car I've ever drove.
3 It's the bumpiest road I ever seen.
4 He's the more intelligent child I've ever met.
5 That's the worst mistake you've ever make.
6 She's the nicest manager I've ever worked for.
7 It was best meal I've ever eaten.
8 It was the wonderful holiday we've ever had.
9 This is the longest book she is ever written.
10 It's the most difficult journey they've ever filmed.

3 Complete the sentences with the word(s) in brackets in the correct form.

1 That's _____ (funny) joke I've ever heard.
2 You're the most helpful neighbour we _____ (ever / have).
3 This is _____ (bad) storm I've ever seen.
4 It was the most boring holiday I _____ (go) on.
5 Jake is _____ (patient) manager I've had.
6 I think I'm _____ (exhausted) I've ever been.
7 That's the silliest thing I _____ (ever / hear) you say.
8 You're _____ (nervous) I've ever seen you.
9 This is the most difficult thing I _____ (ever / have to) do.
10 It's probably the most brilliant film we _____ (ever / see).

4 Make sentences with the correct form of the words in brackets so they have a similar meaning to the first sentence.

1 That film is brilliant! We loved it!
(it / best / see)
It's the best film we've ever seen.

2 That restaurant is terrible. I hated it.
(that / worst / eat in)

3 This is a beautiful song! I love it.
(this / beautiful / ever / hear)

4 We went on a twenty-eight-hour trip.
(it / long / be on)

5 She's an amazing actress!
(amazing / I / ever / see)

6 One of my university students is thirteen years old.
(he / young / I / teach)

7 This city is huge.
(big / I / ever / visit)

8 This campsite is extremely dirty.
(dirty / we / stay in)

9 I love that programme.
(it / good / watch)

GRAMMAR BANK

5A relative clauses

REFERENCE ◀◀ page 58

Defining relative clauses

We use defining relative clauses to give important information about a person, place or thing. The information is essential in the sentence.

We use **relative pronouns** to join the main clause and the relative clause We use:

- *who* for people.
  He's the man **who** took my bag!
- *where* for places.
  This is the building **where** we got married.
- *which* for things.
  This is the bank card **which** she was looking for.
- *when* for times.
  That was the day **when** I graduated from university.
- *whose* for possessions.
  Is that the man **whose** phone you picked up?

We often use relative clauses to describe something we don't know the name of.

It's the thing which you use to hang up the washing.

To make the relative clause we use a relative pronoun + subject + verb.

Main clause	Relative clause
The is the house	where we lived.
They started to feel ill on the day.	when the spider bit them.

We can use *that* instead of *who* or *which*. We can also sometimes use it to replace *when*.

He's the man **that** took my bag!

This is the bank card **that** she was looking for.

2019 was the year **that** we first met.

We can leave out *who*, *which* and *that* when the subject of the verb in the main clause is not the same as the subject of the relative clause.

He's the man **(who/that)** I told you about.

The subject of the main clause is *the man*. The subject of the relative clause is *I* (I told you about him). The subjects are different, so we can leave out *who* or *that*.

He's the man **who** took my bag.

The subject of the main clause is *the man* and the subject of the relative clause is *the man* (the man took my bag), so we cannot leave out the pronoun *who* or *that*.

We can also sometimes leave out *when*.

2019 was the year we first met.

PRACTICE

1 Complete the sentences using *who, which, where, when* or *whose*.

1 That's the office _____ I did my work experience.
2 She's the woman _____ I was telling you about.
3 That's the article _____ he wrote for the magazine.
4 That was the moment _____ I realised my mistake!
5 This is the man _____ laptop I borrowed.
6 She's the girl _____ left the birthday party early.
7 I can't remember the time _____ I last spoke to them.
8 Eva married the man _____ she met online.
9 This is man _____ blog I was talking about.
10 This is the beach _____ I walk every morning.

2 Tick the sentences in Ex 1 where you can use *that* instead of a relative pronoun. In which sentences is it possible to leave out the relative pronoun?

3 Choose the correct option to complete the clues. Then complete the answers.

1 A piece of jewellery **who / which / where** you wear around your neck.
   n _____ e
2 Someone **who / when / which** writes for a newspaper.
   j _____ t
3 The day each year **who / which / when** you become a year older.
   b _____ y
4 Someone **which / who / when** plays sports professionally.
   a _____ e
5 An animal **who / which / where** has eight legs.
   s _____ r
6 Something **when / which / where** you use to find information or communicate with people.
   i _____ t
7 A personal webpage **who / which / where** people can write their own articles.
   b _____ g
8 Someone **which / where / who** works in politics.
   p _____ n
9 The time of year **which / when / where** people like to go to the beach.
   s _____ r
10 A place **where / when / which** people drive their cars.
   r _____ d

5B reported speech

REFERENCE ◀◀ page 60

We use reported speech to report what someone said earlier.

After a past tense reporting verb, e.g. *said*, *told*, etc., the original verb often moves one tense back into the past.

direct speech	reported speech
present simple	past simple
present continuous	past continuous
present perfect	past perfect
past simple	past perfect
am/is/are going to	was/were going to
will	would
can	could
have to/has to	had to

'I always **recycle** my waste.'
He said (that) he always **recycled** his waste.

'I**'ve passed** my exams.'
She said (that) she **had passed** her exams.

'We **saw** her at the station.'
They said (that) they **had seen** her at the station.

'I**'ll** help you.'
He said (that) he **would** help me.

There are sometimes other changes in reported speech, e.g. to pronouns and possessive adjectives.

'I'll go.'
She said (that) **she would** go.

'It's my car.'
He said (that) it **was his** car.

Say and *tell* are the most common reporting verbs. Notice the different verb patterns.

She **said** (to me) (that) she wanted to stay.

He **told** me that (that) he'd be late.

PRACTICE

1 Complete the reported statements. Change the verb tenses and make any other changes that are necessary.

1 'We're going to clean the beach.'
He said that .... going to clean the beach.

2 'I go to the recycling centre every week.'
He said that .... to the recycling centre every week.

3 'We've never donated to a charity before.'
They said that .... never donated to a charity before.

4 'I'd lived there for more than twenty years.'
She .... that she .... lived there for more than twenty years.

5 'I've lost my passport.'
She said that .... had lost .... passport.

6 'I'm feeling a bit stressed.'
He .... me that he .... feeling a bit stressed.

7 'We grew these carrots in our garden.'
They told us that they .... grown the carrots in .... garden.

8 'I can't stay long because I have to go to a meeting.'
She said that she .... stay long because she .... to go to a meeting.

2 Read the pairs of sentences. Then correct the mistakes in the reported speech.

1 'Recycling waste is very important to me.'
She told to me that recycling waste was very important to her.

2 'I'm going to meet a group of activists.'
He told me that he met a group of activists.

3 'Maja called me.'
He said that Maja has called him.

4 'We'll meet you.'
They told us that they will meet us.

5 'We haven't received your application.'
They told her that we hadn't received your application.

6 'I'll see you at the party, Matt.'
She told Matt that she will see him at the party.

7 'I've already sent you an email explaining the situation.'
He said that he already sent an email explaining the situation.

8 'I can collect the documents.'
She told to her manager that she could collect the documents.

5C How to ... give and respond to personal news

REFERENCE ◀◀ page 63

We use these phrases to give good and bad news, and respond to other people's good and bad news.

give good news

Guess what!
I've got some (good/amazing) **news**.
I've got some good news to tell you.
I'm really pleased to tell you ...

give bad news

Bad news, I'm afraid.
Unfortunately, ...
There's something I need to tell you.

give good or bad news

You won't believe this (but) ...
I've got something to tell you.
You know ... ? Well, ...

respond to good news

Wow, that's (amazing/fantastic/awesome)!
That's (wonderful/great) **news**!
I'm so pleased for you.
I can't believe it. That's great!
Well done!
Congratulations!
That is good news.

respond to bad news

That's (terrible/awful).
I'm really sorry.
What a shame.
I'm sorry to hear that.

PRACTICE

1 Complete the conversations with the correct words.

1 A: [1]G_____ what! I'm moving house tomorrow.
   B: Really? Wow, that's [2]w_____ . I'm so [3]pl_____ for you.

2 A: Bad news, I'm [4]a_____ .
   B: What's the matter?
   A: I lost my wallet with more than €200 in cash.
   B: Oh no! That's [5]t_____ .

3 A: There's something I [6]n_____ to tell you.
   B: What's that?
   A: I'm afraid I crashed the car.
   B: Oh that's [7]a_____ . Are you OK?

4 A: I've got some amazing [8]n_____ .
   B: What is it?
   A: I'm going to have a baby!
   B: [9]C_____ ! I can't [10]b_____ it! I'm [11]s_____ pleased for you!

2 Put the words in brackets in the correct order to complete the conversations.

1 A: _____ we're getting married. (this / believe / but / you / won't)
   B: Wow. Congratulations! _____! (good / that / news / is)

2 A: I've _____ (something / tell / you / got / to)
   B: What is it?
   A: _____ my exams. (failed / unfortunately / I)
   B: Oh, I'm really sorry. _____ . (a / shame / what)

3 A: I'm _____ that you got the job. (to / really / tell / pleased / you)
   B: _____! (believe / I / it / can't)

4 A: You passed. Congratulations! Well done!
   B: _____ ! I'm so excited! (amazing / wow / that's)

3 Complete the conversations with the phrases (a–h).

a   I've got some good news
b   I'm really pleased to tell
c   You know
d   I'm sorry to hear that.
e   Well done
f   I'm afraid
g   Congratulations to them both
h   That's wonderful news

1
[1]_____ you that your application has been successful.

[2]_____ . Thank you so much.

2
[3]_____ to tell you. I finally passed my driving test. Third time lucky!

That's wonderful news. [4]_____!

3
Bad news, [5]_____ . I lost my job this morning.

Oh no. [6]_____ .

4
[7]_____ Gian Carlo?

Yes.

Well, he and his partner got engaged last week.

Oh, that's awesome! [8]_____ .

5D *will*, *might* and *be going to* for predictions

REFERENCE ◀◀ page 65

We use *will*, *might* and *be going to* to make predictions about the future.

I think the price of petrol **will** go up.

When I go to university, I **won't live** at home.

I think we **might** win the World Cup.

I'm feeling ill so I **might not** go to college today.

It**'s going to be** a difficult job.

I've got so much to do. It **isn't going to be** easy to finish everything.

We use *will* when we feel certain about a prediction.

I'm sure he **will** get the job.

We use *might* if we are not sure.

They **might** win the game, but they might not!

We use *be going to* when we can see evidence that something will happen.

Look at those black clouds – it**'s going to** rain!

We can use *probably* if we are not sure about our prediction, and we use *definitely* when we are almost 100 percent sure.

He'll **probably** be late (but I'm not sure).

He'll **definitely** be late (he always is).

Notice that we use *probably* and *definitely* after *will*, but before *won't*.

She**'ll definitely** pass the exam.

I **definitely won't** be able to make the meeting.

She **probably won't** call again.

We also use *probably* and *definitely* with *be going to*.

She**'s probably going to** miss the bus.

He**'s definitely not going to** meet us there.

PRACTICE

1 Match the sentence halves.

1 It's probably
2 We definitely
3 The team will
4 The car might
5 Sam and Laura are definitely
6 You might not

a probably win their next match.
b going to snow tomorrow.
c hear from me until the weekend.
d won't have time to get to the shops later.
e not going to bring their kids to the party.
f break down on the way to work tomorrow.

2 Correct the mistakes in the sentences. Two sentences are correct.

1 I'm sure you play well tomorrow.
2 I can see from the look on your face that you're not probably going to enjoy this game.
3 You probably might get a message from Jon later.
4 I definitely will see you tonight.
5 Erika's definitely going to drive us to the cinema.
6 It won't probably be warm enough to swim in the sea.
7 There might definitely be a storm tonight but the weather woman wasn't sure.
8 I'm probably going to have an early night tonight.

3 Complete the sentences with the correct words and phrases in the box.

definitely win   going to   might be   might not
probably   will   will watch   won't

1 I don't think people .... the news on television in the future.
2 Young people .... be very interested in politics.
3 Technological change is .... keep on coming.
4 We .... definitely see more news reports from people in the street, and not just from professional journalists.
5 People probably .... be able to tell which reports are by professional journalists.
6 I think there will .... be a lot of fake news.
7 Politicians who are better at controlling the news will .... more elections.
8 It .... difficult to decide which news reports are real, and which are fake.

4 Complete the sentences using the prompts in brackets in the correct form and with the correct word order.

1 I .... know my results until August. (probably / will / not)
2 They .... invite you to talk at the conference. (probably / going)
3 I think that team .... win the competition. (probably / going)
4 They .... to New York next year. (move / might)
5 I think my flight .... on time after all. (going / arrive)
6 He has done no work, so he .... pass his exams! (definitely, not / going)
7 I think the environment .... an issue in the future. (definitely / going / be)
8 It's very popular, so we .... be able to get tickets. (not / might)

GRAMMAR BANK

6A *used to*

REFERENCE ◀◀ page 70

We use *used to* for talking about past habits and states which are usually no longer true.

As a child, I **used to eat** a lot of sweets.

You can also use the past simple with the same meaning.

As a child, I **ate** a lot of sweets.

+	I/You/He/She/ It/We/They	used to live in France.
-		didn't use to see my parents.
?	Did they use to visit?	

We don't use *used to* for things that happened only once, a specific number of times or a specific length of time. We use the past simple for this.

My family **moved** to the USA last year. NOT ~~My family used to move to the USA last year.~~

We **went** to Italy twice on holiday. NOT ~~We used to go to Italy twice on holiday.~~

I **studied** at university for three years. NOT ~~I used to study at university for three years.~~

In spoken English, we often use the negative form *never used to* rather than *didn't use to*.

I **never used to see** my cousins, except in the summer holidays.

In spoken English, we often leave out the verb or phrase after *used to*, especially in short answers.

A: Do you play tennis?

B: No, **I used to**, but I don't anymore.

PRACTICE

1 Which sentence is correct: a, b, or both? Why?

1 a I used to collect toy animals when I was younger.
   b I collected toy animals when I was younger.

2 a He sang for us last night.
   b He used to sing for us last night.

3 a I worked in an art gallery for three years.
   b I used to work in an art gallery for three years.

4 a She used to be a photographer.
   b She was a photographer.

5 a He used to start composing songs when he was ten.
   b He started composing songs when he was ten.

6 a Last March I used to visit some friends in Mexico City.
   b Last March I visited some friends in Mexico City.

2 Complete the text with one word in each gap.

As a child I never used ¹＿＿＿＿ like art. I was terrible at drawing. I ²＿＿＿＿ to look at my friends' pictures and think, 'They're more talented than me.' Also, I didn't ³＿＿＿＿ to like my art teacher. She was very strict. Later, as a teenager, I started playing video games. I ⁴＿＿＿＿ to play for five hours a day. When I turned sixteen, I designed my first game. My friends used ⁵＿＿＿＿ come to my house to play it. A year later, I sold the game to a big company. They said the details and design were incredible. These days, interviewers often ask me, 'Have you always been artistic? ⁶＿＿＿＿ you use to spend a lot of time in art galleries?' I find it funny. I just say, 'No! I did ⁷＿＿＿＿ use to go to art galleries at all!'

3 Complete the sentences with the correct form of *used to* and the verb in brackets.

1 We ＿＿＿＿ (live) close to the train station, but we moved away from there last year.

2 Elena ＿＿＿＿ (drink) a lot of coffee, but she does now.

3 I ＿＿＿＿ (like) my job, but I love it now.

4 ＿＿＿＿ you ＿＿＿＿ (have) art lessons when you were young?

5 My parents ＿＿＿＿ (watch) a lot of television, but they do now.

6 ＿＿＿＿ Akira ＿＿＿＿ (draw) well when he was a child?

7 It never ＿＿＿＿ (be) so hot in the summers here.

8 I ＿＿＿＿ (do) a lot of walking, but I don't have time these days.

6B comparatives and superlatives

REFERENCE ◀◀ page 72

Comparing people, places and things

We use comparative adjectives to compare people, places or things.

I'm **fitter than** my brother.

This recipe is **easier than** the one I tried yesterday.

I think rugby is **more dangerous than** football.

For one-syllable adjectives, we add -er.

For two-syllable adjectives ending in -y, -y changes to -i.

For adjectives ending in consonant + vowel + consonant, we double the final consonant.

For longer adjectives (two syllables or more), we use more (or less) + adjective.

For one-syllable adjectives ending in -ed, we use more + adjective.

stressed → **more stressed**, bored → **more bored**

Some common adjectives are irregular.

good → **better**, bad → **worse**, far → **further/farther**

We often use (not) as + adjective + as … to make comparisons. As … as means that two things are the same, and not as … as means they are not the same.

This painting is just **as good as** the last one you did. (They are both equally good.)

This is **not as expensive as** you think. (It is cheaper.)

It's **not as easy as** you think. (It is more difficult.)

Comparing actions

We use comparative adverbs to compare two actions.

He listened **more carefully** when the teacher talked about the exam.

I don't speak English **as well as** my sister.

For regular adverbs, we add -er, or more (or less) + adverb.

fast → fast**er**, slowly → **more slowly**, easily → **less easily**

Some adverbs are irregular.

well → **better**, badly → **worse**, far → **further/farther**

We've walked much **further** than I expected.

Superlatives

We use superlative adjectives and adverbs to compare people, places, things or actions with the rest of the group.

This is **the most expensive** museum in the city.

Martha ran **the furthest** of all the students.

For short adjectives and adverbs we add the + adjective/ adverb + est.

strong → **the strongest**, fast → **the fastest**

For short adjectives and adverbs ending in -y, -y changes to -i.

easy → **the easiest**, happy → **the happiest**

For longer adjectives and adverbs (two syllables or more), we use the most/the least + adjective/adverb.

important > **the most/the least important**

This is **the most important** day of my life!

Let's take that one – it's **the least expensive**.

We usually use the before superlatives, but we can also use possessive adjectives.

That's **her** most famous sculpture.

We often use superlatives with the present perfect + ever.

It's **the most beautiful** painting I**'ve ever seen**!

PRACTICE

1 Complete the sentences with a comparative or superlative form of the word in brackets.

1 It was brilliant! It's the .... film I've ever seen. (good)

2 It's a complicated book. I need to read it again .... so I understand it better. (slow)

3 My boyfriend is the photographer – he takes wonderful photographs. He's much .... than me. (talented)

4 I find that organising my workspace can be .... than actually doing my work. (enjoyable)

5 I feel more relaxed and my life is a lot .... when I take time out to enjoy nature or do something creative. (stressful)

6 You'll need to drive .... in the future if you don't want to have another accident. (careful)

7 I get up .... now I have an alarm clock. (easy)

8 We're going to be late. Can you try to get ready a bit .... ? (fast)

2 Complete the second sentence so it has a similar meaning to the first. Use the correct form of the word in bold.

1 This course is more boring than the last one.
   The course isn't as interesting as the last one. **interesting**

2 She doesn't walk as quickly as she used to.
   Nowadays, she walks .... before. **slow**

3 The other hotel is more expensive than this one.
   The other hotel .... as this one. **cheap**

4 I find reading a book is not as relaxing as walking in nature.
   I find walking in nature .... than reading a book. **relaxing**

5 My new job is difficult, and so was my previous job.
   My old job was .... as my new job. **difficult**

6 I make more mistakes when I speak English now.
   I speak English .... before. **accurate**

7 The final lecture was not as important as the others. **important**
   The final lecture was the ....

8 Of all my brothers, the youngest drives the slowest.
   My youngest brother drives .... **quick**

6C How to ... ask for and give opinions and reasons

REFERENCE ◀◀ page 75

We use these phrases to discuss opinions.

ask for an opinion

What do/did you think (of the meal/of the gallery/about what the tour guide said)?

How about you?

How was it?

give an opinion

I think/thought ...

I would say (it was OK/it's too expensive)

In my view, (it wasn't very good/it's too loud).

For me, ...

ask for a reason

Why do you think that?

What makes you say that?

give a reason

It's because ...

The reason is ...

agree to disagree

I suppose we're all different.

I guess it's good we're not all the same.

I guess we all like different things.

PRACTICE

1 Correct the sentences by adding the missing word to each one. A contraction counts as one word.

1 So you went to that new restaurant! How was?

2 What do you think this new design?

3 I just bought his new book; I would it's his best one!

4 I loved his new song. How you?

5 I don't understand why you liked his performance, but I suppose we're different!

6 Me, she's the world's best photographer.

7 My view, it's a fascinating programme.

8 Reason is, I don't like black and white photography very much.

2 A Put the words in the correct order.

a games / interesting/ like that / me, / are / For .

b different / guess / all / things / I / like / we .

c of / did / match / What / you / the / think ?

d think / do / that / Why / you ?

e the end / only one goal / there was / because / near / It's .

f pretty / view, / it / In / was / boring / my .

B Number the sentences in Ex 2A in the correct order to make a conversation.

3 Complete the conversation with one word in each gap.

A: What did you ¹_____ of the art in the museum?

B: I liked it but it's not the best.

A: What ²_____ you say that?

B: In my ³_____ , older styles of art are much better than modern art.

A: Really? I ⁴_____ say that modern art is much more interesting. I like looking at shapes and colours and trying to understand them.

B: Hmm. ⁵_____ me, it's more important to know what the art shows, and then try to understand what it means.

A: Well, I ⁶_____ it's good that we're not all the ⁷_____ .

4 Complete the conversations with the phrases in the box.

for me	how was	isn't very
say that	liked it	my view
what do	you think	

1 A: What did ¹_____ of the show?

B: In ²_____ , it was very original and imaginative.

2 A: ³_____ the film?

B: The audience really ⁴_____ , but I thought it was terrible.

3 A: ⁵_____ , that blog post was fascinating.

B: Really? What makes you ⁶_____ ?

4 A: ⁷_____ you think of that new art gallery?

B: It ⁸_____ good. It's tiny. There isn't enough space to hang the paintings.

6D present perfect + *for, since* and *yet*

REFERENCE ◀◀ page 76

We use the present perfect with *for* and *since* to talk about things that started in the past and are still true now.

We've been married **for** fourteen years. (We got married fourteen years ago and we are still married.)

I've lived in Paris **since** 2016. (I started living in Paris in 2016, and I still live there.)

We use *since* to talk about the specific time when something started, e.g. *last Saturday, 2018, June, last weekend*, etc.

He**'s worked** here **since** 2021.

I've known about the prize **since** Monday.

I've wanted to be an artist **since** I was a child.

We use *for* to talk about the period of time that something has continued, e.g. *ten years, two months, a few weeks, a long time*, etc.

I've lived in Berlin **for** eighteen years.

We **haven't seen** my mother **for** a few weeks.

We use the present perfect with *yet* to talk about 'at any time up to now'. We use it in negative sentences and questions when something hasn't happened up to now, but we expect it to happen soon.

Rosa **hasn't arrived yet**. I hope she gets here soon!

Have you **finished** your homework **yet**?

I **haven't finished** it **yet**. I'll do it later.

Notice that *yet* usually comes at the end of the sentence or question.

PRACTICE

1 Complete the table with the time phrases in the box.

> a few years yesterday 2021 ten minutes
> 2nd November several hours I was at school
> weeks three or four months this morning

for	since

2 Choose the correct words to complete the sentences.

1 He's been a writer **for** / **since** / **yet** about ten years.

2 He hasn't had a book published **for** / **since** / **yet**.

3 They haven't been back to China **for** / **since** / **yet** 2019.

4 I haven't finished all my work **for** / **since** / **yet**.

5 I haven't been to an art exhibition **for** / **since** / **yet** a long time.

6 He's really tired. He hasn't stopped working **for** / **since** / **yet** 5.30 a.m.

7 I haven't done a lot of work **for** / **since** / **yet** my boss left the office.

8 I've lived in this city **for** / **since** / **yet** six months.

3 Complete the sentences using *for, since* or *yet*.

1 I've been here .... about ten minutes, but the film hasn't started ....

2 Martha sent off lots of job applications last month, but she hasn't had any replies ....

3 It's great to see you. It's been a long time .... we last met.

4 'Do you still run a lot?' 'No, I haven't run .... a few months. I'm really unfit!'

5 Have you finished that work .... ? I asked you to do it last week!

6 I have known Kelby .... we were at school together.

7 We'd love to go back to Sicily. We haven't been .... a few years.

8 I've played the piano .... I was a child, but I haven't learnt to play this piece ....

4 Use the prompts to make sentences using the present perfect and *for, since* or *yet*.

1 we / be / here / 2 o'clock.

....

2 you / go / to the shops?

....

3 My aunt / have / her mobile phone / 2012!

....

4 Dani and I / know / each other / we were children.

....

5 I / live / here / a long time.

....

6 We / not / meet / Luka.

....

7 I / feel / ill / a few days.

....

8 you / see / Max's new car?

....

GRAMMAR BANK

7A first and second conditionals

REFERENCE ◀◀ page 82

First conditional

We use the first conditional to talk about possible situations in the future and their consequences.

If you give me your phone number, I'll call you when we're leaving.

When you get to the station, you'll see the hotel is just opposite.

We form the first conditional with *If/When* + present simple + *will*.

If you **go** to Spain, you**'ll** be able to meet my brother.

We can change the order of the sentence, but *if/when* is always followed by the present simple. We use a comma when the *if/when* clause comes first, but not when it comes second.

If my train arrives on time, I'll meet you at 10 a.m.

I'll meet you at 10 a.m. if my train arrives on time.

In first conditional sentences *if* and *when* have different meanings. We use *if* when we are not sure if the situation will happen. We use *when* for a situation which we know will happen.

I'll tell Ben about the party **when** I see him. (I expect to see Ben.)

I'll tell Ben about the party **if** I see him. (I'm not sure if I will see Ben.)

Second conditional

We use the second conditional to talk about an unreal or imaginary situation and its consequences.

If I didn't have to work, I would spend all my time travelling. (I do have to work.)

If tourists spent more time in the city, they would get to know it better. (Tourists don't spend much time in the city.)

We form the second conditional with *if* + past simple + *would*.

If you **had** more free time, what **would** you do? (You don't have more free time.)

If I **didn't have** a job, I **would** spend more time with my children. (I do have a job.)

In spoken English *would* is contracted to *'d* in the positive form and *wouldn't* in the negative form.

I'd be there if I had time.

If you **ate** more breakfast, you **wouldn't** be hungry all morning.

We do not usually contract *would* in the question form.

If you could go anywhere in the world, where **would** you go?

Would you give up your job if she asked you to?

PRACTICE

1 Choose the correct words to complete the sentences.

1 If the weather is terrible, they **will / would** cancel the flights.

2 If I didn't have to work in the city, I **will / would** buy a house by the sea.

3 If they **miss / will miss** their flight, we will have to wait for ages.

4 If the climate **would be / was** better, we wouldn't have to travel in the summer.

5 If the tourists **won't leave / didn't leave** so much mess, it wouldn't be such a big problem.

6 When you **get / got** to the hotel, I will call you to tell you where we are.

2 Complete the sentences with the correct form of the verbs in brackets.

1 When we visit the museum, we .... (buy) a souvenir.

2 If I don't find any cheap tickets, we .... (not go) to Malta.

3 If people .... (want) to improve the situation, they would do something about it.

4 I'll get some money when the bank .... (open).

5 If he .... (enjoy) his job, he wouldn't want to change it.

6 I .... (visit) Australia if I had enough money!

3 Complete the first and second conditional sentences using the prompts.

1 We might go to Cambridge tomorrow. We'll see uncle Rob.

If we .... uncle Rob.

2 I don't have a car, so I won't drive you to the station.

I .... a car.

3 We plan to move out of the city. First, we need to sell our house.

We .... our house.

4 I can't travel around the world because I have a job.

If I .... around the world.

7B quantifiers

REFERENCE ◀◀ page 83

We use quantifiers to give information about the amount of something. They can say
if it's a big or small amount, the right amount or more/less than the right amount.

	meaning	countable nouns	uncountable nouns	positive (+)	negative (–)	questions (?)	examples
much	large amount		✓		✓	✓	How **much** time do we have?
many	large amount	✓		(rarely)	✓	✓	I don't have **many** friends.
lots of/a lot of	large amount	✓	✓	✓	✓	✓	I spend **a lot of** time in Paris.
plenty of	large amount	✓	✓	✓			I have **plenty of** milk and apples.
too much	more than needed		✓	✓	✓	✓	There's **too much** salt on this meat.
too many	more than needed	✓		✓	✓	✓	There are **too many** people here.
enough	the right amount	✓	✓	✓	✓	✓	There isn't **enough** time.
a few	small amount	✓		✓			She knows **a few** actors.
a bit/a little	small amount		✓	✓		✓	I need **a bit of** help.
hardly any	very small amount	✓	✓	✓			I have **hardly any** friends.

Too + adjective means more than you need or want.
This film is **too long**.

Remember *Too* does not mean the same as *very*. When we use *too*, it means there is a problem.

PRACTICE

1 Choose the correct words to complete the sentences.

1 I didn't see **much** / **many** people in the restaurant.
2 Can I have **a bit of** / **a few** sugar in my tea, please?
3 Do we have **a bit** / **enough** water?
4 Does she have **lots of** / **much** friends?
5 There's too **much** / **many** noise in here.
6 I read hardly **any** / **enough** books last summer.
7 We have **too** / **plenty of** time before the flight leaves.
8 I don't know **many** / **a few** songs by that band.

2 Correct the mistakes with quantifiers in the sentences.
Two sentences are correct.

1 There are too much people in here. It's too crowded.
2 If you've got a little time, I'd love your help.
3 There's hardly pasta. How can I make a meal for four people?
4 Put a few cheese on the top, but not too much!
5 Sorry, I have enough money to pay for both drinks, so I'll just pay for mine.
6 There isn't much paper in the printer.
7 We've got plenty people to help us with the cleaning.
8 There's much juice left, so please have some!

3 Complete the text with the words in the box.

a	bit	enough	few	hardly
much	plenty	too		

The worst holiday ever?

I've been on [1]............ of bad holidays, but
[2]............ any as bad as my last one. I'd rented a
house on the coast for a week. I arrived at night
and found the key in a box, as planned. I was a
[3]............ tired, so I went to the bedroom. That's
when I saw the hole in the roof. That night,
there was [4]............ lot of rain, so I moved to the
living room. I didn't get very [5]............ sleep! In
the morning, I discovered the tap in the kitchen
wasn't working. There wasn't even [6]............ water
for a cup of coffee. The brochure said that the
place was only a [7]............ metres from the beach,
but when I went outside I realised the beach
was miles away, [8]............ far to walk. After two
days, I gave up and went home!

GRAMMAR BANK

7C How to … make and respond to recommendations

REFERENCE ◀◀ page 87

We use these phrases to make and respond to recommendations.

make recommendations

There are a few things you absolutely have to (see/do) …

You must (visit/try/see) …

You should definitely (visit/try/see) …

Make sure you …

… is one of the best things to do.

It's a great place to/It's a lovely place to (buy souvenirs/ eat lunch/see old buildings).

You can (eat/see/walk) …

Don't leave without (visiting/seeing) …

respond to recommendations

Great thanks.

OK, that's a good idea.

Oh, wow! How exciting!

Oh, that's a shame.

That sounds good.

That sounds interesting.

PRACTICE

1 Match the sentence halves to make recommendations.

1 Visiting Cancun is one of the

2 You should

3 You

4 It's a great

5 Don't leave

6 There are a few things you absolutely

7 It's a great place

a must try the street food there.

b place to walk around.

c have to see while you're there.

d best things to do in Mexico.

e to buy souvenirs.

f without seeing the palace at night.

g definitely visit the museum before you leave.

2 Put the words in brackets in the correct order to complete the conversations.

1 A: If you go to London, [1]................................. (definitely / should / you / visit) the London Eye.

   B: OK. [2]................................. . (good / a / idea / that's)

2 A: When you're in Lisbon, [3]................................. (sure / make / you) try a *pastel de nata*. They are delicious!

   B: [4]................................. . (sounds / good / that)

3 A: In Rome, [5]................................. (must / you / visit) Trastevere. [6]................................. (to / lovely / it's / place / a) walk around at night.

   B: [7]................................. . (thanks / great)

4 A: When you're in Mexico, [8]................................. . (a / things / few / do / there / to / are / have / you) One of them is visit Frida Kahlo's house.

   B: OK. [9]................................. . (sounds / interesting / that)

5 A: If you come to Beijing, [10]................................. (without / leave / don't) seeing the Great Wall of China. It's the most amazing place to visit and I'd be happy to take you there.

   B: [11]................................. ! [12]................................. ! (wow / exciting / how / oh)

3 Complete the conversation with the phrases in the box.

> And don't leave   How exciting   It's a great place
> Make sure you   OK, that's a good
> That sounds   You can walk   You must visit

A: I'm going to Barcelona next weekend for a few days.

B: Oh, lucky you! [1]................................. to visit.

A: What do you recommend?

B: [2]................................. Las Ramblas. It's a really long street in the middle of the city. [3]................................. over a kilometre down to the sea.

A: [4]................................. good.

B: [5]................................. go to the Sagrada Família. It's such an unusual building. Get there at 9 a.m. when it's not so busy.

A: [6]................................. idea. Thanks for the advice.

B: [7]................................. without going on a boat trip. You can take one in the evening and watch the sun go down.

A: Oh, wow! [8]................................. !

7D reflexive pronouns

REFERENCE ◀◀ page 89

We use reflexive pronouns to show actions that we do to ourselves. The pronoun comes after a verb or preposition.

I hurt **myself**.

They introduced **themselves**.

He made a coffee for **himself**.

By + reflexive pronoun means 'alone'.

She works best **by herself**.

I like travelling **by myself**.

Some verbs + reflexive pronouns are used as fixed expressions.

Enjoy yourself!

Help yourself! (Take something for free.)

Behave yourself! (Be good.)

We sometimes use reflexive pronouns for emphasis. In this case, the reflexive pronoun often goes at the end of the sentence.

Did you make this **yourself**? (without any help)

I did it **myself**. (It's a big achievement and no one helped me.)

object pronouns	reflexive pronouns
me	myself
you	yourself
	yourselves (plural)
him	himself
her	herself
it	itself
us	ourselves
them	themselves

PRACTICE

1 Correct the mistakes in the sentences.

1 I can't believe your brother made all this food by myself.

2 Shall we get the kids to clean the car or do it themselves?

3 That's strange. The light just switched herself on.

4 Mohammed just rode his bike by itself for the first time!

5 I told yourself not to be nervous and that I could do it!

6 You can do it by myself. You don't need my help.

7 Maria painted the whole room by yourself.

8 Maki and Rico wanted to order pizza, but I asked them to make one yourselves.

2 Complete the sentences with the correct reflexive pronouns.

1 Are you OK? Have you hurt .... ?

2 I prefer dancing by ....

3 Did he enjoy .... last night?

4 They have to behave .... at school!

5 Did dad help you or did you do the homework .... ?

6 Can you two introduce .... to the class?

7 Mary cut .... while she was cooking.

8 We made the cake ....

9 My alarm clock switches .... off after one minute.

10 Hi, Jen! The food is over there. Help ....

3 Choose the correct words to complete the text.

I didn't want to travel around Central America by [1]**my own** / **myself**, so I invited a friend. But we soon started arguing. He didn't want to do anything by [2]**himself** / **myself** and he only wanted to visit tourist attractions. Eventually, we decided to travel by [3]**yourselves** / **ourselves** and meet in Honduras in a month. I called and told my mother. She was worried. She said, 'What if you run out of money or hurt [4]**himself** / **yourself**?' I said I was fine. It was true. Without my friend, I really enjoyed [5]**myself** / **my own**. I never got lonely because I introduced [6]**me** / **myself** to local people in El Salvador and learnt about local customs in Nicaragua. When you travel alone, I think you explore more and learn about [7]**yourself** / **myself**. I really grew up that year. After a month, I met my friend in Honduras, as planned. He seemed different. He wanted to stay there and make a new life for [8]**itself** / **himself**. I left and never saw him again.

8A *can, could, be able to*

REFERENCE ◀◀ page 93

We use *can/can't* for ability in the present, and *could/couldn't* for ability in the past.

	present	past
+	I can cook.	I could run fast.
-	I can't drive.	He couldn't do maths.
?	Can you speak Spanish?	Could you cook when you were younger?

We can also use *be able to* for ability in the present and past.

	present	past
+	She's able to write well.	When I was three, I was able to read.
-	He isn't able to drive.	At the age of two, he wasn't able to walk.
?	Are you able to speak French?	Were you able to get a job?

In the present, we can use *can* or *be able to* for a general ability or an ability at one specific time.

I **can/am able to** install a washing machine. (a general ability)

We **can/are able to** offer you a free ticket today. (a specific time)

In the past, we can use *could* or *was/were able to* for a general ability.

For an ability at one specific time in the past, we use *was/were able to*, but NOT ~~could~~.

I **could/was able to** swim when I was four. (a general ability)

When the boat sank, we ~~could~~ **were able to swim** to safety. (a specific time)

We can use *couldn't* and *wasn't/weren't able to* for a general ability in the past and an ability at one specific time.

I **couldn't/wasn't able to** swim when I was four. (a general ability)

I didn't have a bottle opener, so I **couldn't/wasn't able to** open the bottle. (a specific time)

1 Correct five mistakes with *can, could* and *be able to* in the text.

Johnny isn't able make full sentences yet, but he can to say several words such as 'mama' and 'dada', which he couldn't a month ago. He able to understand various commands like, 'No!' and 'Come here' and he recognises his name. His movement is improving, too. Yesterday, he crawled from the living room to the kitchen. He's also getting better with his hands. He can hold a pencil and he is able to drawing simple pictures. Yesterday, he found a red pen and he could draw all over the kitchen wall!

2 Choose the correct words. Sometimes, both options are possible.

1 I **was / wasn't** able to pass my driving test first time, but I did the second time.
2 We **can / 're able to** help you if you like.
3 After ten minutes of trying, we **could / were able to** open the door.
4 I **can / could** speak two languages well when I was four.
5 Rosie **can / could** sing really well these days.
6 I tried to remember where I left my phone, but I **couldn't / wasn't able to**.
7 You **'re able to / can** get a free drink when you order lunch today.
8 I **could / was able to** run 5,000m without stopping yesterday.

3 Complete the second sentence so it has a similar meaning to the first. Use the word in brackets.

1 She knows how to ride a motorbike.
   She _____ a motorbike. (can)
2 I'm not able to play any instruments.
   I _____ any instruments. (can't)
3 Seyi and Denia weren't able to come last night.
   They _____ night. (couldn't)
4 Can you take good photos on your phone?
   _____ take good photos on your phone? (able)
5 Do you know how to make pizza?
   _____ pizza? (can)
6 I can usually sleep for eight hours, even on a plane.
   Usually I _____ sleep for eight hours, even on a plane. (able)
7 Were you a fast runner when you were a child?
   _____ when you were a child? (could)
8 I didn't finish my homework. I didn't have time.
   I _____ finish my homework. I didn't have time. (able)

8B active and passive

REFERENCE ◀◀ page 97

We use an active verb form to talk about things people do.

We **watched** television.

Sam **ate** a sandwich.

We use a passive verb form:

- to talk about what happens to things or people.
  Khaled **was given** a prize.
- when we don't know the doer (the person or thing that does the action of the verb).
  The laptop **was stolen**.
- when the identity of the doer of the action is not important.
  The video **was watched** by more than a million viewers.
- when the doer of the action is obvious.
  The thief **was arrested**. (It is obvious that the thief was arrested by the police.)

If we want to mention who does the action of a passive verb, we use *by*.

The television was invented **by John Logie Baird**.

We sometimes use the passive form to emphasise a particular part of the sentence.

Compare:

Google **bought** YouTube in 2006 for US$1.65 billion.

YouTube **was bought** in 2006 by Google.

In the active sentence, the emphasis is on *Google*.

In the second (passive) sentence, the emphasis is on *YouTube*.

We often use the passive in formal writing, e.g. newspaper reports or scientific reports.

	active	passive
present simple	The shop **doesn't accept** credit cards.	Credit cards **aren't accepted** here.
present continuous	**Is** anyone **using** that computer at the moment?	Is that computer **being used** at the moment?
past simple	Someone **told** us to be here at 8 a.m.	We **were told** to be here at 8 a.m.
present perfect	No one **has asked** us about the video.	We **haven't been asked** about the video.

PRACTICE

1 Choose the correct verb forms to complete the sentences.

1 All the clips **have been uploaded / are upload / uploaded** to the website.
2 We can't use the laptop because **it's being repaired / it's repairing / it was repaired** right now.
3 The video **filmed / was filmed / filming** in Mexico City.
4 Were those documents **be sent / send / sent** by email or by post?
5 Not many houses **are been built / are being built / are being build** at the moment.
6 Are those toys **make / been made / made** by hand?
7 We **weren't employed / didn't employed / weren't employ** by the government until 2018.
8 That piano **isn't been played / hasn't be played / hasn't been played** for years.

2 Complete the text with the correct passive forms of the verbs in brackets.

Charlie Bit My Finger – Again! is one of the most watched videos on the internet. In the video, a little boy, Harry, puts his finger in his baby brother Charlie's mouth and then complains when his finger [1]_____ (bite). The video clip [2]_____ (upload) in May 2007 by the boys' father. Since then, it [3]_____ (watch) over 885 million times, and many *Charlie bit me* products [4]_____ (create). In 2018, the video [5]_____ (put) at number 1 on *Teen Vogue*'s list of the best-ever viral videos. In 2021, the video [6]_____ (sell) to a company for over $760,000, but it's still on the internet for everyone to enjoy.

3 Complete the sentences with the correct active or passive form of the verbs in brackets.

1 This is a popular channel. It _____ (watch) mainly by teenagers and new videos _____ (upload) every day.
2 The book _____ (write) in 2010, when the author _____ (live) in the USA.
3 Today this dish _____ (not cook) in the oven. Instead, we _____ (use) the grill.
4 He doesn't live in Europe, so most of his programmes _____ (not film) in Europe; he usually _____ (work) in Asia.
5 I _____ (not update) the website yet because the software _____ (not install) on my computer yet.
6 I _____ (set up) my first company in 1998, and it _____ (buy) by a multinational company three years later.
7 The office looks great – the walls _____ (paint) recently, and we _____ (buy) some new furniture.
8 I _____ (not buy) the food for the party yet, but the invitations _____ (send out) already.

8C How to … describe a problem and make recommendations

REFERENCE ◀ page 99

We use these phrases to describe a problem and make recommendations.

describe a problem

There's a problem with …
The (wifi/connection/printer) **isn't working.**
I can't (open the attachment/hear you).
It won't (save/open the file).
It keeps (crashing/going wrong).
When/Every time I … , it …
I think it's broken.

make a recommendation

Have you tried + -ing … ?
Try + -ing …
Have you checked … ?
Maybe you need to …
It sometimes works if you …

solve the problem

Yes, I'll try that.
Yes, that works.
Yes, it's working now.

PRACTICE

1 Match the sentence halves.

1	There's a problem with	a	if it's plugged in?
2	The coffee machine	b	if you install the app again.
3	My laptop keeps	c	isn't working.
4	Every time I use my phone,	d	the screen stops working.
5	Have you tried	e	crashing.
6	Have you checked	f	it's working now.
7	It sometimes works	g	switching it off and on again?
8	Yes,	h	this computer.

2 Put the words in brackets in the correct order to complete the sentences.

1 _____ (with / a / my / problem / there's) laptop. It keeps freezing.
2 My phone isn't working. _____ . (on / won't / it / switch)
3 _____ . (file / I / open / can't / this) My computer crashes when I try.
4 _____ (you / off / switching / tried / have / it) and on again?
5 _____ (you / to / maybe / need) download some new software.
6 _____ (works / sometimes / if / it / you) resave it.

3 Complete the conversations by adding the words in the box in the correct places.

> broken   checked   it's   to
> try   when   with   working

1 A: There's a problem my computer. It keeps freezing.
B: Have you the internet connection? Maybe it isn't connected to the wifi.
A: Yes, I'll that.

2 A: My remote control isn't. I press the buttons, nothing happens. I think it's.
B: Maybe you need replace the batteries.
A: Good idea. I've got some batteries here.
B: Is it OK now?
A: Yes, working now.

4 Complete the conversation with the phrases (a–h).

A: [1] _____ get this printer to work.
B: [2] _____ that it's plugged in?
A: Yes, I have. It's on. [3] _____ connect to my laptop.
B: [4] _____ to install some software.
A: I've already done that.
B: [5] _____ the program and opening it again.
A: I've done that but it didn't help.
B: Hmm. [6] _____ you delete the software and install it again.
A: OK, [7] _____ . Give me a few minutes. …
B: Ah, great. [8] _____ . Thanks a lot!

a Have you checked
b I can't get
c Maybe you need
d It's working now
e It won't
f It sometimes works if
g Try closing
h I'll try that

8D -*ing* form

REFERENCE ◀◀ page 100

Sometimes we use two verbs together.
I love singing.

After some verbs we put the second verb into the -*ing* form. We use the -*ing* form after these verbs: *begin, delay, hate, imagine, keep, like, practise, recommend, remember, suggest*.

She **practises listening** to English every day.
I **recommend using** an app.
Keep working!
I **suggest doing** a course.

After some verbs, it is possible to use the -*ing* form or the infinitive with *to*. There is very little change in meaning.
I **like cooking**. I like **to cook**.
I **hate running**. I **hate to run**.
I **began exercising**. I **began to exercise**.

Some expressions with verbs are also followed by the -*ing* form. For example:
can't stand   look forward to   wouldn't mind
I **can't stand listening** to really loud music.
I **wouldn't mind trying** that new restaurant.
I **look forward to meeting** you.

PRACTICE

1 Choose the correct words. Sometimes both are possible.

1 We need to practise **playing** / **to play** the song.
2 I can't stand **doing** / **do** housework. It's so boring!
3 We all hate **seeing** / **to see** Thomas look unhappy.
4 I look forward **hearing** / **to hearing** from you soon.
5 I remember **seeing** / **to see** you for the first time.
6 You keep **repeating** / **to repeat** yourself!
7 I wouldn't mind **getting** / **to get** a new phone soon.
8 We've begun **going** / **to go** for a walk after lunch every day.
9 We should delay **going** / **to go** away until we know Ed is OK.
10 I imagine **starting** / **to start** a new job will be stressful.

2 Complete the conversations with the words in brackets in the correct form.

A: I'm enjoying ¹............ (learn) Chinese. It's fun. It's not easy to remember new words, though.
B: I like ²............ (find) vocabulary games online. It helps me learn Italian.
A: Good idea. Somebody recommended ³............ (download) a vocabulary app, which I've done and it's quite good.
B: If you keep ⁴............ (use) that, I imagine ⁵............ (remember) the words will get easier.
A: I hope so. I've begun ⁶............ (record) myself, too. I can practise ⁷............ (speak) and check my use of language.
B: Sounds good. I wouldn't mind ⁸............ (try) that with my Italian but I hate ⁹............ (listen) to my own voice!
A: There's nothing wrong with your voice! We should try ¹⁰............ (find) someone online to practise with. There are websites that match different language learners.
B: Sounds like a good idea!

3 What words do you think complete these sentences?

1 Can you imagine .... eleven languages?
2 He .... learning French when he was sixteen.
3 I remember .... to my first English lesson.
4 I wouldn't .... watching that video clip again.
5 The teacher .... using that textbook.
6 Magda likes .... her homework with friends.
7 We keep .... the same mistakes.
8 I can't .... watching promotional videos.
9 I look forward .... working with you.
10 I hate .... after that dog!

4 Use the words in the box to complete the sentences in Ex 3.

began   going   looking   making   mind
recommends   speaking   stand   to   to do

VOCABULARY BANK

1A personality adjectives

{ page 9 }

1 A Complete the sentences with the adjectives in the box.

bossy   crazy   easy-going   funny   generous   helpful   kind
noisy   patient   polite   reliable   rude   serious   tidy

1 My parents are pretty .... and relaxed. They don't mind if I stay out late.

2 It's very .... of him to donate so much money to helping homeless people.

3 Jack never says please or thank you. He's so .... !

4 My dad is a very .... and thoughtful man. He doesn't joke very much.

5 At first, my parents thought I was .... when I told them my plans to quit my nice job and travel for six months.

6 I'm not very .... I hate waiting for things.

7 I don't think it's very .... to leave without saying thank you.

8 My brother and I are complete opposites. He's really messy and I'm very ....

9 The teacher was very .... and gave me some good advice.

10 My neighbours are too .... They play loud music all the time!

11 She is such a .... lady, always trying to do things for other people.

12 My sister is really .... She's always telling me what to do!

13 I laugh so much when I'm with Tom – he's really ....

14 I know that if I ask Chloe to do the job, she will do it well. She's very ....

B 🔊 **VB1.01 | Listen and check.**

C Look at the adjectives in the box in Ex 1A again. Are the characteristics positive, negative or neutral? Which words can you use to describe yourself?

1B work

{ page 11 }

1 A Complete what the people say about their jobs with the words in the boxes.

career   part-time   wages

'I'm a student, but I have a [1] .... job in a supermarket. I work every Saturday and Sunday. I'm studying finance and I'd like a [2] .... as a banker one day. I think it's an interesting job and the [3] .... are good. I can make a lot of money.'

full-time   responsible for   run

'I [4] .... a small company that makes furniture. I'm [5] .... the designs and for finding customers. It's a [6] .... job. Sometimes I work fourteen hours a day when we're busy.'

out of work   profession   qualifications   volunteer

'I'm a singer. Unfortunately, I'm [7] .... at the moment. Singing is a very difficult [8] .... because there are loads of singers and a lot of competition. I have no [9] .... because I never did well in exams and I left school when I was fifteen. When I'm not singing, I [10] .... at a shelter for homeless people. We aren't paid, but I love helping others.'

B 🔊 **VB1.02 | Listen and check.**

C Choose six of the words and expressions in Ex 1A. Write true sentences about you.

My qualifications include a law degree and a Master's degree in English.

I work part-time in a restaurant and I also study part-time.

2A adjectives for feelings

◀◀ page 20

1 A Match the adjectives and expressions (1–12) with the pictures (A–L).

1 angry	**5** jealous	**9** sleepy
2 calm	**6** nervous	**10** terrified
3 exhausted	**7** proud	**11** upset
4 in love	**8** silly	**12** worried

  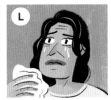

B 🔊 **VB2.01 |** Listen and check.

2 Choose the correct words to complete the sentences.

1 I organised a relaxing weekend and by Sunday evening I felt very **calm** / **jealous**.
2 She is very **in love** / **worried** about her exam results.
3 Tim is **upset** / **proud** because his football team just lost their match.
4 Don't worry too much about him – he's probably just **sleepy** / **jealous** of your success.
5 I'm very **angry** / **nervous** because I bought these shoes last week and they've already broken.
6 They are a beautiful couple and they are very much **in love** / **proud** with each other.
7 I got up really early this morning, so I'm feeling a bit **sleepy** / **calm**.
8 Sam is a really bad driver. I'm always **silly** / **terrified** when I'm in the car with him!
9 Don't worry about my younger brother. He can be very **silly** / **terrified** sometimes.
10 She was so **nervous** / **calm** about her exams that she couldn't sleep.

2B types of film

◀◀ page 24

1 A Match the sentences (1–10) with the pictures (A–J).

1 A **documentary** tells a true story or looks at important issues such as wildlife conservation.
2 A **comedy** has jokes and makes us laugh.
3 A **horror film** is frightening, and often has monsters or very bad people.
4 An **adventure film** often has heroes who travel and have exciting experiences.
5 A **drama** is a serious film with realistic characters in difficult situations.
6 An **action film** usually has fights, escapes and chases.
7 A **romantic comedy** is a funny film about people falling in love.
8 A **mystery** has a big secret that we try to understand or a problem to solve.
9 A **biopic** tells the true story of a famous person.
10 An **animation** is often for children, and uses cartoon pictures.

B 🔊 **VB2.02 |** Listen and check.

2 Work with other students. Discuss the questions.

1 Can you think of an example of each type of film in Ex 1A?
2 Which three types do you like the best?
3 Which do you never watch? Why?

VOCABULARY BANK

3A verbs and nouns

◀ page 32

1 A Complete the table with the words in the box.

> guess   inform   know   memorise   preparation   revision   solution   understanding

verb	noun
1	knowledge
guess	2 ....
revise	3 ....
4	information
prepare	5 ....
solve	6 ....
understand	7 ....
8	memory

B 🔊 **VB3.01 | Listen and check.**

2 Complete the sentences with the correct form of words from Ex 1A.

 1 This is a lovely dish, but it takes a lot of .... !
 2 If you don't know the answer, have a .... !
 3 I'm not sure how we can find a .... to this problem.
 4 It took me ages to .... the whole poem, so I knew every word!
 5 I've got an exam tomorrow, so I need to do some .... tonight.
 6 We are sorry to .... you that this flight has been cancelled.
 7 Thank you for your patience and ....
 8 My .... of geography is terrible – I can't even draw a map of Europe!

3C places in a city

◀ page 38

1 A Match the places in a city (1–15) with the reasons for going there (a–o).

 1 tourist information centre
 2 taxi rank
 3 museum or art gallery
 4 stadium
 5 shopping mall
 6 bus station/railway station
 7 car rental office
 8 doctor's surgery
 9 police station
 10 theatre
 11 garage/petrol station
 12 guesthouse
 13 pharmacy (USA)/chemist (UK)
 14 town square
 15 cycle lane

 a to find a taxi
 b to watch a sports event
 c to visit lots of shops
 d to watch a play
 e to stay for a night
 f to buy medicines
 g to see a doctor
 h to hire a car
 i to catch a bus or train
 j to find information about the city
 k to buy fuel for your car
 l to ride your bike safely
 m to report a crime
 n to learn about the past, or about art
 o to meet friends in an open public space

B 🔊 **VB3.02 | Listen and check.**

2 Work in pairs. When was the last time you went to the places in Ex 1A? Why did you go there?

4B word building: suffixes

◀◀ page 49

1 A Read the sentences (a–f) below and answer the questions (1–2).

  1 Which words in each pair of sentences belong to the same word family?
  2 Which is the noun and which is the verb in each pair of sentences?

  a He'd won the race to invent the mobile phone.
  b The invention weighed more than 1 kg.
Invent is a verb. Invention is a noun.

  c It was the creation of Tim Berners-Lee.
  d William Higinbotham and Robert Dvorak created the world's first video game in 1958.

  e They developed the game to show to visitors at the Brookhaven National Laboratory.
  f The new development grew quickly.

B Complete the table by adding the missing letters.

verb	noun	person
invent	invention	invent_ _
cre_ _ _	creation	creator
educate	educat_ _ _	educat_ _
introduce	introduc_ _ _ _	
develop	develop_ _ _ _	develop_ _
discover	discovery	
lead	leadership	lead_ _
succeed	success	

C 🔊 **VB4.01 | Listen and check.**

D Answer the questions.

  1 Can you think of other words which end with the suffixes in the box?

  | er/or ment ship tion y | organisation, action

  2 Which ending is common to describe types of people? What jobs can you think of that use the same combinations of letters? actor
  3 In your language, are there similar suffixes to make nouns and jobs?

E Complete the sentences with words from Ex 1B.

  1 My uncle is an .... He's always building strange new machines!
  2 I've spent fifteen years in .... : twelve years at school and three at university.
  3 The party was a .... Lots of people came and everyone loved the food.
  4 Jane, I'd like to .... you to my boyfriend. This is Dmitri.
  5 Our president is a good .... Everyone respects her and she has great ideas.

VOCABULARY BANK

4C sport

◀ page 51

1 A Work in pairs. Match the words in the box with the photos (A–P).

ball   bat   court   draw   field   goalkeeper hit   pass   pitch   player   racquet   referee score   shoot   stick   win

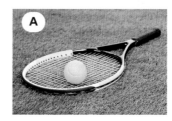
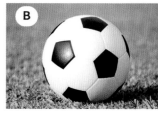

B Complete the table with the words from Ex 1A.

equipment	people	places to play	verbs

C 🔊 **VB4.02** | Listen and check.

D Think about a sport that you know. Can you add words to the table in Ex 1B for that sport?

E Make sentences. Use at least two words from Ex 1B in each sentence.

In tennis, you hit the ball with the racquet.

There are eleven players on a football team, and anyone can shoot.

5B the environment

◀◀ page 59

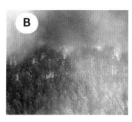

1 A Match the photos (A–H) with the sentences (1–8). Some sentences match more than one photo.

1 People leave their **rubbish** on the beach.
2 **Traffic jams** block the roads and cause pollution.
3 **Public transport** is very bad, so everyone hates using it.
4 **Climate change** means the world is getting hotter.
5 There are more **natural disasters** like fires and hurricanes now.
6 The Amazon **rainforest** in Brazil is disappearing.
7 **Factory smoke** pollutes the air.
8 We need to stop using **natural resources** like oil, which cause pollution.

B Work in pairs. Do you have these problems in your city or country? Have you visited other places where these problems exist?

2 A Choose the correct option (a–c) to complete the sentences.

1 By 2070, there will probably be no oil, but there will be other ___ .
   a climate change **b** factory smoke **c** natural resources
2 The terrible forest fires in California are an example of a ___ .
   a natural resource **b** natural disaster **c** rainforest
3 Many natural disasters are happening because of ___ .
   a rubbish **b** public transport **c** climate change
4 One example of air pollution is ___ .
   a natural resources **b** factory smoke **c** rainforests
5 The environment is cleaner when people pick up their ___ .
   a factory smoke **b** public transport **c** rubbish
6 I was late to work because I spent half an hour in a ___ .
   a traffic jam **b** climate change **c** public transport

B 🔊 **VB5.01** | Listen and check.

6A the arts: people, places, things

◀◀ page 68

1 A Read the sentences. Then put the words in bold into the correct places in the lists below.

1 I went to the **art gallery** yesterday. It's showing a collection of photos by my favourite **photographer**.
2 She was a **dancer** in the 1920s. She danced in lots of famous **venues** in Paris, including some nightclubs that are still there today.
3 The **show** became famous because of its great music. It had hundreds of people in the **audience** every night.
4 The **architect** was working on the plan of the building for years. He drew over fifty sketches for it before he chose the best **design**.
5 You can go to the artist's **studio**, where she worked for thirty years. You can see many of her **drawings** in pencil there.

People

A person who …
dances is a(n) [1] ___ .
designs buildings is a(n) [2] ___ .
takes professional photos is a(n) [3] ___ .
watches an event is part of the [4] ___ .

Places

A place where …
an artist or musician works is a(n)
[5] ___ .
art is shown to the public is a(n) [6] ___ .
people perform plays or live music is a(n)
[7] ___ .

Things

A performance or event for the public is a(n) [8] ___ .
A picture you make with a pen or pencil is a(n) [9] ___ .
A picture that shows how something will be made or how it will look is a(n)
[10] ___ .

B 🔊 **VB6.01** | Listen and check.

7A travel and tourism

◀◀ page 81

1 A Match the words and phrases (1–12) with the photos (A–L).

1 accommodation
2 luggage
3 check-in
4 backpacker
5 exchange rate
6 city break
7 souvenir
8 monument
9 resort
10 nightlife
11 book a tour
12 rent bicycles

B 🔊 **VB7.01** | Listen and check.

A

B

C

D

E

F

G

H

I

J

K

L

2 Complete the sentences with the correct form of the words in Ex 1A.

1 I should be at the airport by 12 o'clock, so I'll meet you at the .... desk.
2 I need to change some money. Do you know if the .... is better here or in the hotel?
3 We've booked a .... for next month. We're going to Venice for a few days!
4 I'm going to look around the shops. I'd like to buy a little .... of the holiday to take home.
5 Are those your bags? You can't take all that .... on the plane with you!
6 If it's a nice day tomorrow, I think we should .... and cycle around the island.
7 It's not easy to find cheap .... All the good hotels are booked.
8 Puerto Vallarta is a beautiful .... on the Pacific coast.
9 We decided to .... of the historical centre to find out about its history.
10 We had a really fun time in the evenings. The resort has a flourishing ....
11 I travelled around Europe with another ....
12 I took hundreds of photos of all the historical ....

7B the natural world

◀◀ page 84

1 A Match the words in the box with the photos (A–J).

> coast   countryside   jungle   mountain range   national park
> rainforest   seaside   stream   valley   waterfall

A

B

C

D

E

F

G

H

I

J

B 🔊 **VB7.02** | Listen and check.

C Complete the sentences with the correct form of words from Ex 1A.

1 The Amazon is the world's largest _____ . It produces lots of the world's oxygen.

2 I love climbing. The biggest _____ I've been to are the Alps and the Andes.

3 I saw elephants, giraffes and other protected animals in the Kruger _____ in South Africa.

4 As a child, I loved going to the _____ . I played in the sand and swam in the sea!

5 We live at the bottom of a _____ , with steep hills on both sides.

6 I used to go fishing by a small _____ near my house.

7 I lived in a big city for years, but it was too noisy. I prefer the _____ now.

8 I'd like to explore a _____ because I love wild animals like gorillas.

9 The _____ near where I live has large rocks and no sandy beaches. It's dangerous for boats.

10 I visited Angel Falls, the biggest _____ in Venezuela. The sound of the water is incredible!

D Work in pairs. Discuss the questions, giving reasons for your answers.

Which type of place would you:

- choose if you wanted to spend time alone?
- like to visit with family or friends?
- choose to live in?
- not like to visit for long?
- completely refuse to visit?

8A abilities: phrasal verbs

◀◀ page 92

1 A Match the phrasal verbs in bold in the sentences (1–8) with the meanings (a–h).

1 My ability is that I **pick up** languages quickly.
2 When I was twenty, I **set up** my own business.
3 My ability is that I can **make up** songs or stories.
4 I'm very practical. I can **work out** how to fix machines easily.
5 I'm good at **looking after** animals. I have six dogs and four cats.
6 My special ability is that I **get on with** people of all types.
7 I **took up** golf when I was ten and now I play well.
8 I'm good at **coming up with** ideas and solutions to problems.

a to invent something make up
b to care for a person or an animal
c to have a good relationship with someone
d to start a company or business
e to start doing a new hobby
f to understand how to do something difficult
g to think of a new idea
h to learn something quickly

B Complete the sentences using a verb from box A and a particle from box B.

A

| come | get | look | make | pick |
| set | take | work | | |

B

after   on   out   up (x5)

1 I can't come out. I have to _____ my little cousin because his parents are away.
2 She wanted to learn an instrument, so she decided to _____ the guitar.
3 We need someone who can _____ with great ideas quickly.
4 That's not true! You shouldn't _____ stories like that!
5 She already spoke Spanish, so it was easy for her to _____ Portuguese.
6 I don't _____ with my boss. He doesn't like me and I don't like him.
7 With the money I've saved, I'm going to _____ my own business, building websites.
8 This text is too complicated. I can't _____ what it means.

C 🔊 **VB8.01 | Listen and check.**

D Choose four of the phrasal verbs. Make true sentences about yourself.

I get on with my brother.
I'm good at making up jokes.

8B technology 1

◀◀ page 95

1 A Choose the correct word(s) to complete the sentences.

1 The first thing you need to do when you get a new computer is **plug it in** / **plug it out** at the wall and **switch it on** / **switch it in**.
2 To make a coffee, you just put the cup in here and then **press** / **give** the button to start it.
3 If you think a machine is broken, you should always **unplug** / **undo** it before you do anything else.
4 Please remember to **switch off** / **take on** the lights at the end of the day.
5 If I have problems with my computer, I sometimes need to **shut it down** / **put it down** and then **restart it** / **press it**.
6 The battery on my laptop is low. Is there somewhere I can **charge** / **pay** it?
7 I wanted to call you, but my phone **ran out of charge** / **charged**.
8 I can't get the software to work. It says I need to **install** / **switch** an update.

B 🔊 **VB8.02 | Listen and check.**

C Answer the questions about the verbs and phrasal verbs in Ex 1A.

1 Which ones relate to starting a piece of technology or making it work?
2 Which ones relate to stopping a piece of technology working?

D Work in pairs and discuss the question. What should you do in the following situations?

1 Your computer has crashed.
2 Your phone has run out of charge.
3 You have put some water in the kettle and you want it to boil.
4 You have not updated the software on your phone or laptop.
5 Your phone or laptop is charging, but it's getting very hot.

8C technology 2

◀◀ page 98

1 A Match the conversations (1–5) with the photos (A–E).

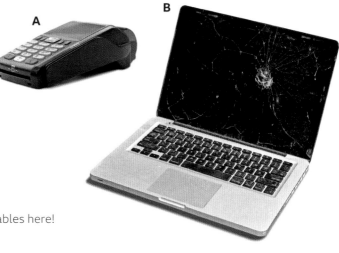

1. A: Where can I **charge** my phone?
   B: There's a **socket** next to the TV.
2. A: This laptop is really old!
   B: I know! The keyboard is fine but the **screen** is broken.
3. A: Can I pay by **credit card**?
   B: Yes, just type in your **PIN**.
4. A: Do you have the electronic files in a folder?
   B: Yes, I put them all on this **USB storage device**.
5. A: Can you plug in the TV?
   B: Yes. Is this the right cable? There are about twenty cables here!

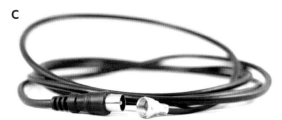

B Complete the questions with the words in bold from Ex 1A.

1. Do you usually pay by cash or .... ?
2. Do you ever forget your .... when trying to take out money?
3. Do you need to .... your phone right now?
4. Do you keep your important files on a .... ?
5. Where's the nearest .... in the room? Is there a plug in it now?
6. How much time do you spend in front of a .... every day (computer, phone or TV)?

C 🔊 **VB8.03** | Listen and check. Then work in pairs and answer the questions.

COMMUNICATION BANK

3A Ex 6A Student B

1 a butterfly / how many legs?
   How many legs does a butterfly have?
2 write / *The Lord of the Rings*?
3 country / Oslo / capital?
4 game / use / two kings, two queens and four castles?
5 British tennis player/win/US Open/in 2021?
6 lead / South Africa / from 1994 to 1999?
7 country / chocolate / come from?

5A Ex 6 Student B

1 Look at the words in the box. Think about how you can describe the things using relative clauses.

   It's a person who …
   It's a thing which …
   It's a place where …

   > athlete   blogpost   desk
   > Facebook   journalist   office

2 Describe the things to your partner. Can they guess the words?

4B Ex 1A

Usain Bolt was the first man to win three Olympic gold medals at 100 and 200 metres.

Tenzing Norgay and Edmund Hillary were the first people to climb Mount Everest.

Indira Gandhi was the first female prime minister of India.

Uruguay was the first team to win the football World Cup, in 1930.

Elon Musk's SpaceX was the first private company to send people to space.

5A Ex 7C

Story A
Whale lands in farmer's field
This story is fake. In the past, hurricanes have picked up small animals like frogs and fish, but never a whale. However, the story appeared online.

Story B
Spider bite!
This story is true.

Story C
Your pizza delivery!
This story is true.

1B Ex 4A Student B

B
The Friend in the Hospital

Zeal Akarawai arrives at a hospital in Lagos, Nigeria, in a black Mercedes. The smartly dressed forty-something is not a doctor and he's not a patient either. And although he's a visitor, he doesn't know the people he visits.

On seeing him, the hospital workers give him a list of names. These are the names of the patients who are well enough to go home, but can't because they can't pay their medical **bills**. Many have little **income** or no family support.

The nurses tell him about these people: who they are and why they are in the hospital. Akarawai, who has a career as a financial consultant, just listens. Then he goes to the bedside of a patient and begins to talk. He doesn't tell them who he is and the patients don't ask. 'What happened to you?' he might say. 'And how will you pay your hospital bill?' The answer is usually, 'I don't know.'

After visiting each patient, Akarawai talks to the nurses. He **makes sure** he understands the patients' stories. Then he pays their bills and the patients leave. They don't need to know who paid, and Akarawai doesn't want to receive any thanks. Helping people is what he does because he's just a kind and caring person. He would like just one thing in return for his **kindness**: that the patients tell people what happened – an unknown friend came and helped to pay their bills. That way, he hopes to see his actions **catch on** all over Nigeria.

7B Exercise 1B

1 b
Eighty-seven million people visit France every year. Spain is the second most popular (eighty-two million).

2 b
Millennials (born 1981–96) travel thirty-five days a year, on average.

3 a
People from Finland travel, on average, 7.5 times per year per person. People from the USA come second, with 6.7 trips (mainly in the USA).

4 c
People from China spend the most on tourism ($257.7 billion). The USA is in second place ($135 billion).

2B Ex 1A

1 *The Lord of the Rings*
2 *Frozen*
3 *Titanic*
4 *Jurassic Park*
5 *Home Alone*

4A Ex 1B

Key

Add up your total score.
Q1: A=3, B=2, C=1
Q2: A=1, B=2, C=3
Q3: A=1, B=2, C=3
Q4: A=3, B=1, C=2
Q5: A=1, B=3, C=2
Q6: A=1, B=2, C=3

Score

14–18

You are competitive, and you just want to win, win, win. That's great, but try to relax a bit sometimes – coming second isn't too bad!

9–13

You are **competitive** and you like winning, but you accept it isn't always possible, so you're also happy to just do your best.

Less than 9

You're not competitive. For you, taking part is the most important thing, and you don't worry about being the best.

6B Ex 1B

10 creative ways to use a paperclip

1 to open an envelope
2 as an earring
3 as a bookmark
4 to hold flowers in place
5 to fix your shirt/glasses
6 as a key ring
7 to make a paperclip chain
8 to hold your money
9 in the kitchen to close a packet
10 as an emergency hairclip

3A Ex 6B Student A

1 How many strings does a violin have? 4
2 Who won the 2018 football world cup? France
3 Which OR What continent is Namibia in? Africa
4 Which OR What animal runs the fastest? cheetah
5 Which OR What medicine did Alexander Fleming discover in 1928? penicillin
6 Who became Chancellor of Germany in 2005? Angela Merkel
7 Which OR What country do/did noodles come from? China

8C Ex 5A Student B

1 **Listen to Student A's problem.**
   - Ask questions to find out more information.
   - Make recommendations.
   - See if you can solve the problem together.

2 **You need to print an important document in the next fifteen minutes. The document is big and has pictures in different colours. The printer isn't working.**
   - Explain the problem to Student A.
   - Respond to their recommendations.
   - Try to solve the problem together.

3C Ex 6 Student B

1 **You work at Ello Language School. Your partner will make some inquiries. Use the information below to answer their questions.**
   - Students usually study for three hours a day, or five hours a day for intensive courses.
   - Students must attend all the lessons if they want to receive a certificate.
   - The school has a study area and a library where students can borrow books.
   - The school offers free wifi to students.
   - There is a department store near the school and a shopping centre about ten minutes away (walking).

2 **You want some more information about a sports centre. Use the prompts to make polite inquiries using indirect questions.**
   - where exactly / the sports centre?
   - need to be / member / to use the facilities?
   - how much / cost / use the gym?
   - a swimming pool?
   - what time / swimming pool / open / in the morning?
   - what time / gym / close / in the evening?

   Can you tell me where exactly the sports centre is?

1B Ex 4A Student C

C

The Fixer

Plumber James Anderson received a call. Could he repair a broken boiler in an old lady's house? Her boiler was broken, so she had no heating and no hot water. Usually, repairing a boiler costs hundreds of pounds. Anderson accepted the job.

After finishing, Anderson sent the **bill**. On it was written 'No charge for this lady … we will be available twenty-four hours to help her.' The lady's daughter posted a photo of the bill on social media and suddenly the world knew about Anderson.

Anderson, from Burnley, UK, saw that a lot of older people needed to borrow money to get basics like hot water. He said many people don't have a lot of **income** and don't like to ask for help. So he decided to start a company that goes to the houses of older people and people with disabilities and does the plumbing for free. He contacted full-time plumbers in several other UK cities, such as Manchester and Leeds, who also agreed to work for free.

Anderson himself is a volunteer. Helping people is what he does. In the winter, especially, his services are very important, because when the plumbing goes wrong, pipes freeze and people get cold. Anderson's plumbers **make sure** this happens less frequently.

After reading about his story on social media, many people called to ask for his services. And many more offered to help the company. The public donated tens of thousands of pounds. Anderson hopes his **kindness** will **catch on**.

3A Ex 6A Student A

1 a violin / how many strings?
  How many strings does a violin have?
2 2018 football World Cup / win?
3 continent / Namibia?
4 animal / run / the fastest?
5 medicine / Alexander Fleming / discover / in 1928?
6 become / Chancellor of Germany / in 2005?
7 country / noodles / come from?

2C Ex 6 Student B

1 A colleague missed a work meeting. You are the manag
• Accept the apology.
• Explain what happened in the meeting.
• Check they know what actions to take.

2 You arrive very late for dinner with a friend.
• Apologise.
• Give a reason.
• Ask if your friend has eaten already.

5A Ex 6 Student A

1 **Look at the words in the box. Think about how you can describe the things using relative clauses.**

It's a person who …
It's a thing which …
It's a place where …

> fact checker fake news headline politician
> social network website

2 **Describe the things to your partner. Can they guess the words?**

A normal day

Now

1 Review Ex 2

Make sentences about Bill's usual life and his life now (on holiday).
Use the verbs below or your own ideas.

| drink | feel | look at | listen to | read | sit | spend time | wear |

Bill usually sits at a desk. Now he's sitting on the beach.

3A Ex 6B Student B

1 How many legs does a butterfly have? 6
2 Who wrote *The Lord of the Rings*? J.R.R. Tolkien
3 What country is Oslo (the) capital of? Norway
4 Which OR What game uses two kings, two queens
  and four castles? chess
5 Which British tennis player won the US Open in 2021?
  Emma Raducanu.
6 Who led South Africa from 1994 to 1999?
  Nelson Mandela
7 Which OR What country does/did chocolate come
  from? Mexico or Central America

1C **A warm welcome**

SPEAKING OUTPUT | a committee meeting
GOAL | agree on a community project
MEDIATION SKILL | managing turn-taking

WARM-UP

1 Work in pairs and discuss the questions.

1 Have you ever moved to a new country, city or area?

2 How do you meet people in a new place?

PREPARE

2 Read the Scenario and answer the questions.

1 What is happening in the town?

2 What is the meeting about?

3 Who are you trying to help?

SCENARIO

You live in a town where there are many people moving to the area. You work for a community group and you want to help new people feel welcome in the town. You also want to help other people in the area who don't have a lot of social contact. The group arranges a meeting to talk about different ideas.

Town meeting agenda
19 February, 19.00, Town Hall

NOTE: what are the **advantages** and **disadvantages** for each activity or event? We also need to think of **who the events would be good for** (age groups, for example).

1 **Cultural activities – art, theatre, music**
• Which activities? Where?

2 **Community events (for example, fairs, markets, food festivals)**
• What events? • When? Who will organise?

3 **Physical activities**
• Which sports or activities?

3 Read the meeting agenda and write notes. Which idea do you think is the best? What are the advantages and disadvantages of each idea?

4 Read the Mediation Skill box. Think of one more phrase for each section.

MEDIATION SKILL
managing turn-taking

When you are working in a group, it's important to get everyone's ideas, share your own ideas and make sure you discuss all the important points. Here are some ways to do that.

Finish someone's turn

A: Some people don't like using technology …

B: So, you think it will be difficult for some people to use social media. Good point!

Bring new people into the conversation

What's your opinion on that, Goran?
What do you think, Gio?

Introduce a new topic

How about social media groups?
What do you think about the idea of cultural activities?

MEDIATE

5 Work in groups of three and discuss the ideas on the meeting agenda. Take turns to introduce each point on the agenda.

Student A: Start the meeting and introduce the first topic: cultural activities.

Student B: Introduce the second topic: community events.

Student C: Introduce the third topic: physical activities.

6 Can you think of any other good ideas to add to the plan? Discuss them with your group.

2C Let's talk about it

SPEAKING OUTPUT | a meeting about a problem at work
GOAL | solve a problem between work colleagues
MEDIATION SKILL | asking questions to deal
with disagreements

WARM-UP

1   Work in pairs and discuss the questions.

    1 Have you ever had a disagreement with someone at work or school?

    2 What happened? Did you solve the problem?

PREPARE

2   Read the Scenario and the article about workplace disagreements. Answer the questions.

    1 Are disagreements between colleagues always negative?

    2 What are the negative effects of work disagreements?

SCENARIO

You are a manager at Finca Bank. You notice that some of the people in your team are not working well together. It's making life difficult for everyone and causing problems on an important project.

You're not sure what to do about it, so you speak to a colleague. Your colleague sends you an article about dealing with conflict at work.

Dealing with conflict at work

In a work environment, people should be able to work out small problems. Some disagreements are natural and can even help people to be creative. However, as a manager, sometimes you need to do something about conflict, especially if it causes difficulties for your team.

Talk to everyone involved. Ask questions, encourage them to be honest and open, and listen.

When you have spoken to everyone and understand the reasons for the problem, think of ways you can solve the problem together. Ask people what they think they can do about it. It will be more successful if people agree to a solution.

Remember that not all conflict is bad. It sometimes happens between people working hard in a busy place. However, when conflict stops people doing their work, asking questions and communicating honestly is the only way to solve it.

3   Look at the list of issues. Discuss them and put them in order from the most to least serious.

- She sends me work messages at five in the morning!
- The way he writes emails is very direct … and it seems rude!
- She interrupts me in meetings – I can't share my ideas.
- He takes my ideas and says they are his.
- I don't like the way she speaks to customers.
- He always leaves everything till the last minute. It's really stressful.

4   Read the Mediation Skill box and think about the advice in the article. Choose one of the statements in Ex 3. What questions would you ask the people involved?

MEDIATION SKILL
asking questions to deal
with disagreements

When you are trying to find a solution to a problem or a disagreement between people, it's important to understand the details about what has happened, the reasons for it and the effects it has had on people. So, you should ask questions to understand what happened and how people feel.

Ask about the disagreement from their point of view

What exactly happened?

What's the problem between you and Sabine?

So Tom, did you interrupt her in the meeting?

Find out the reasons for it

Why do you think she does that?

And why did you do that?

Think about the effects it has

What problems does it cause?

How do you think she feels about that?

MEDIATE

5   Work in groups of three. Take turns to play the role of the manager and ask questions to resolve a disagreement at work. Prepare what you are going to say for each conversation.

Student A: Explain how Student B takes your ideas. Student C is the manager.

Student B: Explain that Student C interrupts you in meetings. Student A is the manager.

Student C: Explain that Student A sends you work messages early in the morning. Student B is the manager.

3C Where in the world?

WRITING OUTPUT | an online post
GOAL | give a friend advice about where to study English
MEDIATION SKILL | describing advantages and disadvantages

WARM-UP

1 Work in pairs and discuss the questions.

Where do you think are the best places in the world to study English? Why? Is it the place, the schools or other activities?

PREPARE

2 Read the Scenario. What does Sakura want to know?

SCENARIO

Your classmate Sakura is thinking about studying English abroad and she posts a question on your online class forum.

Sakura

Hi, everyone! I want to keep studying English next year, but I'm not sure where to go. I want to go somewhere a bit different as I have already been to the UK and the USA. I read something about Malta, which looks nice. Does anyone have any other ideas?

You know that Sakura enjoys eating out, socialising and meeting new people. She is used to living in a big city, but she also enjoys nature and doing things outdoors.

3 Work in pairs. Read about one destination in the text and write notes about the important things to tell Sakura.

Student A: Read about Belize and write notes.
Student B: Read about Iceland and write notes.

4 Read the Mediation Skill box. Think of the country you read about in Ex 3. Write a sentence about an advantage and a disadvantage of that place.

MEDIATION SKILL
describing advantages and disadvantages

When you're giving someone a recommendation, it's useful to think about advantages and disadvantages. Here are some phrases you can use.

It's an interesting place, **but** the transport **isn't great**.

The weather is **pretty good** in the summer – winter is **a different story**!

It's **not the busiest** city, **but** there's **still** a lot to do.

Another good thing is that it's not very expensive.

Belize

It may not be a large country, but Belize has a lot to offer. You can visit Mayan ruins, go hiking in rainforests, visit beautiful beaches to go surfing or diving and enjoy delicious Caribbean food and nightlife. English is the official language of Belize – in fact, it's the only country in Central America where English is the official language and it has some great language schools. Your classmates will be from all over the world. Travelling around Belize isn't always easy because some of the roads are not very good and the buses are sometimes slow! But that's not a problem if you have some time. It's also not the easiest place to get to, but it's well worth the trip!

Iceland

It's true that English isn't the official language of Iceland. However, 80 percent of the country's population speak perfect English and the people are very happy to speak English with tourists, so you'll get lots of practice. There are some excellent English-language schools in Reykjavik, the capital city. Reykjavik also has plenty of things to do: interesting museums and galleries, impressive architecture and fantastic bars and restaurants. Outside the city, Iceland has beautiful scenery, including mountains, waterfalls and lakes. It's true that Iceland is an expensive place to visit, and make sure you prepare for the weather. But whatever the weather, studying in Iceland is an unforgettable experience.

MEDIATE

5 Post a comment to Sakura.

Student A: Tell her about Belize and explain why it would be a good place to visit.

Student B: Tell her about Iceland and explain why it would be a good place for Taki to visit.

6 Read your partner's online post and write a comment to reply. Discuss your posts and comments.

4C Let's play!

SPEAKING OUTPUT | a description of a word game
GOAL | help someone understand a game
MEDIATION SKILL | describing how something is similar or different to something else

WARM-UP

1 Work in pairs and discuss the questions.

1 What word games do you know?
2 Do you ever play word games in English? If not, would you like to try?

PREPARE

2 Read the Scenario. How will you decide which word game to play?

SCENARIO

Your class decides to have a games evening and you decide to include a word game. There are different suggestions for games to play. You will vote to choose the game you want to play.

3 Work in pairs and look at the rules of the games.

Student A: Read about Pronunciation Ships and write notes about the important details. What is the aim of the game?

Pronunciation Ships

Work in pairs. Each player creates an identical grid with words along the top and down the side.

	so	saw	know	now
sheep			🚢	
ship				🚢
cheap	🚢			
chip				

Then draw boats on three of the squares. Do not show your partner where you put the boats.

Take it in turns to read out two words, one from the left side and one from the top, e.g. 'sheep-now'. Your partner will say 'hit' or 'miss' if you hit or missed one of their boats. The winner is the first person to hit all their opponent's boats.

Student B: Read about Sheep and Cows and write notes about the important details. What is the aim of the game?

Sheep and Cows

This is a word-guessing game for pairs or a small group. The first player chooses a word with a set number of letters, and keeps it secret. The other players take turns to guess the word by saying a word with the same number of letters. The first player tells them how many letters match in the right position (sheep) and how many letters are correct but in the wrong position (cows). The first player to guess the word correctly scores a point. Then the next player chooses a word.

A: Three letters.
B: Sad.
A: That's one sheep.
B: Tap.
A: One sheep, one cow!
B: Cat.
A: Correct!

4 Work in pairs. Read the Mediation Skill box. Use the phrases to compare two games or sports you know (e.g. rugby and football, basketball and volleyball).

MEDIATION SKILL

describing how something is similar or different to something else

When you want to help someone understand new information, it's useful to compare it to things they already know. To do that, you can describe similarities and differences.

It's like a crossword, but **instead of** read**ing** clues, you have to write them.

You see other people's letters, **but** not your own letters.

It's different from Scrabble™, you play it on your own.

It's better than the other game **because** you have to help each other.

MEDIATE

5 Work in pairs. Use phrases in the Mediation Skill box to help your classmates understand a new game.

Student A: Tell your partner about Sheep and Cows.
Student B: Ask questions and check that you understand the game.
Student B: Tell your partner about Pronunciation Ships.
Student A: Ask questions and check that you understand the game.

6 Work in pairs. Decide which game to play, and then play it.

5C Change of plans

SPEAKING OUTPUT | an informal discussion about plans
GOAL | agree on a plan
MEDIATION SKILL | agreeing to a change of plans

WARM-UP

1 Work in pairs. Think of a time you had to change plans. Discuss the questions.

1 What happened?
2 What did you do?

PREPARE

2 Read the Scenario and answer the questions.

1 What were your plans and what is the problem?
2 What might you decide to do next?

SCENARIO

You and a group of friends bought tickets to go to a music festival in the summer. A few weeks before the festival, you receive this email from the organisers.

> Dear music fan,
>
> We have some very sad news about the Max Farm MusicFest. Unfortunately, we have to cancel the event this year as there are some problems with the location and we don't have time to arrange a new one. We'll write to you soon with more information.

3 Work in pairs and follow the instructions.

Student A: Read the next email from the organisers and note the important information.

Student B: Read about the City Radio Arts festival and note the important information.

Max MusicFest

We're sorry that the festival is cancelled this year, but we promise to make next year's festival bigger and better and we're giving you tickets! We will have ten more world-famous artists to bring you, so you will get an extra day of entertainment.

You can also upgrade your accommodation for just $30 per person and we'll give you vouchers for some of the great food that will be available.

So don't ask for a refund, just wait another year!

City Radio Arts Festival

The Max festival is cancelled this year, but don't worry … City Radio's annual festival is going to be better than ever this summer.

The festival is famous for its theatre, food and comedy, but this year we'll have a lot of music, too – ten bands that were going to play at Max Farm are booked to play the festival.

We still have some tickets available, but don't wait too long!

4 Read the Mediation Skill box. Think of another phrase for each section.

MEDIATION SKILL
agreeing to a change of plans

When you need to change plans as a group, it's important to listen and understand other people's ideas and think about the options. When you want to decide what to do next, share your ideas and explain the reasons for your ideas.

Show you understand how someone feels

Yes, I see what you mean.
I know how you feel.

Check you understand an idea

So, you're saying you want to wait?

Explain your reasons

They might cancel the MusicFest again next year so let's get our money back. Then we can do something else – like the arts festival.

Deciding what to do

What do you think we should do?
Why don't we … ?

MEDIATE

5 Work in pairs. Discuss your options and decide on a plan.

Student A: You want to wait and go to the MusicFest next year.

Student B: You want to get a refund so you can do something else this year.

6C Book club

SPEAKING OUTPUT | an informal discussion
GOAL | agree on a book to read for a book club
MEDIATION SKILL | describing why something interests you

WARM-UP

1 Work in pairs and discuss the questions.

   1 What was the last book you read? Did you enjoy it? Why/Why not?

   2 Have you ever been part of a book club?

PREPARE

2 Read the Scenario. How will your group decide which book to read?

SCENARIO

You want to a start a book group in your class.

Read some book reviews. Explain to the rest of the group which book interests you and vote to decide which book to read.

3 Read three book reviews and decide which ones might be interesting to read.

The Curious Incident of the Dog in the Night-Time

Genre: detective story

This is not an ordinary mystery novel. The 'detective' is a teenage boy called Christopher, who has Asperger's syndrome, and he finds communicating with people very difficult. One night, his neighbour's dog is killed and Christopher, who has never travelled far from home, decides to investigate what happened. He begins an incredible journey to find the truth.

Freakonomics

Genre: Non-fiction – economics

Freakonomics asks some interesting questions and gives us some very surprising answers: for example, which is more dangerous, a gun or a swimming pool? He uses facts and analysis to make you question what you know. It's great to read just a chapter, but you might find it impossible to stop reading. There is also a great podcast of the same name that you can listen to!

The Hitchhiker's Guide to the Galaxy

Genre: comedy, science-fiction

This is the story of Arthur Dent, a normal man who finds himself going on an extraordinary trip through space. On the trip he meets many interesting characters. For example, there's Zaphod Beeblebrox, the loud president of the Galaxy; and Marvin, an unhappy robot. The only other normal human on the journey is Trillian. They're chased all the way to the Restaurant at the End of the Universe because someone believes Arthur knows the meaning of life! There is also a film version you can watch.

4 Read the Mediation Skill box. Think about the reviews you read in Ex 3 and decide which of the sentences below you would use to describe them.

MEDIATION SKILL
describing why something interests you

If you're trying to persuade someone why they should read a book, film or TV programme, describe why it's interesting to you.

What you like about the book in the review

It sounds fascinating.

It sounds like an interesting story.

Why it's similar to other things you enjoy

I enjoy books about real events.

I've read another book by the author.

Why other people might like it

I think it will give us lots of things to talk about.

I think people will enjoy it because it's quick and easy to read.

MEDIATE

5 Work in groups. Discuss which of the books is best for your group to read and give your reasons.

6 Vote on which of the books you'd like to read.

7C Singapore

WRITING OUTPUT | an informal message
GOAL | tell someone useful information
MEDIATION SKILL | selecting relevant information

WARM-UP

1 Work in pairs and discuss the questions.

1 Have you ever been on a short city break? Where? What did you do?

2 What do you do before you travel to a country or city for the first time?

PREPARE

2 Read the Scenario and the messages. Do Paola and Rui need the same information about Singapore?

SCENARIO

Two friends send you different messages asking for advice.

> Paola: I'm going to Singapore for work. I will have a lot of meetings and I won't have much time to go sightseeing. But do you know anywhere I can go to feel better after a long stressful day at the office? Also, where are the best places to eat? That's very important!

> Rui: I'm going to be in Singapore for two days on the way to New Zealand. I heard that the food is great and you know I love shopping, though I don't want to spend too much money! I also read that there are interesting buildings. I don't have much time, but I want to do as much as possible – things I can't do anywhere else. Any ideas?

You went to Singapore a few months ago and still have a travel guide. Use it to write a reply with some suggestions.

3 Read the Mediation Skill box. Then read the travel guide and find one piece of information that would be useful for Paola and Rui, or both.

MEDIATION SKILL
selecting relevant information

To select relevant information, you need to think about two things. Firstly, think about the important points in the original text or conversation. Then consider the person you are sharing the information with and think about the information they have asked for, or that would be important for them.

Then think about the text or conversation and write a list of the information to answer the questions.

Explain why you're making your recommendations – so the reader understands why something is useful for them.

I know you like shopping. So, you should really go to …

If you don't want to spend a lot of money, go to …

Singapore
What to see and do

Marina Bay is a good place to start any visit to Singapore. Even though it's full of banks and other offices, it has a lot for tourists, too. The iconic Marina Bay Sands towers are an impressive piece of architecture and if you take the lift to the top, you can see the whole of Singapore. The views are amazing and you can get something to drink at the rooftop bar.

Marina Bay also has plenty of fantastic restaurants with a wide variety of international options. If you want to try some of the local dishes, check out the Malay quarter. For a cheaper but still delicious meal, you can go to a 'hawker centre'. There are hawkers (food sellers) all over the city with something for every taste.

You have to see the incredible electronic 'supertrees' in the Gardens by the Bay, just a short distance from Marina Bay. It's a great place to relax away from the heat of the city, and go for a walk along the waterfront. There's also a Children's Garden water play zone. If you take fun seriously, you can also visit Sentosa water and amusement parks.

If you want to take a souvenir of Singapore away with you, check out Orchard Road. In just one street, you can find everything from luxury products to bargain buys. Changi Airport, where you'll arrive, is also a great place to shop. There's something for everyone.

And if fun, food and shopping just aren't enough for you, take some time to visit the National Gallery and National University of Singapore Museum, with its Chinese and Indian artworks.

MEDIATE

4A Work in pairs and read the Scenario again. Student A: Write a message to Paola. Student B: Write a message to Rui.

B Read your partner's message. Does it answer the questions with relevant information for Paola or Rui?

8C Setting up

WRITING OUTPUT | a set of instructions
GOAL | make instructions easier to understand
MEDIATION SKILL | using headings, bullet points and simple sentences

WARM-UP

1 Work in pairs and discuss the questions.

1 How much time do you spend using technology (phones, tablets, laptops)? What do you do (use apps, play games)?

2 Do you ever use technology for learning?

PREPARE

2 Read the Scenario and the instructions. Are the statements True (T) or False (F)?

1 Wize is an app for teachers to use.

2 Users will have to pay for the app.

3 You can use the app on a laptop.

4 The app is only for learning.

SCENARIO

A language school is about to start using a new app called Wize. Wize helps students to learn English, and to communicate with their teacher and other students. They will also use it for homework, and to check their progress. The instructions on the help video are too difficult though. You need to rewrite them so they are easier for students to understand.

1 Before you install the app, you need to decide which device to use: a phone, a tablet or a laptop. We recommend a tablet if possible. Download the program from the link on our website, or get it free from the app store. It is best to download the 'standard' version. You will see an icon called 'Wize'. Click 'open' and 'install'. Then you can log in to your account with the username and password from your teacher.

2 When you have logged in to the app, you're ready to go! But, what can you do with the app? Well, you can do lots of things. You can click on the 'messages' icon to see messages from your teacher or from your classmates. If you want news, you can go to the 'notice board' to see all the news about the school, like events and changes to your class. Finally, there's the 'My homework' icon, and this is very important. It tells you what homework you have to do!

3 Read the Mediation Skill box. Think of headings for the two sections in the text in Ex 2.

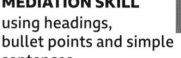

MEDIATION SKILL
using headings, bullet points and simple sentences

To make a text easier to understand, you can break down a text into sections. Then each section should have a list of instructions with bullet points for each step. Each bullet point should be short and simple – you don't even have to write full sentences. You can also use headings to describe the main areas or ideas.

Starting your class
- go to reception
- take the level test

MEDIATE

4A Work in pairs and rewrite the instructions in the Scenario to make them easier to understand. Student A: Rewrite part 1. Student B: Rewrite part 2.

B Show your instructions to your partner and put them together. Give each other feedback on how you can improve them.

- Do they use headings to break the text into sections?
- Do they use bullet points?
- Are the bullets written as short, simple sentences?

AUDIOSCRIPTS

Audio L.01

bar, heart
boat, show
fight, shy
heat, seen
mail, take
oil, toy
put, took
queue, through

UNIT 1

Audio 1.01

Tomasz: Studying is important to me. I'm a student at Manchester University. I'm studying design and I love it! I'm living with a few of the people on my course at the moment and we're really close friends. They're so funny, and great to be with, so we spend a lot of time together. We study during the day and then we usually cook together in the evening. We sometimes go out to eat. The other people that are important to me are my family. My parents live back home in Poland, so I hardly ever see them but I try to stay in touch with them and speak to them every day on the phone. They're getting older, so they need more help nowadays. Luckily, my sister gets on well with them and lives nearby, so she often visits them to make sure they're OK.

Michaela: Hockey is really important to me. I always train twice a week and play matches at weekends. We're training for a big competition at the moment, which is exciting. I'm not the best player in the team, but I do my best to be a reliable teammate. When it comes to the people in my life, my relationship with my grandmother is one of the most important to me. She's such a kind and generous person and she's always cheerful. I spent several years living with her when I was younger. I look up to her because she worked as a nurse for years while bringing up three children. She's amazing. And I also have a very close group of friends. We were all at school together. Now, many of them are living in different parts of the world, but we stay in touch, and when they come home, we always try to meet up.

Jo: I think as we get older, we seem to have a lot of different roles in life. I'm a mum, a partner and a friend. But I'm also a manager in a marketing company. My work is really important to me. It's really busy at the moment because we've got a big project to finish next month. But I'm lucky because I work with a big team of people. They are hard-working and very reliable. When I get home, I have a whole set of other roles. I'm the main chef in the house, as well as the dog walker and sometimes the taxi driver for my teenage son. My roles at home are more exhausting than my job, and I don't get paid!

Audio 1.02

Do you cook for your family?

Audio 1.03

1 What time do you usually start work?
2 Do you enjoy playing sport?
3 Do you get on well with your colleagues?
4 Do you usually get up before 7 a.m.?
5 How often do you see your close friends?

Audio 1.04

1 I help people to make decisions about their money. I give advice on what to do with the money they save.
2 I know all about water pipes, toilets and heating systems. I repair them when they go wrong. I think people are very happy to see me because they need help.
3 I write stories for newspapers and magazines. I try to inform people about the real world.

4 I work in the kitchen at a restaurant, preparing food. We hope to give people a great experience at the restaurant and help them relax.
5 I play in a band. We play in front of live audiences and also record songs.
6 I serve customers. When they ask to see a product I show it to them, and help them buy what they need.
7 I work in a garage and repair cars when they have a problem.
8 I grow and sell fruit and vegetables. We help people by providing healthy, natural food.

Audio 1.05

assistant
consultant
journalist
mechanic
musician

Audio 1.06

1
A: Excuse me, is anyone sitting here?
B: No, go ahead.
A: Thanks.
B: No problem.
A: Are you going to the music festival?
B: Yes, I am!
A: Me, too. Have you been to the festival before?
B: Yes, I go every year. How about you?
A: Oh, it's my first time. I'm really excited.
B: Yeah, it should be good fun. Are you meeting some friends there?
A: No, I'm meeting my sister.
B: Ah, right. Well, have a good time.
A: Thanks. You, too.

2
A: Excuse me, do you know where I can get a cup of coffee?
B: Yes, there's a machine over here, but the coffee is much better in the café downstairs.
A: Oh, thank you.
B: No problem. Are you new here?
A: Yeah, I just started yesterday.
B: Oh right. How's it going?
A: Not too bad, thank you. What about you? How long have you worked here?
B: Me? I've worked here for a couple of years. I'm Kate, by the way.
A: Hi, Kate. I'm Justine.
B: Great. Well, Justine, I've got to go. Nice to meet you.
A: Yes, nice to meet you, too.

3
A: Excuse me, do you mind if I charge my phone here?
B: Not at all. Be my guest.
A: Thanks. That's very kind. It's a lovely morning, isn't it?
B: Yes, it is. It's beautiful. Are you here on holiday?
A: No, I live locally. And you?
B: I just came here for the weekend, visiting a friend.
A: Really? Was it your first time here?
B: Yes. It's such a beautiful city. I don't want to go home!
A: Oh, that's my train. Nice talking to you.
B: Safe journey home!

Audio 1.07

Woman: Excuse me, is anyone sitting here?
Man: No, go ahead.
Woman: Thanks.
Man: No problem.

Woman: Have you been to the festival before?
Man: Yes, I go every year. How about you?
Woman: Oh, it's my first time.

Kate: I'm Kate, by the way.
Justine: Hi, Kate. I'm Justine.
Kate: Great. Well, Justine, I've got to go. Nice to meet you.
Justine: Yes, nice to meet you, too.

Man: Excuse me, do you mind if I charge my phone here?
Woman: Not at all. Be my guest.
Man: Thanks. That's very kind.

Woman: Oh, that's my train. Nice talking to you.
Man: Safe journey home!

Audio 1.08
Not at all.
Go ahead.
Help yourself.
Be my guest.
No problem.

Audio 1.09
See you later.
Nice to meet you.
I've got to go.
Enjoy your weekend.

UNIT 1 VOCABULARY BANK

Audio VB1.01
1 My parents are pretty easy-going and relaxed. They don't mind if I stay out late.
2 It's very generous of him to donate so much money to helping homeless people.
3 Jack never says please or thank you. He's so rude!
4 My dad is a very serious and thoughtful man. He doesn't joke very much.
5 At first, my parents thought I was crazy when I told them my plans to quit my nice job and travel for six months.
6 I'm not very patient. I hate waiting for things.
7 I don't think it's very polite to leave without saying thank you.
8 My brother and I are complete opposites. He's really messy and I'm very tidy.
9 The teacher was very helpful and gave me some good advice.
10 My neighbours are too noisy. They play loud music all the time!
11 She is such a kind lady, always trying to do things for other people.
12 My sister is really bossy. She's always telling me what to do!
13 I laugh so much when I'm with Tom – he's really funny.
14 I know that if I ask Chloe to do the job, she will do it well. She's very reliable.

Audio VB1.02
I'm a student, but I have a part-time job in a supermarket. I work every Saturday and Sunday. I'm studying finance and I'd like a career as a banker one day. I think it's an interesting job and the wages are good. I can make a lot of money.

I run a small company that makes furniture. I'm responsible for the designs and for finding customers. It's a full-time job. Sometimes I work fourteen hours a day when we're busy.

I'm a singer. Unfortunately, I'm out of work at the moment. Singing is a very difficult profession because there are loads of singers and a lot of competition. I have no qualifications because I never did well in exams and I left school when I was fifteen. When I'm not singing, I volunteer at a shelter for homeless people. We aren't paid, but I love helping others.

UNIT 1 REVIEW

Audio R1.01
VSO
VSO (Voluntary Service Overseas) is an organisation that sends people to foreign countries to work as volunteers. They work on community projects and spend time learning about the culture and language of the host country. Quite a lot of them help to build houses or public buildings or work in education or healthcare. The wage they earn is small, but it's enough to live in the country. The people on the programme often end up becoming close friends. When they return to their country, their time abroad is like a qualification that they have gained. The skills they have learnt can help in many different careers. An employee who has been responsible for organising a project in another country often has an open mind and good problem-solving skills. One VSO volunteer said, 'A lot of what I know about the world comes from my time living in Mozambique. It was amazing.'

UNIT 2

Audio 2.01
I had a very memorable trip to India thirty years ago. I was travelling there with Jane, an Australian friend, for two months. We spent the first week staying by a lake in the mountains, which was very beautiful and relaxing. From there we planned to travel by train to Varanasi and visit Nepal before returning to India and spending a couple of weeks exploring Rajasthan. We knew the journey to Varanasi would be long and tiring, but we had no idea that it would change everything.

The train journey usually takes twenty-four hours. We had booked a standard ticket and the train was very busy. It was hot and crowded. People were everywhere – they were sleeping on the floor, crowded into all the seats and even sitting on the roof. We tried to sleep, but it was difficult. By early morning, the family who were sitting next to us got off the train and my friend and I moved into some seats next to an open window. We were exhausted, our clothes were dirty and we were thirsty and hungry. It was already very hot and there was no air conditioning. Anyway, Jane said she didn't feel well and needed to go to the toilet. I decided to stay with the backpacks so we didn't lose our seats by the window. I waited and waited, but Jane didn't come back. I was beginning to get really worried. Suddenly, the train stopped in the middle of nowhere. The next thing I knew, I was taken off the train to meet a group of officials who told me my friend had fallen off the train ten kilometres further back, and she was going to be taken by another train to Bareilly station, where I would meet her. I was terrified. I got on the train and travelled another hour to Bareilly station. I thought I would never see Jane again.

Jane remembers that she woke up on the railway track. She had fallen off the train. She was standing near the open door of the train to get some fresh air when she fell out. A railway worker found her and carried her to lie under a tree, out of the sun. She obviously needed to drink some water, so he set off on his bicycle and returned carrying a kettle of boiled water and gave her some to drink. Luckily, she still had her passport in her money belt as she was terrified she would be lost forever! When I met her a few hours later at Bareilly station, her knee was in a bandage, her clothes were torn and she had no shoes! We went straight to the hospital, where a doctor treated her. We changed all our travel plans and spent the next ten days resting as Jane couldn't walk properly. She had injured her knee.

In the end, we arrived in Rajasthan much later than our original plans because of Jane's accident. In Jaipur we stayed in a beautiful old hotel called the Bissau Palace. We met another traveller there who had just been looking at elephants. I married him two years later. And Jane came over from Melbourne for the wedding and was the guest of honour!

Audio 2.02

1 I was beginning to get really worried.
2 They were sitting on the roof.
3 She had fallen off the train.

Audio 2.03

1 They were travelling around Greece.
2 She was waiting at the airport.
3 She had forgotten her passport.

Audio 2.04

1: I think having an exciting plot is important. The story should surprise you. Also, you need a hero that you like. Maybe the hero's funny or strong. And I like a happy ending, too!

2: When I was a child, my grandmother told me fairytales and I loved them because I like the fight between good and bad. It's the same with TV shows and films. That battle or fight between the hero and the bad guys.

3: What makes a good story? Everything depends on the storyteller, and the way they tell the story. If someone tells a story well, it comes alive. That's why I prefer to watch plays and films to reading books. I love the actors' performances. They bring the characters to life.

Audio 2.05

1 I've never played a video game.
2 Have you ever performed on stage?
3 What have you learnt today?
4 I haven't seen the show.

Audio 2.06

1 A: Hi, everyone. Sorry to keep you waiting! There was a problem with the wifi.
   B: That's OK. Are we ready to start?

2 A: Sorry – I have to leave the lesson early today. I got the time wrong. Sorry about that.
   B: That's fine.

3 A: John, sorry, I'm going to be late. First, there was a delay at the airport, then the taxi driver got lost! I'll be there as soon as possible.
   B: Don't worry. I've only just got here.

4 A: Yes, you were right. It was our fault. We sent the wrong one. There was a problem with the boxes – they look the same. I apologise. We'll deliver it this afternoon.
   B: OK, no problem.
   A: I'll call you back when we know the exact delivery time.

5 A: I'm really sorry I didn't return your call. My battery was dead.
   B: Never mind. You're here now.

6 A: Sorry I missed you yesterday. My train got cancelled.
   B: It's fine. Don't worry.

Audio 2.07

1 Sorry! I made a mistake.
2 I apologise. It was my fault.
3 Sorry I'm late. I got the time wrong.
4 I'm really sorry. There was a problem with my ticket.

Audio 2.08

1 A: Sorry to keep you waiting. My flight was delayed.
   B: That's OK.

2 A: Sorry, this line's really bad. I'll call you back.
   B: No problem.

3 A: I'm really sorry! There was a problem with my wifi.
   B: It's fine. Are you ready to start now?

4 A: I apologise. I made a mistake with the address.
   B: That's fine.

5 A: Sorry! I got the time wrong.
   B: Don't worry. I've just arrived, too.

Audio 2.09

When I first visited Barcelona, it wasn't busy at all. You could walk around the old streets and a lot of the time it was quiet and empty. Then, during the 1990s, Barcelona held the Olympic Games and there was a lot of investment in the city. It became much more popular as a tourist destination. Barcelona is well known for its amazing architecture, fantastic food and relaxed way of living. It has a wonderful atmosphere and a fantastic history. You can explore the city's old Gothic quarter, and see the narrow streets where artists like Picasso and Joan Miró once lived, which haven't changed with time. You can visit the Boqueria – Barcelona's famous food market – and you will see that this is still a place where locals go to enjoy their lunch with friends. But the city is changing. Barcelona is much busier than before. It is now one of the most popular tourist destinations in Europe. People are buying property in the city centre and renting out rooms as accommodation for tourists. This means prices are increasing and many local people can't afford to live there. The shops and businesses are changing, too, with many now selling things for tourists. Barcelona is still a wonderful city to visit, though, and the people are very friendly. I really recommend it, especially for a weekend break.

UNIT 2 VOCABULARY BANK

Audio VB2.01

1 angry, B
2 calm, I
3 exhausted, D
4 in love, E
5 jealous, J
6 nervous, A
7 proud, G
8 silly, K
9 sleepy, H
10 terrified, C
11 upset, L
12 worried, F

Audio VB2.02

1 H, documentary
2 I, comedy
3 D, horror film
4 E, adventure film
5 B, drama
6 G, action film
7 F, romantic comedy
8 C, mystery
9 J, biopic
10 A, animation

UNIT 2 REVIEW

Audio R2.01

How to tell better stories

Have you ever told a story about something that happened to you and found that by the end of the story, nobody was listening to you? They were checking their phones instead. Me, too. Here are a few things that I have learnt to help me become a better storyteller.

Before you start telling your story, you need to get the listener's interest. Use strong adjectives to introduce the story. Try things like, 'The most amazing thing just happened to me.'

Tell your story as if you were the hero in a film. Make it dramatic. Use eye contact and hand gestures. Say things like, 'I was terrified of what was happening to me.'

Ask the listener if they can guess the ending of the story. For example, 'I met Adam Sandler in the gym the other day. Guess what he said to me?'

UNIT 3

Audio 3.01

A: So are you ready? This is a general knowledge quiz – seven questions. You just choose A or B. OK?

B: OK. I'm ready. My general knowledge is terrible so this could be bad.

A: Don't worry about it. And I have the answers here with a bit of extra information.

B: OK.

A: First question. Can fish live out of water?

B: I'm going to guess A: yes.

A: Correct. Most fish die quite quickly out of water but some types of fish can breathe air and move on land. And by the way, there are about fifty types of flying fish.

B: Oh wow.

A: Moving on to the next one, why do we have eyebrows?

B: Because they look nice? Maybe option B, to protect our eyes?

A: Correct. Eyebrows protect our eyes. They keep them clean. For example, when it rains, the water stops on the eyebrow. Number three. Why is red used in stop signs?

B: I'm not sure. Is it A?

A: No, B. Red has been the colour of danger for thousands of years as it's the colour of blood. It's also a colour that we can see from far away, so red is good for stop signs.

B: Oh, that's interesting.

A: Number four. Who wrote the Sherlock Holmes stories?

B: Sir Arthur Conan Doyle.

A: Correct! The first Sherlock Holmes story was published in 1887. That reminds me: I think there's going to be a new film version of one of the books soon.

B: Oh really? I loved his books when I was younger. And I love the TV series, too.

A: Ready for number five? How many different materials does a smartphone contain?

B: I really don't know this one. Um … I'll guess option B.

A: It's A. Smartphones contain about seventy different materials, but mainly plastic, gold, silver and copper. OK, number six. Where was paper first invented?

B: Hm, not sure. In France?

A: No, in China. This is completely off-topic, but I read recently that people in China were the first to drink tea.

B: Oh really?

A: Yep. And the last one. What did Tim Berners-Lee invent?

B: That's easy. The internet, or the World Wide Web, as people used to call it.

A: Correct!

B: I told you my general knowledge was terrible. What was my score?

A: Your score was … four out of seven. Not bad!

B: Yes, not bad at all!

Audio 3.02

1 By the way, there are about fifty types of …
2 Moving on to the next one, …
3 That reminds me: I think …
4 This is completely off-topic, but …

Audio 3.03

1 Do you have a good memory for names?
2 Did you always revise for tests at school?
3 Where do you study?
4 What do you know about India?

Audio 3.04

1 A: When did people first land on the Moon?
   B: People first landed on the Moon in 1969.
2 A: Who played the Black Panther in the 2018 film?
   B: Chadwick Boseman stars as T'Challa, Black Panther.

3 A: Where is the Pink Palace?
   B: It's in Jaipur, in India.
4 A: What object related to weather did Benjamin Franklin invent?
   B: He invented the lightning rod, which protects buildings from damage caused by lightning.

Audio 3.05

1 A: What are you planning to do next year?
   B: I'm not really sure what to do at the moment. I'm planning to go to university to study politics, but I don't know whether to start this year, or next year. My friends are going travelling in a couple of months. They're going to travel around South America and I'd really like to go, but at the moment I don't have enough money for the flight. I might get a job in a local restaurant for the summer.
2 A: What are you going to do this summer?
   B: My husband and I are planning to move. We live in a small, noisy flat in the city centre. We're thinking of moving outside the city. Next week we're looking at a house in a village. It'll be bigger, and it'll be cheaper. Another advantage is that it might be better for the children. We'll see if we can find somewhere nice, then we'll make our decision.

Audio 3.06

1 What are you planning to do next year?
2 What are you going to do this summer?

Audio 3.07

1 What are you doing later?
2 What are you cooking for dinner tonight?
3 Are you going to have a holiday soon?
4 What are you going to do after this lesson?
5 What are you planning to do next year?

Audio 3.08

1

A: Hello. WorkAbroad applications office, can I help you?

B: Hi. Yes, thank you. I'm organising my work placement and I'd like to know if I need to apply for a work visa.

A: OK. Could you tell me which country you're planning to work in?

B: Yes, I'm going to Malta.

A: Right. Are you an EU citizen?

B: Yes, I am.

A: Great. As an EU citizen you don't need to apply for a work visa for Malta.

B: That's good. Thank you.

A: Can I ask if you're going to register for an English course while you're there?

B: Yes, I'm planning to do a language course in the evenings.

A: OK, so when you complete the application form …

2

A: Oh, hi. Is that the accommodation office?

B: Yes. How can I help?

A: I'd like to ask some questions about my accommodation.

B: Yes, go ahead.

A: OK, firstly can you tell me where the university halls of residence are? How far are they from the campus?

B: It's about a twenty-minute walk.

A: Twenty minutes? Oh. Do you know if there's a bus?

B: Yes, there's a regular bus service to and from the campus.

A: Also, I'd like to know if the accommodation is near a beach.

B: Yes, the accommodation is just a short walk from the beach.

A: OK, that's perfect. Thank you. And could you tell me if I can …

3

A: Hi, I wonder if you could help me. I wanted to ask about the university sports centre.

B: Yes, what do you want to know?

A: I'd like to know if the facilities are free. Also, do I have to book?

B: Can I ask if you're a student at the university?

A: Yes, I am.

B: OK, that's fine. Most of the facilities are free to students, so you can use the swimming pool and the gym. But you have to book the tennis courts and exercise classes.

A: That's great. Thanks. Do you know what time the gym opens in the morning?

B: It opens at 6 a.m.

A: Great. Thank you.

Audio 3.09

1 Could you tell me which country you're planning to work in?
2 Can I ask if you're going to register for an English course?
3 Can you tell me where the university halls of residence are?
4 Do you know if there's a bus?
5 I'd like to know if the facilities are free.
6 Do you know what time the gym opens in the morning?

Audio 3.10

1 Can you tell me where the swimming pool is?
2 I'd like to know what time the accommodation office closes.

Audio 3.11

1 Can you tell me where the swimming pool is?
2 I'd like to know what time the accommodation office closes.
3 Can I ask you what time the bus leaves?
4 I'd like to know whether there is free wifi.
5 Could you tell me if I can use the gym?
6 Do you know if I need a visa?
7 Can you tell me where the university campus is?
8 I'd like to know how I can apply for a job.

UNIT 3 VOCABULARY BANK

Audio VB3.01

know, knowledge
guess, guess
revise, revision
inform, information
prepare, preparation
solve, solution
understand, understanding
memorise, memory

Audio VB3.02

1 j, You go to a tourist information centre to find information about the city.
2 a, You can go to a taxi rank to find a taxi.
3 n, You go to a museum or art gallery to learn about the past, or about art.
4 b, You go to a stadium to watch a sports event.
5 c, You can go to a shopping mall to visit lots of shops.
6 i, You go to the bus station or railway station to catch a bus or train.
7 h, You go to the car rental office to hire a car.
8 g, You go to the doctor's surgery to see a doctor.
9 m, You go to the police station to report a crime.
10 d, You can go to the theatre to watch a play.
11 k, You go to a garage or petrol station to buy fuel for your car.
12 e, You can go to a guesthouse to stay for a night.
13 f, You go to a pharmacy or chemist to buy medicines.
14 o, You can go to the town square to meet friends in an open public space.
15 l, You can use a cycle lane to ride your bike safely.

UNIT 3 REVIEW

Audio R3.01

1 A: What are you doing later today?
   B: After this lesson, I'm going to the library.
2 A: What time are you going to get up tomorrow?
   B: At about 6 a.m.
3 A: Are you doing anything interesting this weekend?
   B: Yes! I'm going to see a film with my partner.
4 A: Where are you going on your next holiday?
   B: Maybe to a small town by the sea.
5 A: How are you planning to celebrate your next birthday?
   B: This year I'm going to invite my friends to a party!

UNIT 4

Audio 4.01

A: Hello and welcome. Why do some people reach the top of their profession and others don't? What do a top tennis player, a famous actor and a millionaire film producer all share?

B: Yes, in this episode we're talking about what you need to do to be successful. Is there a recipe for success that we can all follow? Let's look at advice from some of the world's most successful people. What are their rules for success?

A: Great. OK, so first of all, advice from Novak Djokovic, the world-famous tennis player. He said that one of the first things you need to do is set goals. You have to know what you want to achieve. Djokovic decided that he wanted to be a number-one tennis player when he was just seven years old. He knew he wanted to win Wimbledon – he had a clear vision in his mind. He even made himself a Wimbledon trophy out of plastic and newspaper, to motivate himself. Seventeen years later, he won Wimbledon.

B: That's amazing. I think that having goals is important. Another rule is: 'Act now!'. You mustn't delay and think that the perfect moment will come one day. You can't sit around waiting for the right moment to do something. That moment might never come. You need to start right now.

A: I'm not sure about that. I think sometimes you need to wait. Sometimes you have to do some preparation first, do some research. You mustn't rush into things.

B: Yes, I see what you mean, but it's important that you don't spend all your time doing the research and never actually start to do the job.

A: That's true. I agree. Also, you must work really hard. You don't have to be more talented than everyone else, but you have to make more effort. The actor Will Smith said when other people were sleeping, he was working. He worked harder than everyone else, and that's how he got to be successful.

B: Good point. Also, you mustn't give up when things get difficult. Walt Disney was fired from his job at a newspaper because his boss said he had no imagination. But he didn't give up – he carried on doing what he loved.

A: So, set goals, then work hard, and don't give up.

B: Exactly! You needn't work all the time though. You should know when to stop work, take a day off and enjoy your free time.

A: Right. And there's another really important thing to remember.

B: What's that?

A: You should be nice to people. There's a saying, 'Be nice to people on the way up because you might meet them on the way down.'

B: Oh that's really true! … So, now we know …

Audio 4.02

1 Mustn't. You mustn't give up.
2 Should. You should be nice to people.
3 Shouldn't. You shouldn't wait for the perfect moment.

Audio 4.03

1 the flight
2 the Brazilian
3 the plane
4 the aeroplane
5 the earliest
6 the inventor

Audio 4.04

A: Today we're looking at a sport that's becoming very popular, especially in Europe: floorball. It's fast, it's fun and anyone can play. Margaret Kleist tells us more.

B: Floorball is a version of indoor hockey which is mostly played in Europe and Asia. The aim of the game is to score more goals than the other team. As you can guess by the name, floorball is a ball sport. It uses a small plastic ball, and each player uses a stick.

There are six players in a team, including the goalkeeper. The goalkeeper is the only player who doesn't have a stick. The other players pass to a teammate or control the ball while running. Like hockey, you score by shooting the ball into the goal. Except for the goalkeeper, the players can't touch the ball with their hands.

The rules are quite easy. To start the game, there's something called a 'face-off', where two players compete for the ball. Then the game continues until someone scores a goal. After that, the game restarts with another face-off.

Floorball is played on a court that's about 40 metres long and 20 metres wide, and a match lasts an hour, three periods of twenty minutes. Fans of floorball come from all over the world, but especially from Sweden, Switzerland and Finland, who have all been world champions.

A: Thank you, Margaret. It sounds really good and the type of sport …

Audio 4.05

1 You can score points.
2 You can't catch the ball.
3 You can play inside or outside.
4 You can't use a stick.
5 You can hit the ball with any part of your body.
6 Your team can't hit the ball more than three times in one point.
7 You can hit the ball after it touches the net.

Audio 4.06

The most memorable journey I've ever been on was when I drove around southern Africa with three friends a few years ago. We went in this old car on all these bumpy roads. It was my first time driving across a desert and in such wild places, and it was one of the most amazing experiences I've had.

We took tents and stayed in campsites every night, and we went to these tiny towns and farming communities in Namibia, Botswana, South Africa and Eswatini. We also saw a lot of wildlife like horses and deer.

It was memorable because that part of the world is so beautiful and also because one day our car broke down. We had to stay in a small town in Botswana for a few days while we waited for a car part to arrive. Everyone was so friendly. Southern Africa is definitely the most interesting place I've been to. It has the nicest people you'll ever meet. I'd recommend it.

UNIT 4 VOCABULARY BANK

Audio VB4.01

invent, invention, inventor
create, creation, creator
educate, education, educator
introduce, introduction
develop, development, developer
discover, discovery
lead, leadership, leader
succeed, success

Audio VB4.02

Equipment: ball, bat, racquet, stick
People: goalkeeper, player, referee
Places to play: court, field, pitch
Verbs: draw, hit, pass, score, shoot, win

UNIT 4 REVIEW

Audio R4.01

A police officer stops a man driving a car. He notices two penguins sitting on the back seat of the car. He asks the driver, 'Hey, why have you got two penguins on the back seat of your car?'

The man says, 'I found them. I like animals, so I put them in my car. What should I do with them?'

The police officer says, 'Well, why don't you take them to the zoo?'

'Great idea!' says the man, and he drives away.

The next day, the man drives past the same place. The same police officer stops him again. He sees that the penguins are still there.

'Hey', he says to the driver. 'You've still got the penguins. I told you to take them to the zoo.'

'Yes, I took them to the zoo yesterday and we had a great time,' says the driver. 'Today I'm taking them to the beach.'

Audio R4.02

Fascinating Nobel Prize Winners

Cambridge University has produced ninety-six Nobel Prize winners over the years. We take a look at two of them.

Ernest Rutherford was born in New Zealand in 1871 and is one of the best-known scientists who has ever studied at Cambridge. He's known as the 'father of nuclear physics' for his discoveries around radioactivity. Under his leadership the neutron was discovered by James Chadwick in 1932.

Dorothy Hodgkin won a Nobel Prize in chemistry. She was very strict about her studies and during her career she had a lot of success; she invented advanced techniques of X-ray crystallography, and she worked on the structure of penicillin and Vitamin B.

UNIT 5

Audio 5.01

1 Christopher Blair is a journalist who writes fake news.
2 Schenk checks news stories when they are shared on social media.

Audio 5.02

1 Christopher Blair is a journalist who writes fake news.
2 Schenk checks news stories when they are shared on social media.
3 He writes news stories which are completely fake.
4 This is the room where Maarten Schenk works.
5 This is the politician whose story went viral.

Audio 5.03

campaign
character
colleague
environment
friend
mechanic
plumber
scientist

Audio 5.04

David: Hello, I'm David Salter and I'm with Marina Smith reporting for the *Young people in the news* podcast. Marina, you have some amazing young people to tell us about.

Marina: I certainly do. Our first is Yash Gupta from California. Yash started wearing glasses at the age of five. One day in High School he broke them and had to go to school without glasses for a week.

David: And how was it?

Marina: Terrible! He realised he couldn't study without them. So he did some research and learnt that thirteen million children around the world needed glasses and didn't have them.

David: Wow.

Marina: So he started a campaign to collect used glasses.

David: What a great idea. Glasses for children?

Marina: Glasses for children. After he collected them, he donated these glasses to children all over the world.

David: It's a simple idea, isn't it, but probably makes a really big difference to people's lives.

Marina: That's right. And he started a charity called Sight Learning.

David: Sight Learning?

Marina: Yes. So far this charity has collected more than one million dollars' worth of glasses. They've sent them to students in Mexico, Honduras, India, the USA and many other countries. I spoke to one child in Mexico, and he said that it had completely changed his life.

David: Incredible.

Marina: Next up is a pair of sisters, Melati and Isabel Wijsen, from Bali.

David: Tell us more.

Marina: These amazing girls were only ten and twelve when they became activists for the environment. First, they wanted to do something about the high levels of plastic pollution in the sea and on the beaches. So they started a campaign to clean up all the rubbish.

David: That's fantastic. And they were young, too.

Marina: Ten and twelve. Then they spoke to the government and worked with like-minded organisations to stop the use of single-use plastic bags. And in 2019 the governor announced that Bali would ban single-use plastic bags.

David: So, because of their work, Bali is now free of single-use plastic bags? That's amazing. And do they recycle …

Marina: They recycle shopping bags which use different materials, not plastic. And yes, that's right – no single-use plastic bags since 2019.

David: Now that's really doing something for the environment. And we have one more …

Marina: Our final young person in the news is Kelvin Doe.

David: What's Kelvin done?

Marina: He's from Sierra Leone and he's an amazing inventor. He started working with technology when he was just eleven years old, playing around and experimenting. His childhood friends all claimed that he was a genius! Then he found a way to provide power and lighting for his local community. And he also built a radio station.

David: He sounds incredible. Again, through recycling?

Marina: Yes, he's done it all by recycling waste products. He collects things like batteries and plugs, things he finds in rubbish bins, and recycles them and makes these wonderful machines.

David: Wow.

Marina: And, basically, he taught himself.

David: What amazing young people.

Marina: Yeah. Inspiring, aren't they?

David: Very inspiring. I think they …

Audio 5.05

1 A: Guess what! I've got some amazing news.
  B: What is it?
  A: You won't believe this, but Greg and I got engaged.
  B: Wow, that's amazing! Congratulations! I can't believe it!
  A: I know. I can't believe it either … it's just so exciting …

2 A: I've got some good news to tell you.
  B: What is it?
  A: You know I applied for the manager's job?
  B: Yes.
  A: Well, I got it!
  B: That's wonderful news! I'm so pleased for you.
  A: Thank you.

3 A: You won't believe this!
  B: What?
  A: I just broke my phone.
  B: Oh no! That's awful. What happened?
  A: I was holding a cup of coffee and I dropped it.
  B: Oh. I'm really sorry. Let's see if we can fix it.

4 A: Hi, Mum. I've got something to tell you.
  B: What is it?
  A: I passed my exams …
  B: Well done! That *is* good news. I bet you got top grades, too!
  A: Well, yes I did actually.
  B: I'm so happy for you.

5 A: Guess what! I've just won a competition!
  B: Really? What did you win?
  A: I got two tickets to the music festival next weekend, for Saturday *and* Sunday! There are some great bands playing.
  B: I can't believe it! That's great.
  A: Do you want to come with me?
  B: I'd love to. Are you sure? That would be fantastic.

6 A: Bad news, I'm afraid.
  B: What? What's happened?
  A: You won't believe this, but I failed.
  B: Failed?
  A: I failed my driving test again.
  B: Oh no! What a shame. I'm sorry to hear that. What happened this time?
  A: Well I was doing really well but then there was this bus in front of me and …

Audio 5.06

Wow, that's amazing!
That's awesome.
Congratulations!
I'm so pleased for you.
Oh no! That's awful.
I'm really sorry.

Audio 5.07

1 A: I managed to get tickets for the festival!
  B: Wow, that's amazing!
2 A: I left my phone on the train last night.
  B: Oh no! That's awful.

3 A: We've just had a baby!
   B: Congratulations! I'm so pleased for you.
4 A: I failed my exams.
   B: I'm really sorry.
5 A: I got a new job.
   B: That's awesome.
6 A: I missed my flight.
   B: Oh no! That's terrible.

UNIT 5 VOCABULARY BANK

Audio VB5.01

1 By 2070, there will probably be no oil, but there will be other natural resources.
2 The terrible forest fires in California are an example of a natural disaster.
3 Many natural disasters are happening because of climate change.
4 One example of air pollution is factory smoke.
5 The environment is cleaner when people pick up their rubbish.
6 I was late to work because I spent half an hour in a traffic jam.

UNIT 5 REVIEW

Audio R5.01

WORLDCHANGE is a new monthly magazine that looks at issues related to the environment. The idea is to cover all the breaking news in this field. Our journalists will find out what's really going on and write detailed articles to educate the public. The focus of the magazine will be on issues like the recycling of waste and climate change. In addition to the print magazine, our website will include daily blog posts. These will probably be about new campaigns to save the environment, and the work of activists like Greta Thunberg. Our managing editor, Laura Grundwig, said that the magazine would be a torch that shone a light on the biggest issue of our times.

UNIT 6

Audio 6.01

1 I used to collect toy cars when I was a child.
2 We used to live in the countryside.
3 I didn't use to like vegetables.
4 I didn't use to like playing sports at school.

Audio 6.02

talent – talented
imagine – imagination – imaginative
create – creativity – creative
art – artist – artistic
photograph – photo – photography – photographic
skill – skilful

Audio 6.03
Roza

Interviewer: How important is creativity to you?
Roza: For me, creativity is the most important part of my job. But I don't think that's true just for writers and film-makers, like me. I think it's a vital human need, like we need water and food, and the company of other people. I think being creative is just as important as these other things. Being creative makes us feel happier, more satisfied and less stressed.
Interviewer: OK, and what do you do to bring creativity into your daily life?

Roza: One thing I often do is I try to put myself in new situations, go to new places or talk to strangers. You know, I might just start a conversation with someone on the bus, or in a café. When you talk to someone who has different ideas to you, it opens your mind and you start to see things differently. It forces you to think more carefully about your ideas, and see things from a different point of view. I use that a lot in my work. I think it makes my films more interesting.

Joshua

Interviewer: How important is creativity to you?
Joshua: It's very important to me. I'm a designer, and when I'm looking for a new design, I usually start by going for a walk in nature. I find it helps my imagination, and it's easier for me to get ideas when I'm outside, especially in woodland. I notice the trees and the leaves and the shapes that they make. I also notice butterflies and smaller insects, even though I don't know their names. These things give me ideas for patterns and colours. I think all of my best ideas come from nature. For me, an important part of creativity is just taking time to notice what's around you, and think about what you can do with that.

Fabio

Interviewer: How important is creativity to you?
Fabio: Well, I'm a chef, so obviously, creativity is important because I'm always trying to come up with new ideas for recipes. That's the hardest thing about cooking. I experiment with mixing different ingredients together to see what happens. I take a recipe and think, 'Can I find a better way to do this, maybe cook it more slowly, or try to make it healthier?' But also, in my business, I'm always learning from other people's ideas. Maybe my website is not as good as I want it to be, so I look at how other people use photographs and this gives me ideas. Or I try filming myself making some of my recipes, or offering cooking courses online. I'm always looking for ways to grow the business and reach a bigger audience.

Meera

Interviewer: How important is creativity to you?
Meera: I don't think I use creativity very much in my work. I'm an accountant, so I work with numbers and I have to be very accurate. I'm also not very interested in the arts, or painting. But I guess now that I'm a parent, I have to be a lot more creative than before. I need to entertain my daughter, and help her to learn about the world. I find she quickly gets bored with traditional toys, so we spend a lot of time making things together, like we made a robot out of a cardboard box last week, and we invent games together. I think sometimes I have to work harder when I'm at home than when I'm in the office!

Audio 6.04

1 Creativity is the most important part of my job.
2 I think being creative is just as important as these other things.
3 It forces you to think more carefully about your ideas.
4 I think it makes my films more interesting.
5 It's easier for me to get ideas when I'm outside.
6 All of my best ideas come from nature.
7 That's the hardest thing about cooking.
8 I have to work harder when I'm at home than when I'm in the office!

Audio 6.05

1

Marc: Why do you have this app on your phone?

Serge: I love it! I think it's a fantastic app.

Marc: Why do you think that? All it shows is pictures of oranges falling from a tree.

Serge: The reason I like it is that it makes me feel calm. The oranges fall so slowly and …

Marc: But for me, it has no meaning. It has no purpose.

Serge: I don't agree. I really enjoy using it.

Marc: Well, I guess we all like different things!

Serge: Yeah.

2

Alice: What did you think of her new book?

Nick: I thought it was terrible!

Alice: Really? What makes you say that?

Nick: It's because the story was so boring. I mean, nothing happened! How about you? Did you like it?

Alice: Yes, I think it's a fascinating story!

Nick: Why do you think that?

Alice: Because it develops so slowly, and none of the characters are simple. It's impossible to know what's going to happen next.

Nick: Well, I can't quite understand why you like it, but I suppose we're all different.

Alice: That's true.

3

Louise: What do you think of the new library building?

Steve: Oh, I hate it! I think it's horrible!

Louise: What makes you say that?

Steve: Because it's a really strange shape, and I think the huge round roof looks awful! How about you? Don't tell me you like it.

Louise: Like it?! I love it! In my view, it's a really new and exciting design. I would say the roof is beautiful!

Steve: Well, I prefer more traditional buildings, but I guess it's good we're not all the same.

Louise: You're right about that.

Audio 6.06

1 For me, it has no meaning.

2 In my view, it's a really new and exciting design.

3 I think it's a fantastic app!

Audio 6.07

I'm going to nominate my friend Jake Martin for the creative genius award. Jake is the most amazing graffiti artist and he creates these fantastic, brightly coloured designs on walls or on the sides of buildings. His work is brilliant. Just looking at it makes you happy because of all the bright colours and shapes. Jake has always been creative. He has enjoyed art since he was a kid, when he used to spend all his time drawing. He's also creative in his life. He's always looking for something different to work on, for example he's done a lot of sports like roller-skating, skateboarding and surfing. So now he creates his artwork in skate parks. For the last few years he has worked in fashion, helping brands with their new designs. He hasn't worked on a big building yet, but I know he plans to. I think Jake deserves the award as he is definitely the most creative person I know.

UNIT 6 VOCABULARY BANK

Audio VB6.01

People

1 A person who dances is a dancer.

2 A person who designs buildings is an architect.

3 A person who take professional photos is a photographer.

4 A person who watches an event is part of the audience.

Places

5 A place where an artist or musician works is a studio.

6 A place where art is shown to the public is an art gallery.

7 A place where people perform plays or live music is a venue.

Things

8 A performance or event for the public is a show.

9 A picture you make with a pen or pencil is a drawing.

10 A picture that shows how something will be made or how it will look is a design.

UNIT 6 REVIEW

Audio R6.01

David Hockney – a life of colour

David Hockney is considered by many to be one of the most creative artists. His work is very colourful and imaginative. When Hockney was a young boy, he used to watch his father painting old bicycles. He knew immediately that he wanted to spend his life doing art. However, at school art was not considered a serious subject, and it was only taught to students who weren't very talented in other areas. But Hockney was determined to study art. He spent a lot of time doing drawings with pencils and pens, in order to develop his skills. At the age of sixteen, he decided to go to art school. He worked hard all his life, often spending days and nights in his studio painting. He wrote a sign at the end of his bed which said, 'Get up and work immediately.' He worked in different styles and using different media. Later in his career, he used technology, like iPads, to produce his images. His works have been enjoyed by art lovers for many years now, and they are shown in art galleries around the world.

UNIT 7

Audio 7.01

1 If you learn the language, you'll be able to communicate with people.

2 If you leave rubbish everywhere, somebody'll have to clear it up.

3 If the city charged a tourist tax, they'd reduce the numbers of tourists.

4 If we stayed in a small hotel, we'd help the local economy.

5 If the hotel gets a good review, it'll encourage more tourists to visit.

6 If tourists had more respect for local customs, it'd be better.

Audio 7.02

1 A: Were there lots of people?
   B: There were hardly any.

2 A: Did you see any wild animals?
   B: We saw a few.

3 A: Are there any free seats?
   B: There are plenty.

4 A: Did you eat enough?
   B: I ate too much!

Audio 7.03

When the plane landed in Rio, it felt as if we were landing on the edge of the world. I showed my passport, re-checked my bags, and sat and waited. One more plane journey, then a taxi ride, and I reached my new home: a town in the south of Brazil.

In those first weeks, everything was surprising to me. I felt a bit like a newborn baby. It was strange to see a mango tree in my garden, strange to go into a shop that sold lots of fruits I'd never heard of, strange to realise this heat was normal for a Brazilian summer. And then there was the noise: samba music on the buses, the shouting every time someone scored a goal on TV, families sitting outside laughing late into the night. The sounds of a country in love with life.

I walked along the coast every morning and explored the town and came across a few cafés that served the strongest coffee you've ever tasted. They served it in a tiny cup and called it a *cafezinho*. They didn't seem to notice the stranger with the funny accent. Or maybe they noticed but didn't care. They accepted me and I accepted my new life. The town had hardly anything, no cinema, no theatre, not even a library. But it had soul and it had the sea.

Some say the people of the world are the same everywhere you go. Maybe it's true, but it wasn't for me. I'd expected to be lonely, but I made plenty of friends, enough for a lifetime: the lady who brought bananas to my door, the teenager who fixed my fridge, the fisherman who sold me crabs straight from his boat. And the dogs! Those dogs on the beach were my friends, too, walking the same routes as me, hunting for crabs under the sand. Maybe that's what living by the sea does: makes everyone closer. I don't know, but as I lie in my hammock every day, all I hear is the sound of the waves saying 'live your life, live your life'.

Audio 7.04

Mark: Hi Sam, it's Mark here.

Sam: Hi Mark. How are you?

Mark I'm fine, thanks. I'm calling because I'm going to Shanghai next month. I wondered if you could give me some recommendations for things to see and do while I'm there.

Sam: Sure. I know the city really well.

Mark: Great, thanks.

Sam: So, you've never been to Shanghai?

Mark: No, I haven't.

Sam: Oh, you're going to have a great time. It's an amazing city! There's so much to see and do!

Mark: Oh, wow! How exciting! I'm taking my dad with me. Is there anything in particular you think we should do?

Sam: Yes, of course. There are a few things you absolutely have to see.

Mark: Right.

Sam: First of all, when you arrive at the airport, make sure you take the Shanghai Maglev Train from the airport to the centre of Shanghai. It's the world's fastest train. It's exciting because it's so fast. It only takes you seven minutes to get into the centre, and taking the train is a really fantastic experience.

Mark: OK, that's a good idea. Thank you.

Sam: Yeah, it's great. You must visit the Shanghai Tower. It's a great place to see views of the city and going up in the lift is really exciting.

Mark: Er … I'm not sure about that one. Dad's afraid of heights!

Sam: Oh, that's a shame. Going up the towers is one of the best things to do in Shanghai.

Mark: Ahh … yeah … well.

Sam: It doesn't matter. Maybe you can just go to the area. You can enjoy it even if you don't go inside – it's beautiful from the outside, too.

Mark: That's a good idea.

Sam: You can also enjoy the views of the city from the Bund, along the river. It's a lovely place to walk in the evening and see the skyline, and you can eat at one of the fantastic restaurants while you're there.

Mark: OK. That sounds good. Anything else? What about different areas of the city?

Sam: Oh yes, you should definitely visit Tianzifang.

Mark: Sorry?

Sam: Tianzifang – it's the tourist shopping and café area in the old French district. It's full of narrow streets with little shops. It's a great place to buy souvenirs and to drink tea, of course. And it's beautiful to walk around and enjoy the historical European architecture.

Mark: Right … that sounds interesting.

Sam: Oh, and one other thing you have to do.

Mark: What's that?

Sam: Don't leave Shanghai without visiting the Yu Gardens.

Mark: Yes, I've heard about the gardens.

Sam: It's a beautiful green space and it's very relaxing to walk around and take photos. You can see the amazing Jade Rock …

Audio 7.05

1 There are a few things you absolutely have to see.

2 You must visit the Shanghai Tower.

3 You should definitely visit Tianzifang.

4 Make sure you take the train from the airport.

5 It's one of the best things to do.

6 It's a great place to buy souvenirs.

7 You can eat in one of the fantastic restaurants.

8 Don't leave without seeing the Yu Gardens.

Audio 7.06

1 Great, thanks.

2 OK, that's a good idea.

3 Oh, wow! How exciting!

4 That sounds good.

5 That sounds interesting.

Audio 7.07

1 There are a few things you absolutely have to see.

2 You must visit the Shanghai Tower.

3 You should definitely visit Tianzifang.

UNIT 7 VOCABULARY BANK

Audio VB7.01

1 accommodation – H

2 luggage – D

3 check-in – C

4 backpacker – I

5 exchange rate – K

6 city break – A

7 souvenir – L

8 monument – B

9 resort – E

10 night-life – F

11 book a tour – G

12 rent bicycles – J

Audio VB7.02

A coast

B jungle

C countryside

D seaside

E mountain range

F national park

G rainforest

H stream

I valley

J waterfall

UNIT 7 REVIEW

Audio R7.01

The best job in the world?

Travel writer. It sounds perfect. A magazine pays you to go to beautiful destinations. You learn local customs. You visit tourist attractions and come across amazing things you'd never expected to see. You write about your experiences, and you become rich and famous.

That's the dream. Unfortunately, there isn't much chance of it coming true. Firstly, hardly any travel writers make enough money to live on. Secondly, editors have plenty of writers sending them stories. What makes your story different? If you don't have anything special to say, you'll be just another tourist with a laptop.

Finally, you have to know your market. Make sure you read the magazines you want to write for. What's the style? If you do your research, you'll have a better chance of getting published.

UNIT 8

Audio 8.01

Ahmed: As a child, I could draw quite well. I remember going to the zoo when I was about four years old, and my mother was amazed because when we got home, I was able to draw the elephant. I could remember everything about it: its huge ears, its trunk and its rough grey skin. Years later, I was able to use my skills to design clothes and shoes, and that's what I do now. I work for a big fashion company, and I love it! And it all started with an elephant.

Candace: I learnt to be very practical a few years ago when I went to live in a tiny village. There weren't many services and you had to do everything yourself. Right now I can fix a roof, I'm able to install a washing machine, replace broken pipes, that kind of thing. I couldn't do any of that a few years ago. Anyway, I started doing odd jobs for people, got some qualifications and turned it into my business. I work with lots of different clients: people in their homes, restaurants, even public buildings. The best thing is being independent. The worst thing is when it's cold and wet and I'm on someone's roof and I have to finish the job.

Dan: I was always good at organising parties. When a friend had a birthday or a graduation, they always called me. I could make cakes and arrange live music and I always had fun ideas. A few years ago, I was able to arrange a party on the roof of an old factory. It was amazing, and I started thinking, 'I love doing this.' So that's how I became a party organiser. I don't do it for the money. It's a great job because it's creative and practical and you see people at their happiest.

Maxine: I started young with technology. When I was fourteen, I used to build and repair computers just for fun. Luckily, it was a hobby that I was able to turn into my job. Now I can build websites, design apps, do almost anything related to computers. I've never designed a video game but I love playing them!

Audio 8.02

1 A: Can you put up a shelf?
   B: Yes, I can.
2 A: Could you swim when you were six?
   B: Yes, I could.
3 A: Were you able to speak English as a child?
   B: Yes, I was.
4 A: Could you play an instrument when you were a child?
   B: No, I couldn't.
5 A: Were you able to relax last weekend?
   B: No, I wasn't.

Audio 8.03

1 A: I watch a lot of short video clips on social media. I love anything that makes me laugh, especially anything with cats or dogs. Some of those are so funny! If I like a video, then I'll share it with friends.
   B: How about video games?
   A: Oh yeah, I play those, too.

2 A: I enjoy making short videos. I'm in a band so we record our own videos, and then I edit them and upload them to our website or social media, so hopefully our fans will like them, comment on them and share them with their friends. We also have a vlog where we talk about our latest songs.

3 A: I watch lots of different types of video – I like keeping fit, so I watch a lot of fitness videos online. I also like cooking videos, and video podcasts in which people just chat about things. I use video a lot in my work, so I watch a lot of educational videos. And if I need to do something in the house, like repair something, I watch one of those instructional videos to show me how to do it. Then, in the evening when I want to relax, I watch films!
   B: Do you ever watch promotional videos for new products?
   A: No, I hate those! I always skip them.

Audio 8.04

1 These kinds of videos are watched every day.
2 A lot of teenagers watch these kinds of videos.

Audio 8.05

1 A: The camera was sold for 200 euros.
   B: Alfie sold his camera for 200 euros.
2 A: The video was shared more than 6 million times.
   B: People shared the video more than 6 million times.
3 A: The students are given homework every day.
   B: The teachers give the students homework every day.
4 A: The clip was uploaded to YouTube.
   B: Jenna uploaded the clip to YouTube.

Audio 8.06

1
A: Hi, Bill. Are you all ready for the meeting this afternoon? You look a bit stressed. Is there a problem with your presentation?
B: No. My presentation's fine, but there's a problem with the internet connection. I need the internet to show some of my slides.
A: Have you checked that everything's switched on?
B: Yes. It's all switched on – all the lights are on, but every time I try to go online, it tells me I don't have a connection.
A: Oh, it's so annoying, isn't it? It sounds silly, but it sometimes works if you switch it off, then switch it on again.
B: Yeah. I'll try that. … Yes, it's working now! Thanks, Nicola.

2
A: Hi. Do you want a cup of coffee?
B: Er … Yeah, that would be nice.
A: Is everything OK?
B: Not really. Oh, why is it doing that?
A: Problem with your phone?
B: Yeah. I downloaded a new fitness app, but it keeps crashing.
A: Have you tried closing other apps before you open it?
B: Yep, I tried that but it still isn't working. It lets me add my personal details, but it won't save them.
A: Maybe you need to delete it and then install it again. That sometimes works.
B: Yeah, I'll try that, thanks.
A: Here's your coffee.
B: Oh, thanks. Install.
A: So, you're going to get fit?
B: That's the idea. … Yes, that works now. Great. My fitness journey starts here!

3
A: Hi, Dave. Problem with your laptop?
B: No, it isn't my laptop, it's the printer. It isn't working. When I try to print documents, it makes a noise, but nothing happens.

A: OK. Let me have a look. Have you checked the paper?

B: Yeah, there's plenty of paper.

A: What about the ink cartridges?

B: Well, that's part of the problem. I can't get the lid open to check the cartridges. I think it's broken.

A: OK, I think we'll need to call IT and report it as out of order. You can print your document in the front office in the meantime. There's a printer there.

B: That's true. Thanks!

A: No problem.

Audio 8.07

1 There's a problem with the internet.

2 I downloaded a new fitness app, but it keeps crashing.

3 Every time I try to go online, it tells me I don't have a connection.

4 I think it's broken.

5 Have you tried closing other apps before you open it?

6 Maybe you need to delete it and then install it again.

7 It sometimes works if you switch it off, then switch it on again.

8 Yes, it's working now.

Audio 8.08

1 A: Is there a problem with your presentation?

 B: No. My presentation's fine, but there's a problem with the internet connection.

2 A: Problem with your laptop?

 B: No, it isn't my laptop, it's the printer.

Audio 8.09

I started learning Arabic two years ago. I've been to Egypt three times, and I absolutely love it! At some point, I intend to go back, so it seemed like a good idea to learn the language. I have lessons once a week with a teacher – she's really good – and I spend an hour a day studying the language from a book.

I practise listening a lot. There are some excellent podcasts in Arabic, especially BBC ones, and I also like watching videos on YouTube of Arabic speakers.

Obviously, the Arabic alphabet is different from English and the pronunciation is tricky. It takes a long time to learn the language, but I think the most important thing is not to give up and not to worry if you make mistakes.

UNIT 8 VOCABULARY BANK

Audio VB8.01

1 I can't come out. I have to look after my little cousin because his parents are away.

2 She wanted to learn an instrument, so she decided to take up the guitar.

3 We need someone who can come up with great ideas quickly.

4 That's not true! You shouldn't make up stories like that!

5 She already spoke Spanish, so it was easy for her to pick up Portuguese.

6 I don't get on with my boss. He doesn't like me and I don't like him.

7 With the money I've saved, I'm going to set up my own business building websites.

8 This text is too complicated. I can't work out what it means.

Audio VB8.02

1 The first thing you need to do when you get a new computer is plug it in at the wall, and switch it on.

2 To make a coffee, you just put the cup in here and then press the button to start it.

3 If you think a machine is broken, you should always unplug it before you do anything else.

4 Please remember to switch off the lights at the end of the day.

5 If I have problems with my computer, I sometimes need to shut it down and then restart it.

6 The battery on my laptop is low. Is there somewhere I can charge it?

7 I wanted to call you, but my phone ran out of charge.

8 I can't get the software to work. It says I need to install an update.

Audio VB8.03

1 Do you usually pay by cash or credit card?

2 Do you ever forget your PIN when trying to take out money?

3 Do you need to charge your phone right now?

4 Do you keep your important files on a USB storage device?

5 Where's the nearest socket in the room? Is there a plug in it now?

6 How much time do you spend in front of a screen every day (computer, phone or TV)?

VIDEOSCRIPTS

UNIT 1

Opener: BBC Vlogs

1 People would describe me as creative, artsy, humorous, bearded and most importantly caring and genuine.
2 Hi I'm Jo, and my friends would describe me as funny, most of the time, loud and slightly chaotic.
3 How would my friends describe me? I'd hope that they'd say that I'm friendly, funny and reliable.
4 How would my friends describe me? They'd probably say I'm kind and I'm caring, but that I'm always late.
5 My friends would describe me as caring and funny, I hope, erm, and also smiley.
6 My friends would describe me as happy, caring and fun.
7 My friends would describe me as energetic because I'm always full of energy. They would describe me as smiley because I'm always smiling, and they would describe me as funny because I love making jokes.
8 My friends would probably say that I'm generous, kind, honest and reliable. Definitely reliable.

1D: BBC Street Interviews
Exs 2A and 2B

Alice: I would describe my lifestyle as, er, quite normal really. Erm, I … I go to work, er, I come home … I live with my parents. I think it's quite normal.

Elliot: I have quite a normal lifestyle. I wake up early in the morning, I go to school, I have lunch outside, I do my homework and then I see my friends. And, I do that every day.

Saffi: I'd say because we're students, erm, we live quite alternative lifestyles, erm, normally we'd be going out at the weekend, and always, like, together making dinner and things like that.

Vambai: Er, my lifestyle is pretty normal. I wake up in the morning, go to work, er, come back home, cook for myself, eat dinner and go back to sleep.

Kayla: I'm probably in the more alternative side of things.

Tom: I'd say alternative as well.

Jack: Yeah, alternative, yeah. Same.

Philip: Er, I think my lifestyle is relatively normal and conservative. I have a regular type of job – I work in an office in finance – erm, I live quite near to work, I commute, er, to work by bicycle.

Lotte: Er, yeah, probably the same – quite alternative. Um, mostly, yeah, just hanging out with friends on the weekends, er, doing quite a lot of studying for university. Erm, nothing that exciting really. Just quite normal, but, yeah.

Adam: I guess my life is, is fairly comfortable. Erm, I live in … I have my own house. Erm, I have two children, a wife and two children. Erm, and, er, yeah – it's not too bad.

Ex 2C

Elliot: Erm, if I could change something about my lifestyle, I would do more exercise, would get … maybe go for a run every day – that would be nice.

Vambai: I would like to go out more. Erm, I would like to explore the country a bit more. And visit different places a bit more.

Tom: Er, I would like to save more money. Yeah, and stop spending it all the time.

Kayla: I want to travel a bit more. Erm, I seem to work quite a lot so, yeah, it would be nice to go travelling [to/around] different places.

Jack: Er, work less for me as well. I'm sick of work, basically. So, yeah.

Philip: Erm, it would be nice to have a more exciting job, not working in an office. Erm, maybe live somewhere a little bit warmer than the UK, with less rain.

Adam: Erm, I'm pretty happy with the way that things are. Erm, I look forward to my children growing up, just seeing how they change, erm, and my life changing as, as they become adults, seeing how they get … become, and then maybe having a bit more time to myself as well.

UNIT 2

Opener: BBC Vlogs

1 Er, I remember a summer holiday, erm, I spent with my family in the north of Spain in the mountains, and we had a fantastic time, hiking, canoeing and also I had my first camera so I took plenty of photos as well.
2 Happy memory, getting my first car, which was a tomato-red Mini.
3 When I was nine years old my father gave me as a birthday present a small kitty cat. At the beginning I was a little bit nervous because I thought that it was going to be very difficult to take care of it, but I was also very excited to have it between my arms.
4 I remember when I was about eight, I went to Spain with my family and it was really exciting because I got to try lots of traditional Spanish food. I also learnt how to swim and got to stay up late, which I found really fun.
5 A few years ago I was about to travel to Argentina. I was so excited about that trip. Unfortunately, the day before my flight, my bag was stolen with my passport in it. I thought I was not going to be able to make it. Luckily, a neighbour found my passport on the street and returned it to me just a few hours before my flight, so I was able to travel and had an amazing experience. I was so lucky and so grateful to my neighbour.

2D: BBC Documentary
Exs 2A and 2B

Simon: In living memory, thousands of residents in the town of Matera were so poor they lived in damp, dark caves. People were living in the caves here until the 1950s, when the Italian prime minister declared this poverty a national scandal, and everybody was moved out, forcibly moved out of the caves, into public housing, and so a whole way of life ended. Matera is now turning its once shameful caves into an asset. Many of them are being refashioned as holiday homes and fancy hotels. Marco?

Marco: Yeah, it's me. This is your cave.

Simon: This is my … Look at this! It's astonishing! This was a home!

Marco: Family share the house with donkeys, cow, big animals.

Simon: People lived with their animals inside the cave? I sense that you're turning this from something that is shameful or embarrassing, or people feel that way about it, into something to be incredibly proud of.

Marco: Exactly. We start to understand that there is a way to live again. We need to be proud of this.

Simon: Isn't it totally spectacular? Something and somewhere I won't ever forget. I'll enjoy a good night's sleep tonight, I think.
Ahhh …
Wow! I mean, look at this. Come on, now!
Oh, look. Italian wedding! Fantastic. What a completely splendid sight. Any wedding, anything like this, it represents rejuvenation, regeneration. It's so good to see, because too many towns and villages in southern Italy have been completely depopulated in recent generations, but here, this is … this has got a future.

UNIT 3

Opener: BBC Vlogs

1 I'm interested in a lot of things so I could probably say that I'm curious about everything. I've always enjoyed learning new things about science, nature and I still really enjoy reading popular science books and articles.
2 I'm really interested in history, especially middle eastern history, erm, it's just something that I've always found interesting and I like to read about it, I like to watch documentaries about it and find out more.
3 I am curious about language learning and what happens to the brain when you learn more than one.
4 I'm curious about things that affect the environment, particularly global warming, climate change and what we can do to stop it.

5 I'm curious about food and how what we eat affects how we feel and how we behave.

6 Oh, I'm curious about so many things. I love music, I love art, I love history.

7 I'm really curious about what cats think. They act in such strange ways most of the time, and I always want to know what's going on in my cat's head.

3D: BBC Street Interviews
Exs 2A and 2B

Nikki: Erm, the things that're important in my life are friends, family and food.

Lily: To me, friendships and my family are very important. But at the same time, doing things I'm interested in, such as art and writing, and anything creative, are also very important to me because I think it's very important to follow your dreams and do what you enjoy, and what makes you happy.

Saffi: I'd say, erm, friends is a big thing because most of our friends are uni students so we can't see our families, so being together and eating dinner, and seeing each other lots [is] definitely a big thing.

Lotte: Yeah, making time to socialise as much as you can, erm, looking out for each other, making sure that everyone's healthy …

Saffi: And mentally OK.

Lotte: … Yeah. Yeah.

Natalia: Erm, I quite like music because I believe it is able to change your mood a lot. You know, if you're feeling depressed or sad, erm, putting on a certain song can make you … kind of uplift you.

Mon Zer: Succeeding and providing for my family.

Devante: Er, my family, my friends, er … what else is important to me? Having a freedom of thought, being able to learn, being able to teach each other, friends, family everyone, living a good life and keeping tidy, putting things away after I use them, I think is important to me. So, a… structure is really important to me nowadays.

Gerard: I'd say [the] most important [thing] is … for me is, will probably be friends and family. I think spending time with them, erm, making sure that there's a good balance between my work and my, like, personal life, my free time, make sure I've always got time for them.

Ex 2C

Nikki: Erm, money. I'm not particularly, … I don't find a career that important.

Lily: For me, other people's opinions are not very important and, erm, they shouldn't be because you shouldn't, er, care a lot about what other people think about you.

Lotte: Erm, for me, social media I don't care about too much. Erm, sort of keeping up with, kind of, current trends and Instagram, Facebook. I'd rather, sort of, socialise in the real world. [I'm] more interested in current events and the news, I guess.

Mon Zer: I … I don't care about, er, like, er, new trends that much.

Gerard: So, things that aren't that important for me personally, erm, I'm not interested in sport at all. I've no interest in it, I don't really know anything about it. Erm, and probably brands. I'm not … like, brand names, or … I'm not really into brands at all or, sort of, status symbols.

UNIT 4

Opener: BBC Vlogs

1 Last year I won a really big golf tournament. I'm very proud of myself. I shot my best score of the year, a seventy-nine, which is a really good score in golf, especially for me.

2 Yes, I've won one thing in my life, which was an award for best classwork when I was ten years old.

3 Actually, I won a contest a few months ago, it was an opportunity to watch my favourite singer performing live, Alicia Keys, in London, and I loved it, it was such a good experience.

4 So, I've won quite a few awards, erm, I used to dance when I was younger, so I won quite a few competitions for dancing and I also won a couple of trophies as well. Erm, I've also won a few professional awards for writing, and that's about it really.

5 I usually never win anything, but I won these two turtles in Bali for showing up first to a party. It pays to be on time!

6 I don't often enter competitions, so I haven't won a lot, but I did enter a competition on Twitter last year and I won a television, and that was pretty cool. I think I won it because I was the only person who entered the competition. It wasn't a big Twitter account, but hey, I got a free TV.

4D: BBC Entertainment
Exs 2A and 2B

Narrator: Nepal. An ancient, mystical land. A land that's home to the world's highest peaks, and now also to a very important *Top Gear* test.

Presenters: Hello.
Thank you.
Thank you.
Challenge.
What have we got?
You and your city cars will now undertake the ultimate commute – from Kathmandu to the Forbidden City of Lo Manthang.
Wow!

Narrator: First, we'd have to escape Kathmandu.

Presenter: A little bit, uh, chaotic round these parts.

Narrator: The next thing to do was leave Kathmandu behind, pick up the highway and start our trek west.

Presenters: Tell you what, Paddy, it's about to get really bumpy up here.
It can't get any worse, can it?
I think it just might be.

Narrator: But then things got even tougher.

Presenters: Oh, my …
Up-up-up!
Could someone get back here quite quickly, please?
Great!

Narrator: Miles from anywhere, our next job was to find somewhere to camp for the night.

Presenters: This is nice, innit?
This is the worst camp spot I've ever seen.
Goodnight!
Seriously, boys. This is, this is … frightening up here. I mean, literally, there was just enough room to get the car through.
Fred, I can't believe I'm saying this, but please can you give me a push?
That's literally all I've got. I think the engine's dying.
Fred, hook me up and just tow me. This is ridiculous.
Whoa, whoa!
Paddy!

Narrator: So, this was it. After five days of punishment, and now just ten miles short of the finish, the Renault 4's journey was done.

Presenter: Come on, Chris. Get in.

Narrator: In the five days since leaving Kathmandu, our cars had covered the most arduous miles of their lives. They'd suffered breakdowns and failures. But working together, they'd claimed victories we had no right to expect of them. In the end, the journey had proved too much for some. But we'd come to Nepal to find the ultimate city car.

Presenters: I'm through!
No, you're not!
The finish line!
Technically, Fred, you're not in.
I'm in! I'm in! I'm in!

Narrator: He wasn't. And, ultimately, the Forbidden City had made its choice.

Presenters: Crowned the winner! It's got the gold scarf on it, Chris.
On that, Paddy, I give it to you. I can't argue with you, man.

UNIT 5

Opener: BBC Vlogs

1 I always read the BBC site in the morning first thing, starting with the sport news, in particular football, erm, then I work through world news because I like to know what's happening in the world, and kind of work my way down to national, UK news and then what's happening in my local area.

2 Well, I listen to the radio a lot, I like to get the news from the radio, because they also tend to discuss issues further and interview people regarding current affairs.

3 I read a lot of news every day, I either read it online or I read, erm, a newspaper.

4 Erm, I try to be up to date with current affairs, so I read the news on my phone on an app and I try to read the news on my lunch break at work.

5 I get my news online. (I go) When I wake up I go online and I go straight to BBC news, and then … I also like to read other news sites on the same article to make sure everyone that is saying the same thing.

6 I go to a few different sites, different sources, erm, because usually the truth just lies somewhere in the middle, erm, so I like to get different points of view.

5D: BBC Street Interviews
Ex 2

Isabelle: I think the kind of news that interests me the most must be, erm, international politics.

Matt: Er, people doing well in life. Erm, good news stories. Erm, er, I'm tired of seeing negative stuff on the news.

Natalia: Erm, I like, quite like things to do with crime because [it] just adds a bit of entertainment to my life.

Rob: Erm, I follow politics in the news. Erm, as well as news about sport and, erm, culture.

Devante: News about things I care about. I love news on technology, so I'm really into business development and I'm into technology helping us do things in a more efficient and, hopefully, cheaper way. Erm, I'm really into learning about the arts, I love musicals, I love news about music.

Henry: Er, the news that I'm interested in is world news. I'm from Australia, so I really like, er, international politics, international relations, er, local news is also interesting.

Exs 3A and 3B

Isabelle: I think print media will disappear over time and I think, er, the new generation might focus more on social media and get their news through different social media platforms, erm, and I think it might be hard then to distinguish real news from fake news.

Matt: Er, it probably won't. It probably won't! But I hope it does. Erm, there's too much negativity on the news. There's far too much negativity.

Natalia: I think the younger generation will be more interested in the news, but I think the way we access the news or, erm, information that would be included in the news will change from the traditional BBC website or the newspaper to social media, such as, like, Instagram and even Snapchat.

Rob: Erm, hopefully people will stop getting their news from social media. Erm, yeah.

Devante: Hopefully, it'll be a bit more selective so that you can click on the things that you're most interested in and just watch those rather than things that are quite depressing, quite sad, that are repeated every day, that get worse and worse, i.e. news that's out of your control, that's negative.

Ayesha: Erm, I definitely think that celebrities are going to be more prominent in the news and that their role will be much more influential as well.

Henry: Yes, I think the news will be online a lot more, including on social media. I think the news will be represented by younger people and mostly on social media platforms, such as Instagram, Facebook, er, and other internet things.

UNIT 6

Opener: BBC Vlogs

1 I think I'm a pretty creative person, but the things that I do aren't works of art, obviously. I love to dance, to sing, I sing quite a lot to be honest.

2 I'm not very creative in the literal sense. I can't play a musical instrument or sing, or, I'm not very good at art either, but I do enjoy creative writing, erm I always enjoyed that at school.

3 I really like baking cakes and bread. I started baking with a friend who I live with at university this year. Oh, and I'm also teaching myself to play the guitar.

4 Well, I'm not very good at art, and I don't play any instruments either, but I am creative in other ways, for example I love crafts and I have recently started knitting as well, and I really enjoy it.

5 The creative things that I'm interested in are drawing – I like to sketch things, I'm not very good but I do enjoy it. I also like gardening because I love to watch things grow.

6 I draw a lot and I paint a lot, but mainly digitally. I have a tablet which I can take with me wherever I want so I can draw whenever I want.

6D: BBC Documentary
Exs 2A and 2B

Narrator: Yinka Shonibare is a British–Nigerian artist working in the UK. His art takes many different forms: sculpture, painting, photography and film-making. Yinka is designing a sculpture for the Stephen Friedman Gallery. It's the art gallery's 20th anniversary, and it has supported Yinka since the start of his career.

Yinka: So, I'm doing this rather surreal piece. I'm doing a sketch of this kind of man celebrating and he's got all these balloons pulling him up. So, that's *Balloon Man* I'm actually doing.

Narrator: Yinka works with a team of craftspeople across the UK. They help him create his art works. His sketches for Balloon Man go to a studio in south London. Nigel Schofield has worked with Yinka for more than ten years.

Nigel: We get the sketch from Yinka and you try and get the flavour of what he's trying to get across. This is a guy who's being lifted off the floor by balloons.

Narrator: First, Nigel photographs himself hanging in the air like *Balloon Man*. Next, Nigel and his team use the photographs to help them create the basic structure of the sculpture. This helps them make sure the figure is realistic. Once Nigel has finished, the sculpture is sent to costume maker, Miranda Curran.

Miranda: What's great is that … there's a lot more sort of artistic freedom for me as a maker because I can … You know, I'm given the fabrics and then I can work with them and do what I like with them, which is a really lovely way to work.

Narrator: Like many of Yinka's sculptures, *Balloon Man* is dressed in brightly coloured African fabric. Yinka hasn't seen the finished sculpture yet, so the team move it into the main studio.

Yinka: I'll just stand back a bit. Let's have a look. Yeah, that's looking … That's looking good. I'll just have a look here.

Narrator: After some last-minute changes, *Balloon Man* is finished and ready to go to the gallery.

Stephen: Welcome.

Yinka: Ah, Stephen. OK.

Stephen: Here we are.

Yinka: Wow.

Stephen: What do you think?

Yinka: That's looking good.

Stephen: Right at the centre in the front room, of course. Where you belong.

Yinka: It's really great, actually, that you've got it just on its own in the middle. Yeah. It's a celebratory piece.

Stephen: It's exciting, it's fun, it's engaging. It's everything a work of art should be.

UNIT 7

Opener: BBC Vlogs

1 I think I feel happiest in the garden, either planting new plants or looking after the older ones. I also love to walk in nature and to be able to hear the birds singing.

2 The place that I feel happiest is on my bike. I like to ride through the countryside, I find it helps me think about complicated things and they become simpler, so it helps me solve problems. I enjoy seeing the flowers and the trees and the rivers, sometimes I even ride my bike to the sea which is about 30 kilometres from where I live.

3 I'm happiest either at my home in Brighton or when I'm visiting my family on a lovely sunny day.

4 I feel happiest sat around a dinner table with my friends and family.

5 I feel happiest in every place where I can be with my friends, just hanging out in the street, sharing our thoughts and having a lot of good moments, or even watching a film at home.

6 My favourite place is here. I'm in Northumberland by the ocean on the north-east coast of England and the sky is huge and the sea is beautiful, so this is where I feel the happiest.

7D: BBC Street Interviews
Exs 2A and 3B

Dan: Erm, probably India. Erm, because it's such a fantastic, big, diverse country, amazing food, amazing people. I'd love to go back.

Saffi: Budapest, I think, because there's so much … you can see so much in one city, you can go to … you can be in Buda or Pest, and I didn't know that before I went there. Erm, and it's a really beautiful city and the people are really lovely and the food is amazing as well.

Lotte: Yeah, I really love New Zealand. Erm, I went to Auckland two years ago, erm, and stayed there for about a month and the scenery was amazing, the people were so friendly, erm, and it was just a really beautiful place.

Will: Erm, I think the most amazing place I've ever visited is, er, Mount Kilimanjaro. Just being at the top when sunrise is coming and you've got snow and there's very, very few people up there. It's quite a special place.

Lumi: I think the most amazing place I've ever been to currently is Iceland. I went there to do … shoot a film and to capture some of the Northern Lights and just general culture, but Iceland.

Osaid: The most amazing place I've ever visited would probably be Syria a couple of years ago. Er, this is because there's so much history behind it and so many different … and, such a wide variety of foods to try, and was really different from any food that I've tried in this country.

Anabel: Erm, I think London because there's so many things to do here and each part of London is so different and diverse. Erm, and it just feels so lively. I just really enjoy spending time here.

Exs 2C and 3C

Molly: I'm going to say by myself because I'm more of a … I prefer my own company.

Dan: Bit of both. Er, I like the freedom of travelling by myself, but, erm, ultimately, it's nice to travel with someone else because it can get a bit lonely on your own.

Saffi: With other people.

Lotte: I … I'd say by myself. I think it … you've got more room to do what you want, umm, and be more flexible with your plans.

Nikki: I actually prefer going by myself because I'm a bit selfish and … could do whatever I want without worrying if someone else is having a good time as well. But obviously there are some … some times where you want to be in a big group and be with all your friends. But if you want to go somewhere specifically, just go on your own I'd say.

Lumi: Preferably, probably by myself, but I do enjoy, er, travelling with people. But I like probably, like, small groups, so probably like, four max, maybe.

Osaid: I prefer travelling with other people, just because I feel the experience is shared with my friends or family. Because when I'm travelling alone, whatever happens is mostly on my own and I find it safer to travel with other people.

Anabel: Erm, I enjoy spending time with other, er, travelling with other people because, erm, then you can talk about the experience with them and enjoy it with them and share the memory with them, rather than just yourself.

UNIT 8

Opener: BBC Vlogs

1 Generally speaking, I'm pretty terrible at fixing things. If it's got anything to do with electronics, a motor or an engine then I haven't got a clue.

2 I try and fix something before getting help, erm, so with computers I'm quite good, but anything with cars, I'm pretty bad.

3 I think, generally, I'm good at fixing things, at least I always try before throwing something away or asking for help.

4 I'm really bad at fixing things – never ask me to fix something for you. I don't even know how to change a lightbulb, so when something breaks in my house, either I ask someone for help or I live with it.

5 Am I good at fixing things? Not really. I'm more of a project manager than a DIY expert if you know what I mean. So, I always have big plans, and then I need to find someone to do the actual work for me.

6 I am not very good at fixing things: I would say I'm quite good at breaking things. I am quite clumsy.

8D: BBC Documentary
Exs 2A and 2B

Narrator: Finely tuned ears and a wonderfully versatile voice have allowed humans to invent over 7,000 different languages.
          And each of us, as we grow, pick up over a thousand new words every year. By your early teens, you have a working vocabulary of over 10,000 words. From an early age, Wendy Vo's brain has been bursting with languages.

Wendy: When I was one, I spoke Vietnamese only, like, it was just like baby words. When I was two, I spoke English, Vietnamese, Spanish and Chinese, so four languages when I was two years old. Well, at least I started learning them.

Narrator: She hasn't stopped at just four languages. Wendy spends an hour every week talking to a range of different people in their native tongues.

Winita: I am Winita from India, and I teach Wendy Hindi.

Rashida: My name is Rashida and I teach Wendy Arabic, from Yemen.

Woman 1:   And I teach Wendy Spanish. She speaks Spanish a lot better than some Hispanic kids do.

Woman 2:   At the Russian languages, she is very good.

Woman 3:   Portuguese.

Woman 4:   She is at the top because she can switch very … in few seconds, from one language to the other one. And she can think, speak, write. It's unbelievable.

Wendy: Vietnamese, English, Spanish, Chinese, French, Japanese, Hindi, Arabic, Russian, Cantonese and Portuguese.

Narrator: Add them all up and Wendy has eleven different voices packed inside her head.

IRREGULAR VERB TABLE

Verb	Past simple	Past participle
be	was	been
become	became	become
begin	began	begun
bite	bit	bitten
blow	blew	blown
break	broke	broken
bring	brought	brought
build	built	built
burn	burnt/burned	burnt/burned
buy	bought	bought
catch	caught	caught
choose	chose	chosen
come	came	come
cost	cost	cost
cut	cut	cut
do	did	done
draw	drew	drawn
drink	drank	drunk
drive	drove	driven
earn	earned/earnt	earned/earnt
eat	ate	eaten
fall	fell	fallen
feed	fed	fed
feel	felt	felt
find	found	found
forget	forgot	forgotten
freeze	froze	frozen
get	got	got
give	gave	given
go	went	gone
grow	grew	grown
have	had	had
hear	heard	heard
hit	hit	hit
hold	held	held
hurt	hurt	hurt
keep	kept	kept
know	knew	known
learn	learned/learnt	learned/learnt

Verb	Past simple	Past participle
leave	left	left
let	let	let
lie	lay	lain
lose	lost	lost
make	made	made
mean	meant	meant
meet	met	met
pay	paid	paid
put	put	put
read	read	read
ride	rode	ridden
run	ran	run
say	said	said
see	saw	seen
sell	sold	sold
send	sent	sent
shine	shone	shone
show	showed	shown
shut	shut	shut
sing	sang	sung
sit	sat	sat
sleep	slept	slept
speak	spoke	spoken
spend	spent	spent
spill	spilled/spilt	spilled/spilt
stand	stood	stood
stick	stuck	stuck
swim	swam	swum
take	took	taken
teach	taught	taught
tell	told	told
think	thought	thought
throw	threw	thrown
understand	understood	understood
wake	woke	woken
wear	wore	worn
win	won	won
write	wrote	written

Pearson Education Limited
KAO Two
KAO Park
Hockham Way
Harlow, Essex
CM17 9SR
England
and Associated Companies throughout the world.

pearsonenglish.com/speakout3e

First published 2022

ISBN: 978-1-292-35953-3

Set in BBC Reith Sans

Printed in China (GCC/04)

Acknowledgements
Written by Antonia Clare and JJ Wilson
The publishers and authors would like to thank the following people for their feedback and comments during the development of the material: Maria de la Paz Giglio, Charlotte Rowe, Isela Fernández Shipton, Alper Topbaş.

Image Credits:
123RF.com: bowie15 140, chrisga 143, Enrique Miguel Borque. 143, oneinchpunch 140, Steve Collender 140, Teoh Chin Leong 142, William Rodrigues dos Santo 142; **Alamy Stock Photo:** Granger Historical Picture Archive 47, PA Images 47, Pictorial Press Ltd 69; **Apex News and Pictures:** David Morris 57; **BBC Studios:** 7, 16, 17, 19, 28, 31, 40, 41, 43, 52, 53, 55, 64, 65, 67, 76, 77, 79, 88, 89, 91, 100, 101; **Bye Bye Plastic Bags:** Erik Ginanjar Nugraha 60; **Getty Images:** 10'000 Hours 144145, Adam Gault 145, Alexander Haase / EyeEm 82, Alexander Spatari 142, Alistair Berg 92, Anders Blomqvist 25, ansonmiao 86, apomares 140, 141, Ariel Skelley 105, Ashley Corbin-Teich 8, Atlantide Phototravel 73, Axelle/ Bauer-Griffin / Contributor 45, Benoit BACOU 102, Bettmann / Contributor 68, 69, BJI / Blue Jean Images 50, Brais Seara 86, Cavan Images 143, Cecilie_Arcurs 94, chabybucko 91, Chainarong Prasertthai 145, dalomo84 60, 61, David Madison 140, Deepak Sethi 96, Digital Vision 141, Dmytro Ponomarenko / EyeEm 67, Drazen_ 8, Elena Eliachevitch 95, Enis Aksoy 48, Erik Pronske Photography 108, Erika Stone / Contributor 68, fi ladendron 26, Fran Polito 132, Francesco Carta fotografo 72, franckreporter 7, Frederick M. Brown / Stringer 60, Gonzalo Azumendi 37, Grant Faint 86, Hendrik Sulaiman / EyeEm 95, Hinterhaus Productions 142, Hulton Archive / Stringer 45, Ippei Naoi 22, izusek 95, James O'Neil 56, Jessica Jin / EyeEm 79, Jetta Productions Inc 36, Kareri 140, JGI/Jamie Grill 99, jldeines 145, John Harper 143, 156, JohnnyGreig 8, 84, 84, Jordi Salas 70, Jose Luis Pelaez 31, Jose Luis Pelaez Inc 8, Juan Silva 95, Juanmonino 6, kali9 63, 135, Karl Weatherly 154, Kathrin Ziegler 142, Kyodo News / Contributor 47, LeoPatrizi 95, 157, Linda Raymond 58, Lottie Davis 94, Luis Alvarez 8, 36, 81, 109, Luis Mauricio Hernández Meyer / EyeEm 10, m-imagephotography 62, © Marco Bottigelli 143, Maremagnum 28, 29, Marilyn Nieves 70, Mario Forcherio / EyeEm 117, Maritza Salazar / EyeEm 118, martin-dm 114, Mascot 34, Maskot 93, Morsa Images 8, myriam meloni 46, narvikk 142, NurPhoto / Contributor 47, ohishiistk 32, olaser 155, Paparwin Tanupatarachai 128, Paul Bradbury 43, pawel.gaul 100, 101, Peathegee Inc 37, PeopleImages 8, Peter Cade 11, 26, Philartphace 35, pixelfi t 45, Posnov 152, Pyrosky 93, R.M. Nunes 80, 81, rebelml 142, recep-bg 85, Reinhard Krull / EyeEm 140, Roy James Shakespeare 70, Sean Gladwell 97, skynesher 45, Sollina Images 36, 70, SolStock 37, South_agency 103, 124, Srdjan Stevanovic / Contributor 45, StefaNikolic 20, stockstudioX 15, Suhaimi Abdullah / Stringer 51, Sushiman 150, Sylvain Sonnet 38, Symphonie Ltd 142, Tascha Rassadornyindee / EyeEm 71, 147, Thanasis Zovoilis 115, The Good Brigade 62, Thomas Barwick 37, Tim Graham / Contributor 47, Tim Robberts 22, 36, 62, 106, Toni Baki / EyeEm 14, Tony Anderson 32, TPopova 86, Trevor Williams 70, valentinrussanov 95, vgajic 142, We Are 71, Westend61 8, 10, 37, 83, 121, Witthaya Prasongsin 56, 57, XiXinXing 32, Yagi Studio 142, 152, yangna 130, 131, Zu Sanchez Photography 112; **Guzelian:** 19; **Jacki Gordon:** © Totie Photies by Jacki Gordon 75; **Paul Jeffers:** 12, 13; **Paula Aguilera:** 61; **Shutterstock. com:** AlessandroBiascioli 95, Alexander Steamaze 133, Anan Kaewkhammul 141, Andrey_Popov 140, aslysun 96, Benoit Daoust 139, BlackCat Imaging 143, Burben 143, Columbia Pictures/Kobal 23, Coprid 145, Dennis van de Water 75, Dilara Mammadova 24, EGHStock 26, FCG 141, Fpskiller 59, Gary Murray 140, Hadrian 145, Halfpoint 49, Igor Iakovlev 141, ilozavr 141, K-Kwan Kwanchai. 140, Kevin Eaves 143, kkphotography2 74, Krasul 110, LeonoraKohanec 55, MH STOCK 140, Milosz Maslanka 126, NDT 142, New Africa 96, Oxana Militsina 143, Photo Smoothies 26, Rawpixel.com 142, RCPPHOTO 140, RealCG Animation Studio 140, Rich Carey 141, S_ Photo 116, Shawn Pecor 140, Simon Dannhauer. 152, Skreidzeleu 33, STILLFX 143, tanatat 108, Tom Wang 140, Tony Skerl 141

Cover Images: Front: **Alamy Stock Photo:** LightField Studios Inc.; **Getty Images:** valentinrussanov, We Are, Westend61

Illustrated by
Stephen Collins (Central Illustration Agency) 20, 63, 137l, 149, 153; Ben Hasler (NB Illustration) 11,137r; Norbert Sipos (Beehive Illustration) 25; Szilvia Szakall (Beehive Illustration) 21

(Key: l-left; r-right)